CW00505761

THE POWER WITHIN

THE POWER WITHIN

Eric Butterworth

JAMES CLARKE & CO. LTD
Cambridge & London

© *Eric Butterworth*
First published in
Great Britain 1969

Published by James Clarke & Co. Ltd,
7 All Saints Passage, Cambridge,
England & distributed by
Book Centre, 110 North Circular Road,
London, N.W.10

Reproduced and printed by
Latimer Trend & Co. Ltd., Whitstable

Dedicated to Charles and Myrtle Fillmore, and to the influence which their lives and teachings have had upon me through their "lengthened shadow"—the Unity School of Christianity, at Lee's Summit, Missouri

Contents

Introduction

This is a great day for unity. Daily we read accounts of the continuing ecumenical efforts of the worlds' religions. Dialogue between philosophy or science and religion is commonplace. The leaders of atheistic Russia are even making new efforts toward communication with the Vatican and with church groups of the West.

There is much to be enthusiastic about in all this. But I find much to be unhappy about, too. As a minister-teacher in the Christian stream of thought, I have a feeling that the Christian movement does not adequately represent itself in such unity discussions. It seems to me that the dynamism of the Christian teaching, which is so greatly needed in our contemporary world, is most often unexpressed.

My concern is certainly not lessened by the confusion of many of our modern theologians who are proclaiming that God is "truly dead"—not merely rejected by modern culture but irrevocably absent. We are hearing terms like "Christian atheism," "eclipse of God," "secular gospel," "religionless Christianity," etc. I herald the efforts of even radical reappraisal of the Christian teachings. But it saddens me that so many have caught so little of the message of Jesus Christ.

This book will ask the question, "What did Jesus *really* teach?" It will cut through theologies and dogma and ritual, and show how Jesus of Nazareth, two thousand years ago, grappled with the problems that beset men and found some profound and yet simple

answers. We will not preach in a tone that suggests that Christianity
alone can save the world. Yet we are confident that Jesus could make
a vital contribution in our time, if He were only given an unbiased,
nonsectarian hearing.

There are whole libraries of books written about Jesus, and about
the great Christian movement that sprang up in His name. However,
little space is given to the concepts He set forth and the techniques
that He outlined.

Theologians have been preoccupied with the religion *about* Jesus,
and it is the modification and even rejection of this religion that
has produced the "Christian atheists." But what of the religion *of*
Jesus? The Christian has long preached about the saving of society,
but Jesus called for a society of saviours. Preachers have emphasized
the Divinity of Jesus, but Jesus taught the Divinity of Man. Stress
has been upon the miracles wrought by Jesus, but Jesus said, "He
that believeth on me, the works that I do shall he do also; and greater
works than these shall he do. . . ." (John 14: 12)

In his recent book, *Cosmic Humanism*, Oliver L. Reiser of the
University of Pittsburgh has written, "In the long course of social
evolution man has sanctified many things as the source of ultimate
power, the object of veneration and worship; but he has seldom
touched upon man's essential divinity. Never have societies deified
the creative force, the divinity in man. Yet if there is one thing the
Christian mystery sought to teach, it was the divinity within man,
the "Christ-in-you," undeveloped and unheeded."[1]

The philosophy of Jesus is a workable philosophy, a way of life.
Jesus taught of the depth potential of man and of his spiritual unity
with God. Perhaps He was ahead of His time. Only recently have
scientists, philosophers, psychologists, and educators begun to catch
the idea of an integrated whole as the guide for studying man or life
or the Universe. This is the concept of spiritual unity that is found
between the lines in all Jesus' teachings. Strangely, religious groups
have been the slowest of all to catch this vision. This is especially
remarkable because the very word "religion," from its Greek root,
has a strong connotation of *unity*.

It is difficult to talk or write about Jesus Christ or the Christian
teachings without coming into direct conflict with deeply rooted attitudes. This is because the whole flow of Western civilization has

been so completely involved in the organization of the Christian church and the outreach of Christian ideals. Leaf through the works of Western philosophers, and in practically every case, whether they show a bias *for* or *against* Jesus and Christianity, they invariably talk about them. It seems to me that both the proponents and the antagonists have been arguing about the wrong things.

Let us admit at the outset, in our study of the Gospel of Jesus we will not be articulating a "social Gospel," nor will we try to substantiate any political views by a rationalization of His teachings. Ours will be a complete *you*-centered approach—since we believe this to be Jesus' approach.

If you can find the consciousness of your spiritual unity with the Infinite and with your fellow man, and if you can become established in the conviction of the Divinity of Man, you will become an intuitively guided and effective instrument for social and political action within the framework of your interests, abilities, and responsibilities.

The Power Within will introduce you to the Gospel of Jesus in a new context, with repeated emphasis upon the great idea of "Christ in *you*." When you understand this emphasis, you will be able to roam wide into the four Gospels — which we will deal with only synoptically — with interest and understanding. The Gospel message will begin to make a lot of good sense. It will cease to be a restrictive and sectarian message. It will become a message for the ages, a universal message of Truth for all people everywhere.

PROLOGUE

ACCORDING to an old Hindu legend there was a time when all men were gods, but they so abused their divinity that Brahma, the chief god, decided to take it away from men and hide it where they would never again find it. Where to hide it became the big question.

When the lesser gods were called in council to consider this question, they said, "We will bury man's divinity deep in the earth." But Brahma said, "No, that will not do, for man will dig deep down into the earth and find it." Then they said, "Well, we will sink his divinity into the deepest ocean." But again Brahma replied, "No, not there, for man will learn to dive into the deepest waters, will search out the ocean bed, and will find it."

Then the lesser gods said, "We will take it to the top of the highest mountain and there hide it." But again Brahma replied, "No, for man will eventually climb every high mountain on earth. He will be sure some day to find it and take it up again for himself." Then the lesser gods gave up and concluded, "We do not know where to hide it, for it seems there is no place on earth or in the sea that man will not eventually reach."

Then Brahma said, "Here is what we will do with man's divinity. We will hide it deep down in man himself, for he will never think to look for it there." Ever since then, the legend concludes, man has been going up and down the earth, climbing, digging, diving, exploring, searching for something that is already in himself.

Two thousand years ago a man named Jesus found it and shared its secret; but in the movement that sprang up in His name, the Divinity in Man has been the best kept secret of the ages.

THE POWER WITHIN

1 The Eternal Quest

THE HOPE of mankind today lies in the great undiscovered depths within. The time is at hand when men everywhere must forsake the fruitless search of the world at the circumference of being and embark upon a courageous quest into inner space. It is a very real world, and its depths can be sounded, its potency released. It is not a conquest but a bequest. It is not as much something *within* man as it is the deeper level *of* man. "Come, ye blessed . . . , inherit the kingdom prepared for you from the foundation of the world" (Matt. 25:34).

The history of man on the eternal quest has been a strange odyssey. In his search for the "holy grail" man has looked everywhere and in vain, but he has failed to look within himself. Occasionally, a prophet came, telling of the world within. But instead of following him into the deeper experience, men invariably made a god of the prophet—worshiped him and built monuments to him. They then trapped themselves in a religious practice that had no *within*. How many times has this happened? How many religions are there in the world?

The pages of history tell and retell the story of mystic teachers who found it and of the ensuing religions that lost it. And the earth is dotted with monuments that tell of inner-space flights that never quite got off the ground.

Yet somehow man has always known with Walt Whitman that not all of him is included between his hat and his boots. He has felt, with Wordsworth,

A sense sublime
Of something far more deeply interfused,
Whose dwelling is the light of setting suns,
And the round ocean and the living air,
And the blue sky, and in the mind of man;
A motion and a spirit, that impels
All thinking things, all objects of all thought,
And rolls through all things.[1]

There is a strange paradox in the world today. The pressing social problems—warfare, the struggle for equality between races, and the exploding population and lagging production of foods—are framed between two contrasting spectacles: (1) the research and exploration into outer space, and (2) the psychedelic "trips" into the inner depths of consciousness. The one, meticulously scientific; the other, about as unscientific as you can get.

Both of these activities may well be symbolic of a sense of frustration with the world of today—an attempt to "stop the world, I want to get off." And the amazing thing is that both of these completely unrelated and contrasting quests may well have deep spiritual implications.

For one thing, space research has enabled man to achieve a breakthrough into another dimension. The more he sees of the Universe around him, the more he realizes that space and time are relative, and that the whole cosmos is like a great thought in the Mind of God. He begins to see that the Universe exists, as far as he is concerned, because he sees it. The center of the Universe, as far as you are concerned, is within you. As far as you are concerned, the Universe exists as an extension of you. The sun and moon and stars are there because you see them.

In Zen Buddhism this point is made in the image of the "moon and the water." The moon-in-the-water phenomenon is likened to human experience. The water is the subject, and the moon the object. When there is no water, there is no moon-in-the-water, and likewise when there is no moon. But when the moon rises, the water does not wait to receive its image, and when even the tiniest drop of water is poured out, the moon does not wait to cast its reflection. But the water does not receive the moon's image on purpose. The event is caused as much by the water as by the moon and, as the water manifests the brightness of the moon, the moon manifests the clarity of the water.

Viewing the vastness of the Universe, we tend to become confused when we seem to be losing our identity. But we must remember that the Universe has meaning because we have meaning, and we have meaning because the Universe has meaning. All discovery is self-discovery and all knowledge is self-knowledge. Thus the greatest discovery in science is not the outward accomplishments, but the inward revelation and the Truth that sets us free to take the outer step.

Nations today may be pouring billions into the hardware needed for outer-space flights, but it is seldom realized that this is all being made possible because of the discoveries within matter, which are actually spiritual discoveries. We have come to know that matter, in the sense of something occupying space, does not exist. We can no longer view the Universe as a vast collection of nebulae, stars, and planets scattered about in empty space. All through the universe there are "force potentials." What we have called "space" is really a *presence*, for there is one continuous, unified, intelligent, and inexhaustible potential that here and there precipitates itself as that which we call matter.

Thus the ultimate of our research into the Universe around us must come in the knowledge of the Mind that sustains it, the Mind in which it actually has its only existence. And the study of Mind can only be done through introspection, self-contemplation, and spiritual research. In the words of Tennyson:[2]

> Self-reverence, self-knowledge, self-control,
> These three alone lead life to sovereign power.

The other activity that along with space research is forming a frame around the world's serious problems is that of the group, perhaps only caricatured by the "hippies," attempting to forsake the decadent civilization of contemporary times by psychedelic flights into the world within. Much has been written on the subject of LSD and the newer STP—the so-called "consciousness-expanding" drugs. On the one hand, Dr. Timothy Leary leads a group who insist that the drugs are here to stay and that it is but a matter of time until everyone will be having his religious experiences synthetically. On the other hand, a growing number of medical scientists warn of the dangers of the drug in terms of permanent physical and mental damage that may result from continued or even occasional use.

However, one fact stands out that cannot be overlooked. Psychedelics have helped to prove the existence of a nonmaterial world of spirit within man. There is serious question whether LSD is the way to reach this world or to release this inherent potential. Perhaps we will ultimately agree that it is an illicit picking of the lock of the door to the superconscious, or at best an improper window-peeking glimpse of the depths of the world within. The method of apprehension is all wrong, but the basic motivation is spiritual and the object of the quest is pure Spirit.

An interesting account of a personal encounter with LSD appears in a book entitled *Exploring Inner Space*, by Jane Dunlap. She tells how it seemed to open the door and allow her to look into the core of life. She says:

People who had such experiences usually agreed that deep within each of us lie goodness unimagined, wisdom, music, talents of every variety, joy, peace, humility, love and spirituality. Hidden away in each individual is a vast gold mine but, as yet, only a few puny and thread-like veins have been discovered. . . . Our fault lies, not in our lack of talent or potentials, but in our refusal to believe that it exists. Only after we can accept such a belief and have thus gained enough confidence to look within ourselves can our development go full steam ahead.[3]

Does that mean we should all take LSD? Certainly not, any more than we should all send rockets out into space. Descriptions of psychedelic illusions do seem to support the spiritual discoveries of the mystics of the ages. There is obviously a great depth of splendor within us, but it must be unfolded through self-realization and self-discipline. There is no synthetic short cut to the Kingdom.

If you have a rosebud in your garden, you may be anxious to see its beauty in full bloom, and so you may force the bud open. For a moment you see the loveliness of its interior, but then it quickly fades and dies. By law, growth is an unfoldment—"first the grain, then the ear, then the full-grain in the ear." The quest for reality through psychedelics is a misguided quest. Man is a spiritual being with infinite possibilities within himself. If he must take psychedelics to prove it, he will find that even the momentary experience of heavenly visions will not endure long enough to make him really believe it over the long haul.

The grievous problems facing mankind today can be solved. However, the solution must be a spiritual one, for material and intellectual ones have been tried and found wanting. And "spiritual things can only be spiritually discerned." The time is ripe, and rotten-ripe, for a serious and concerted drive to educate people in self-knowledge, self-reverence, and self-control. This has been the historic role of religion, but, as we have noted, religions have historically failed to get off the ground in terms of the quest into the world within.

This book calls for a rediscovery of the teachings of Jesus Christ, a reappraisal of the achievements of His life, and a renaissance of the Christian faith. Two thousand years ago, Jesus made the great breakthrough into the world *within,* when He demonstrated the miracle-working implications of letting that inner kingdom come in earth as it is in heaven. It is a strange and yet simple story that is old and yet ever new. Certainly the concept of the great *within* has inspired philosophers and poets and mystic teachers through all the ages. None has put it more eloquently than Robert Browning in his poem "Paracelsus":[4]

> Truth is within ourselves; it takes no rise
> From outward things, whate'er you may believe.
> There is an inmost center in us all,
> Where truth abides in fulness; and around,
> Wall upon wall, the gross flesh hems it in,
> This perfect, clear perception—which is truth.
> A baffling and perverting carnal mesh
> Binds it, and makes all error; and to know
> Rather consists in opening out a way
> Whence the imprisoned splendor may escape,
> Than in effecting entry for a light
> Supposed to be without.

2 The Great Discovery

ABOUT a hundred generations ago in far-off Palestine, something happened that may well be the greatest event in human history. It was the great break-through in man to the world of the spirit within. It happened to a young lad, the son of a simple carpenter.

His name was Jesus, the son of Joseph and Mary of Nazareth. This was no ordinary boy, though He was not unusual in the eyes of his neighbors. Many years later, He returned to Nazareth and was rejected by the people. In essence they said, "What's so special about Jesus? We knew him as a boy in the carpenter shop" (Matt. 13:54).

Much has been made over the manner of His birth. The Bible seems to indicate that His fellow townspeople knew nothing unusual about the incident. Thus the great event was not the birth of Jesus, but a kind of awakening that took place within Him during the years of His growth "in wisdom and stature, and in favor with God and men" (Luke 2:52).

We don't know when it happened or even what happened. We only know that sometime between His birth and the beginning of His miracle-working ministry at thirty years of age, He achieved a unique relationship with God and became the channel for the expression of powers no one had ever before dreamed of. Many believe it was the result of His education. And this is puzzling, too, for we have little knowledge of His life. Some have conjectured that He must have had some exposure to the "masters" of the world of the intellect, in India or Egypt, or even some contact with the Druids in England! However, I believe that what happened had nothing to do with tuition, but was an intuition, an insight, a revelation. It could not have been taught, for there was no precedent.

I like to believe that it happened to him as a youth of about eleven or twelve. It could not have been experienced in the formed intellect of an adult. Jesus Himself later said that to achieve this experience one had to turn and become as a little child.

I can imagine the young boy, Jesus, spending many hours in the hills of Galilee, like any normal youth pondering the wonders of the heavens—the sun and drifting clouds by day, the moon and stars by night. I can visualize Him asking the question posed by the shepherd Psalmist a thousand years before, "What is man?"

And then—one day it happened. Into the consciousness of this thoughtful lad came an idea so great, that He probably didn't catch its full implications at first. It was the concept leading to the full realization of His unity with God. The philosopher, Fichte, once said that an insight into the absolute unity of man with the divine is the profoundest knowledge that man can attain. It was this, but it was more. It was the great discovery of the world within, the breaking down of the "middle wall of partition" between man and God.

This was the beginning of the Age of the Christ, the Divinity of Man. Up to this point, man had existed in the consciousness of separation from God. He could pray *to* God, he could talk *to* God, and receive help and guidance *from* Him. But God was always "out there" and man was "down here." Now Jesus knew what the Psalmist had implied when he said, "Be still, and know that I am God" (Ps. 46:10). Now He knew Himself to be an expression of God, or the activity of God-life and intelligence pressing itself into visibility. Now He knew that the Kingdom of God, the wealth of the Universe, was within the depth-potential within Him.

We don't know how this great break-through was actually accomplished in Jesus, how long the process took, or when He achieved self-mastery. But we know when He made His appearance at the Jordan River to be baptized by John (Matt. 3:13 ff.), He was a committed and polished teacher with the amazing message that "The Kingdom of God is within you."

The Gospels of our Bible record the story of this man, Jesus, and the miracle-working powers He revealed. The message of the Gospels has been misunderstood. They have been made to appear to say that Jesus was really God taking the form of man, standing astride the world like a great Colossus, with the bolts of heaven in His hands. All this fails to take into account His great discovery. It fails to catch the real theme of His teaching: the Truth of the Divinity of Man.

Jesus was not a worker of magic, a performer of feats of the miraculous. He was essentially a teacher. True, He demonstrated unusual power, even over the elements; but He explained that this was an evidence of the power that comes to any man when he makes the discovery in himself of the great within. Jesus' goal was to help everyone—you and me—to understand the great potential within the Adam man, and to help us make the break-through for ourselves. His entire teaching, shorn of the theological embellishments that have been added, is a simple outline of techniques by which we can release our own innate potential and be transformed by the power of our own divinity.

He said: "He that believeth on me, the works that I do shall he do also; and greater works than these shall he do; because I go unto the Father" (John 14:12). In other words, "If you have faith in the God-potential locked within the Adam man, which is yourself, as I have faith in that power within Me, then you can do all I have done and more . . . because I have made the great discovery."

Unless we catch this point, unless we can appreciate and accept this greatest discovery of all time, we lose the thread of the tapestry of the Gospels, and we build our churches and our personal faith on shifting sands. If we recognize this vital and dynamic Truth of man's spiritual unity with God, if we know that man is God's beloved child, endowed with His intelligence, His life, His substance, and that he is the inheritor of a kingdom prepared for him from the foundation of the world, then all the rest of the Gospel story—the miracles and teachings, even the final overcoming in the resurrection—become purely academic, for they are all an outgrowth of this great discovery.

This basic principle—the Divinity of Man—is the dynamism of Christianity that can save the world and lead mankind to a new level of "peace on earth, good will toward men." Without this principle, the Christian church may eventually deteriorate into a monument to a man never understood and a message never applied, and its churches and cathedrals may become gaudy museums where tourists may see displayed the lavish ends to which man has gone in his eternal quest for Truth and reality. The amazing thing is that in each Christian church can be found a Bible that contains Paul's speech on Mars Hill, in which He said:

The God that made the world and all things therein, He, being Lord of heaven and earth, dwelleth not in temples made with hands; neither is He served by men's hands, as though He needed anything, seeing He, Himself, giveth to all life, and breath, and all things . . . that they should seek God, if haply they might feel after Him and find Him, though He is not far from each one of us: for in Him we live, and move, and have our being; as certain even of your own poets have said, for we are also His offspring [Acts 17:24–28].

Jesus discovered His own divinity, His unique relationship with the Infinite. He discovered that through faith He could open doors into the inexhaustible Mind of God, finding renewed creativity, a flow of powerful ideas, a perception beyond the comprehension of the Adam man of His day or ours. And yet He realized that this is a Universe of law and order. He knew, as no other man had, that *what God has done God can do*, that what was true of Him must be potentially true of all men.

Charles Fillmore, one of the great spiritual giants of this century, had this to say about Jesus:

He was more than Jesus of Nazareth, more than any other man who ever lived on earth. He was more than man, as we understand the appellation in its everyday use, because there came into His manhood a factor to which most men are strangers. This factor was the Christ consciousness. The unfoldment of this consciousness by Jesus made Him God incarnate, because Christ is the Mind of God individualized. We cannot separate Jesus Christ from God or tell where man leaves off and God begins in Him. To say that we are men as Jesus was a man is not exactly true, because He had dropped that personal consciousness by which we separate ourselves from our true God self. . . . He became consciously one with the absolute principle of Being. He proved in His resurrection and ascension that He had no consciousness separate from that of Being, therefore He was this Being to all intent and purpose. *Yet He attained no more than what is expected of every one of us.*[1]

When Jesus says, "Follow me," He is referring to our acceptance of the high level of consciousness that He achieved. And, because consciousness often runs in streams, we can follow the trail of His radiant consciousness. We must see Jesus as the great discoverer of the Divinity of Man, the pioneer and way-shower in the great world of the within. We must carefully study and then emphatically reject our historical tendency to worship Jesus. When He becomes the object of our worship, He ceases to be the way-shower for our own self-realization and self-unfoldment.

Jesus came at a time when the wall of separation between man and God was high and wide. Man was living in the darkness of spiritual ignorance. He had an intuitive feeling about a higher power, a greater life. This feeling has lit the fires on every altar through the ages, built every temple, made every creed articulate, and supported every prayer. But there was always a great void separating man and God.

Jesus' discovery created a breach in the wall, "the middle wall of partition." In a way, He created a window in the wall, a great picture window through which man can view the vast and beautiful panorama of the spiritual dimension of life. When He said, "Come unto me," He was inviting His disciples of all times to come and sit with Him and view the infinite reality of things from the perspective that He had found. His finger is pointing out through the window, not at Himself. "Don't look at me," He is saying, "but look to the Spirit as I am looking to the Spirit. See yourself in the light of the Christ as I have seen myself in this light. Believe on me and the actual demonstrations of the Divinity of Man which I have made, and realize what this really means: that you have this same potential within you. What I have done, you can do. I have created the window—let us look through it together. Never forget this window, for it is your 'inlet and outlet to all there is in God.' "

The window was something to be seen through, not to be looked at. The disciples were slow to comprehend; but most of them did eventually see the picture. They, in turn, gathered other disciples, who came to the window to see through to the ultimate reality of unity with God. Generations passed. The contagious influence of Jesus' initial discovery slowly faded. Oh, people still came to the window, for in time it was a ritual of worship. A few still looked through the window, but the majority simply stared at the window in all its austerity.

In time, the window became old, dusty, and opaque. Now almost no one sees through the window. It is the object instead of the medium. It is adorned with gold and gems. It is made into an altar. It is the focal point of worship in every home or cathedral. Millions upon millions of devotees through the ages have come and knelt before this window, but only occasionally does a clear-minded thinker clean the darkened glass and see *through* the window. It is still there, and the great discovery made by Jesus is still as relevant to the life of the individual as it was two-thousand years ago. Anyone may wipe away the dusty concepts and have a firsthand and immediate experience of unity with God. You may know the Truth and find your freedom to become what God has created you to be.

Paul, the Great Christian leader whose awakening involved some window-washing of his own, seems to point to Jesus' great discovery when he says:

For we know in part, and we prophesy in part; but when that which is perfect is come, that which is in part shall be done away. When I was a child, I spake as a child, I felt as a child, I thought as a child: now that I am become a man, I have put away childish things. For now we see in a mirror, darkly; but then face to face: now I know in part; but then shall I know fully even as also I was fully known [I Cor. 13:9–12].

The verse of scripture most commonly uttered by Christian preachers has been John 3:16: "For God so loved the world that he gave his only begotten Son, that whosoever believeth on him should not perish, but have eternal life." This has been cited as positive proof of the divinity of Jesus, and of His special dispensation as *the* Son of God. However, note how this takes on new meaning when we see it through the perception of Meister Eckhart, one of the great mystics of the Middle Ages. He says that God never begot but one Son, but the eternal is forever begetting the only begotten.

The "only begotten" is spiritual man, the Christ principle, the principle of the Divinity of Man. The "only begotten son" is that which is begotten *only* of God. There is that in all of us that is begotten of many sources. One person may be begotten of an alcoholic father and thus may appear to repeat his traits of weakness. Another may be begotten of ancestors who have a history of a certain disease, so he accepts this as his lot in life. And many of us are subliminally begotten of the exploitation by advertising in newspapers, magazines, radio and television—so that we develop the motivations that business is cultivating for its own profit.

But John 3:16 is saying, "God's love is so great, His wisdom so infinite, that He has given unto man that which is pure and perfect, that which is begotten *only* of Him. No matter what a man may experience, he is after all a child of God, and he always has within him the infinite potential of the Christ. Whoever believes this about himself—really believes that he is 'the inlet and may become the outlet of all there is in God'—will not die but will have everlasting life." This is not a proof of Jesus' divinity. It is rather a restatement of His discovery of the Divinity of Man, which He proved. He discovered *that* in Himself which was begotten only of God, and He believed it so completely that even death and the tomb could not hold Him.

Ralph Waldo Emerson says: "Alone in all history. He estimates the greatness of man. One man was true to what is in me and you. He saw that God incarnates Himself in man, and ever more goes forth anew to take possession of the world."[2]

Historically, the Gospel story commences with the birth of Jesus and the tender story of Christmas. However, when one is interested in the spiritual and metaphysical keys, he must begin with the first chapter of John, which starts with the mystical words: "In the beginning was the Word, and the Word was with God, and the Word was God. The same was in the beginning with God." Confusing *Jesus* and the *Christ*, confusing the aspiring man with the principle by which He conquered, theologians have assumed that John refers to Jesus when he uses "the Word." The Greek *logos*, the Word, as used here means Divine Mind in action, the divine archetypal idea of perfect man.

"Christ" is not a person. It is *not* Jesus. Christ is a degree of stature that Jesus attained, but a degree of potential stature that dwells in every man. Paul said, "Christ in *you*, the hope of glory" (Col. 1:27).

In Him was life; and the life was the light of men. [John, in the first chapter of his Gospel, is still referring to the *logos*, the principle of divine sonship, the indwelling Christ-potential.] . . . There was the true light, even the light which lighteth every man coming into the world. [If any man does anything creative or dynamic, he does it "not of myself but through Christ who strengthens me."] He was in the world, and the world was made through Him, and the world knew Him not. [This is the world of your own thinking, the world of your experience that is shaped by consciousness. No matter how you may have perverted the God-potential in your experience, the Christ in you is still your creative genius.] He came unto His own, and they that were His own received Him not. But as many as received Him, to them gave He the right to become children of God. [You are a perfect son of God by right of the Christ-principle by which you are created and sustained. But this potential does not become a conscious influence and a practical power until you "receive Him," or come to believe and act as if you believed that you are the limitless expression of the Infinite Life, Substance and Intelligence of God.]

And then in John 1:14 we read, "And the Word became flesh, and dwelt among us." Now for the first time John is talking about Jesus. But even here the reference is to Jesus after He had made the break-through within Himself to the spirit, after He had made the great discovery of the Divinity of Man and had consciously fulfilled Paul's admonition, "Let the word of Christ dwell in you richly" (Col. 3:16). Jesus had lifted Himself to the complete consciousness of the Word, and thus, in His mountaintop moments, He *was* the Word to all intent and purpose.

In the ultimate, every man must fulfill this mystic utterance for himself: "And the Word became flesh, and dwelt among us." We, too, like Jesus, must make the great discovery of the Divinity of Man, and make the ideal of the Christ in us real in the flesh. For this principle of the Divinity of Man, realized by the young lad on the hills of Judea, is a universal principle—it is the law of life, the law of *your* life. By this law, by this principle of the Christ indwelling, you can do all that you need to do. You can even do all that Jesus did, "and greater things than these shall you do."

Obviously, this is a long-range goal. We are not going to achieve this divine fulfillment in a day or a year, or in one lifetime. But we are challenged to "press on toward . . . the high calling of God" (Phil. 3:14). Along the way there is freedom for us and abundant living. The important thing is to be faced in the right direction—moving forward. We will discuss this direction in our next chapter.

3 The Great Decision

Know this, O man, sole root of sin in thee
Is not to know thine own divinity!
Author unknown

RECENTLY, while driving on a winding mountain road, I came to a crude sign painted on the mountainside. Its message was simply, "Repent, the end is near." The sign was well placed if the purpose was to motivate the traveler to turn to God out of the fear of the treacherous hairpin turns and the thousand-foot-drop embankment. I am always a little saddened at this form of Christian evangelism. I have a feeling that it turns more people from "the way" than toward it. It is an evidence of how far man has strayed from the simple open-sky-and-hillside teachings of Jesus.

What did Jesus really teach? The answer is not easy to formulate, simply because we have been so conditioned by the religion *about* Jesus. For the religion *of Jesus*, we can only turn to the four Gospels of the New Testament and read the words as they have been recorded.

Jesus did not come to found a new religion. He said, "Think not that I came to destroy the law or the prophets: I came not to destroy, but to fulfill" (Matt. 5:17). He sought only to upgrade the teachings of the prophets, to interpret the ancient truths in the light of contemporary experience. He formulated no creeds. He created no ritual, He developed no theology. The alpha and omega of His

14

teaching was the Divinity of Man. He said to the people, "Is it not written in your law, I said, ye are gods?" (John 10:34). His was a vitalizing religion of the Spirit, leading men and women to a direct, personal, intimate relationship with the Father, where the element of immediacy is primal, and not through the intermediary of some other person or agency.

Occasionally we hear someone say that he has "gotten religion." What does this mean? Does it mean he has developed a new feeling toward life, or that he has simply subscribed to a new set of "custom-made convictions?" Can a person's religion be defined by the church he attends or the creed he accepts? Or is Christopher Morley right when he says that you have to guess at it by how you find yourself acting?

Christianity is not an end in itself. You cannot complete the work of salvation or enter the Kingdom of Heaven merely by joining a church or professing a creed. What is called "conversion" is not the end of the road. Maybe it is simply finding *a* road on which to travel. To Jesus, religion was not simply a way of believing or worshipping—it was a way of living.

A traveler in ancient Greece had lost his way and, seeking to find it, asked directions of a man by the roadside who turned out to be Socrates. "How can I reach Mt. Olympus?" asked the traveler. To this Socrates is said to have gravely replied, "Just make every step you take go in that direction."

It is probably true that every man intuitively knows that there is a highway of right living and that he is never completely satisfied with himself or his world until he finds the road to his own "Mt. Olympus." And it may be that this dissatisfaction leads to the indefinable yearning and hunger and thirst that causes the excesses that plague mankind. He feels the inner urge but he usually moves in the wrong direction to fulfill it.

Jesus said, "Enter ye in by the narrow gate: for wide is the gate, and broad is the way, that leadeth to destruction, and many are they that enter in thereby. For narrow is the gate, and straitened the way, that leadeth unto life, and few are they that find it" (Matt. 7:13, 14).

This has been a familiar theme of fundamental Christianity. The "straight and narrow" path has been presented in a manner that has left the individual "strait-laced and narrow-minded." Today, there is an open rebellion from that kind of religion.

Consider the extent to which the word "broad" has become popular. It is a glittering adjective. To many people, it means freedom from crippling confinements. The best thing you can call a man today is "broad-minded"— and the worst thing you can call him is "narrow-minded."

I have heard people rejoice in the fact that they have found a religion that is "broad-minded," by which they mean a religion that will take them as they are and make no effort to change them, a religion that gives them freedom—the freedom to do as they please. But religion that does not promote transformation is no religion at all. You might as well say, "I have found an engineering school that is broad-minded, that will make no effort to change me." If there were such a school, it would be a waste of time and money to enroll in it.

There is only one way under the sun by which man can achieve his "Mt. Olympus"—that is to say, achieve the realization and the unfoldment of his own innate divinity (salvation, in the truest sense of the word)—and that is by bringing about a radical and permanent change for the better in his own consciousness.

There is no other way. Through the ages, man has been trying in every other conceivable way to attain happiness and security. An infinite variety of schemes have been designed to bring about happiness by making changes in external conditions while leaving the inner man unchanged. Always the result has been the same—complete and total failure.

Now we know that the nature of our being is such that it is only by a change in consciousness that outer conditions can really be altered. And this change in consciousness is the "narrow gate" and "straitened way" that Jesus speaks of. And, as He says, the number of those who find it is mighty small. Why is this? Because of the "pull" of the way of the world about us.

Paul says, "Be not conformed to this world: but be ye transformed by the renewing of your mind . . ." (Rom. 12:2, av). Here in just sixteen words, Paul reveals both the greatest problem facing mankind today and also the key to man's salvation. Why do we not turn back even if we sense that the "end is near"? Because we are conformed to "this world."

THE GREAT DECISION | 17

A French painter by the name of Daumier was often criticized by his friends because, talented though he was, he had obviously resigned himself to doing the kind of work that would sell. He defended his "potboiler" work with the remark, "One must be of one's time." But a good friend, also a notable painter, stunned him with the question, "What if one's time is wrong?"

This is a challenging question for all people today. There is a higher standard of excellence and of right than that of contemporary fashion. Again and again, the apology for one's conduct, for questionable ethics, or for indolence in work is in effect the same statement, "after all, one must be of one's time."

A businessman confided to me: "There are certain things about my business practice that I greatly dislike. I dare not analyze them too closely in the light of what I know in my heart to be right or I would not sleep at night. But what can I do? In the business world you are forced to meet competition if you would survive. The times declare that it must be dog eat dog. I don't like it but I can't do anything about it. It's just the way things are today."

Much of what we might think of as the sordid aspect of life originates in conforming to "what is being done." How many young people fall into habits of smoking and drinking and other excesses simply because "everyone is doing it"? And how many parents passively accept these things in their children's lives with the rationalization, "What can you do? It is just the way things are today."

There are few persons who are not in some way swept into conformity with the times. How many of us succumb to the subtle appeal of the advertisers and thus invest needless money in cars, houses, lawnmowers and all kinds of gadgets that are far more than our simple needs require, simply because "One is not socially acceptable unless he lives 'graciously.'" In essence we are saying, "One must be of one's time."

But what if one's time is wrong? What really counts in the individual life and the life of society is not the passing fancy but the ultimate level toward which we are moving. The important consideration should not be, "What is being done this season?" but rather what should be done toward the unfoldment of the individual and collective divine potential.

It has been said by a number of contemporary thinkers that the age in which we are living is an age without standards, an age without a philosophy, an age in which man is much more concerned with the means than the ends, more concerned with the tools than with the ultimate goal, more concerned with materialism than with spiritual things.

Jesus said, "What shall a man be profited, if he shall gain the whole world, and forfeit his life?" (Matt. 16:26) In the hour of personal decision, there are times when each of us must ask himself the question, "Shall I conform to the human standard of what is being done, even if this standard is not in keeping with the divine standard as I have intuitively sensed it?" We are not simply referring to religious ethics and moral standards, important as these things are. The great problem today lies not in getting religion into business and into human relations, but in getting life and light into our personal religion.

When one's religion consists chiefly of a packaged philosophy to which one has given a perfunctory assent, it is comparatively easy to handle without getting too involved. Religion in this form can be conveniently set aside when it might be awkward or embarrassing, or it can be conspicuously worn as a badge of conventional respectability where it might lend us prestige. A Sinclair Lewis character sums up his religion by saying that it is respectable and beneficial to one's business to be seen going to services.

Robert Sheldon's classic novel, *In His Steps*, tells the story of a community of people who resolved to meet all life's experience by asking the question, "What would Jesus do in this situation?" This is a laudable practice. But Jesus did not set the Christ standard—He simply followed it. The Christ standard is not a series of hard and fast rules for behavior, not simply an analysis of what Jesus did for men to see. It is, instead, a principle that Jesus revealed through His discovery of the Divinity of Man. His teachings are the revelation of certain fundamental principles pertaining to the individual, along with illustrations as to how these principles can best be applied in practice.

We all succumb at times to the temptation to condone our mistakes and weaknesses with the thought, "After all, I am only human. The divine standard is too lofty. It is more than I can attain. Besides, why should I lose any sleep over it? Everyone makes mistakes." But the greatest mistake is in believing that we are "only human." Our humanity is but the degree to which we have given expression to our divinity. We are human in expression but divine in creation and limitless in potentiality.

The Christ standard is not a restraint. It is an inherent potential, it is the law of man's higher self. It is the ascending urge within man that keeps him unsatisfied with what he is and does and drives him on to higher goals of living and being. True fulfillment, the goal toward which all men bend their efforts and shape their struggles, can only be achieved through "opening out a way whence the imprisoned splendor may escape" in every experience in life.

To "repent" and turn back, does not mean to forsake all hope of abundant living and resign oneself to sackcloth and ashes. It means to turn from the "broad way" of worldly pursuits that feed the hungers of the human man but starve the soul. It means to realize that life is lived from within out, and to determine to "cleanse first the inside of the cup and of the platter, that the outside thereof may become clean also" (Matt. 23:26).

Perhaps we have been living superficially, pursuing artificial goals, living under false standards, conforming to acceptable patterns in the world around us. To repent means to open the eyes of spiritual perception and see life in a new dimension, to see hidden realities behind every appearance, to resolve to face toward our Mt. Olympus and make every step we take go in that direction.

Jesus said, "Ye shall know the truth and the truth shall make you free" (John 8:32). What is this freedom? It is not license to live without restraints but the inward motivation to tame the raw spiritual power that is within us, to harness our divine potential, and to move in the direction of our highest good. Schiller holds that freedom is not doing as we like, but becoming what we should. This is a meaning of the word that should be broadcast widely today.

Occasionally, the student of Truth with a Christian orientation will become "hung up" on the concept of "accepting Jesus Christ as his personal Saviour." He may ask, "Is there any way that I can follow the Christian path without making a decision for Christ?" I must reply, "No, there is no possibility that we can either understand or demonstrate what Jesus is teaching unless we make the 'great decision.' "

However, let us be mighty sure of our terms. What is meant by a

"decision for Christ"? It is possible that many who hear the evange-
list exhort his listeners to "confess the Lord, Jesus Christ, as your
personal Saviour" are thinking of a picture of the man, Jesus, and are
emotionally prostrating themselves before Him. Yet Jesus said, "Why
callest thou me good? there is none good but one, that is, God"
(Matt. 19:17, av.).

Emilie Cady helps us to bring the idea of the Christ into the
context of our own experience:

We all must recognize that it was the Christ within which made Jesus
what He was; and our power now to help ourselves and to help others,
lies in our comprehending the Truth—for it is a Truth whether we
realize it or not—that this same Christ lives within us that lived in Jesus.
It is the part of Himself which God has put within us, which ever lives
there, with an inexpressible love and desire to spring to the circumference
of our being, or to our consciousness, as our sufficiency in all things.[1]

The Christ in you *is you* at the point of God. It is your "hope of
glory" for it is your true root in Divine Mind. However, you must
become conscious of this root of your being, you must make the
decision to act as though you are a spiritual being in potential. In a
way, making the "decision for Christ" is as fundamental as turning
on the light. You may be interested in the electrical energy in the
circuits. You may have a conviction that it can glow in the bulb and
make light in the room. But in the end you can have light only if and
when you make the decision to turn the switch.

With all the studies of Jesus, few have caught the real significance
of His life and teaching. He was man on the quest, man making the
great discovery of His divinity, man breaking through the psychological barrier between man and God, man proving the Christ in man
and his inherent potential for overcoming, for eternal life.

We have been misled by the focus on *His* divinity. We have
overlooked the fact that He focused on our divinity. He said, in
effect, "You can do what I do, if you have faith"—*if* you make the
decision, the decision for Christ. But this is simply a decision to
accept the Christ in yourself, to follow Jesus' guidance and make the
same discovery of the *unity* in yourself that He had found in Himself.

An English noblewoman was for years in mental torment as to
whether there was a God. Because of her uncertainty in the matter

she could find no peace of mind. On one occasion, leaving her home and many babbling guests, she went alone into the forest. There she cried aloud, "Dear God, if there be a God, reveal thyself to me." And at once she seemed to hear a voice, saying, "Act as if I were, and thou shalt know that I AM." This changed her whole life, and she found great peace.

This is an important key to understanding Jesus' teachings that have been so greatly confused. Jesus knew that He must realize His unity with God, and that He must act the part of this unity—actually act as if He were "the only begotten son of God." So we find Him saying, "I and the Father are one . . . I am the bread of life . . . I am the light of the world . . . I am the door of the sheep . . . I am the good shepherd . . . I am the resurrection and the life . . . I am the Way, the Truth and the Life . . . I am the true vine."

And in John 8:24 we read, "Except ye believe that I am he, ye shall die in your sins . . . then shall ye know that I am *he*." But here the word "he" is not found in the original manuscript at all. The early translators were puzzled by the absence of an object and thus they simply assumed that a word was missing. They changed the statement, "Except ye believe that I AM . . ." to read, "Except ye believe that I am he. . . ." Thus did the translators unwittingly seal off the true meaning, making the Gospels infer that Jesus was a special dispensation of God.

To the unillumined it just didn't make sense. But Jesus knew that "I AM" makes the only kind of sense. It is man's attempt to relate himself with the absolute, to affirm his basic unity with the Infinite. And Jesus made this basic affirmation over and over. Jesus did not affirm "I am the resurrection and the life" because He knew He was greater than death. He became victorious over death because He affirmed "I am the resurrection and the life." He was, after all, man becoming God, man on the quest, man in the process of overcoming. He was climbing the ladder of Truth on the strength of His repeated declaration of *unity*—"I AM the Truth."

Jesus was saying (John 8:24 again), "If you do not realize your basic unity with the Infinite, if you do not consciously identify yourself with the Truth through affirming 'I AM,' you will be relating yourself to all the material things and conditions of the world, which will bring a focus of confusion that will lead to deterioration and death. If you declare, 'I am tired, I am fearful, I am afraid, . . .' you will 'die in your sins.' "

To make this great decision to relate yourself to the Infinite and to act as if you were the "only begotten son" requires a complete change in your way of thinking. As the sign says, you must "repent"—turn back and be transformed completely in consciousness. This is the theme of Jesus' discourse found in John 3:1–15—Jesus' discussion with Nicodemus, a strict Pharisee and a member of the Sanhedrin, the ruling body at the time of Jesus.

Nicodemus said, "Rabbi, we know that you are an inspired teacher, for no one can do the things you have done, except God be with him." And Jesus answered, "Verily, verily, I say unto thee, except one be born anew, he cannot see the kingdom of God." Then Nicodemus posed the arguments of the intellectual man, "How can a man be born when he is old? Can he enter a second time into his mother's womb, and be born?" Jesus is shocked that a man so versed in the religion of the prophets would not understand this principle of rebirth.

Don't miss this important point in the Gospel teaching. It is the foundation on which the whole religion *of* Jesus is built. Jesus later said, "Except ye turn, and become as little children, ye shall in no wise enter into the Kingdom of Heaven" (Matt. 18:3). He was preceded by John the Baptist who preached, "Repent ye, for the Kingdom of Heaven is at hand" (Matt. 3:2). And he was followed by Paul who said, "Be ye transformed by the renewing of your mind" (Rom. 12:2).

A careful study of word origins reveals an amazing similarity between the words "born again," "repent," "turn," and "transform." *Conversion* is the term usually used, but unfortunately its meaning is normally limited to the simple canceling of membership in one sect and subscribing to a new set of custom-made convictions. The essential unity of meaning in all these terms is in the context of "change," "thinking differently," or "awakening." Perhaps nothing expresses it quite as meaningfully as "Ye must be born anew."

It is not easy for man to contemplate something as abstract and nonmaterial as Jesus' "Kingdom of Heaven." We find ourselves thinking in terms of time and space. Where is it? When will it come? It is not easy for man in human consciousness to conceive of himself as a spiritual being. He may well have been conditioned through his early years to accept Jesus as divine, *the* Son of God. But to make the "decision for Christ" in himself, to believe in his own divinity, to determine to think and act from the standpoint of his own innate spiritual unity with God—this is not easy.

So Jesus says, "You must be born anew." The physicist is eventually born anew into a world of atoms and particles. The medical researcher is born anew into a world of white corpuscles and hemoglobin and DNA. An actor is born anew into a world of the theater, of stage and lights and greasepaint and make-believe. Man must be born anew if he is going to achieve a meaningful realization of his own divinity and of the Kingdom of God within him.

Everyone who turns to religion is motivated by the deep-seated urge to let his divinity transcend his humanity, to express more of what he inherently is. Jesus' role, if we see it in the context of this great idea of the Divinity of Man, was to prove to man what *man* can be. And he says: "Don't delude yourself. There is only one way that you can release your potential. You must be changed. You must be born anew."

What is the principle of this change? If this new life, this new birth could come to one person, then it must be possible to all. And it is possible to all because all men are spiritual beings, whether they know it or not, and whether they act the part or not. Man is born as a physical being, but the physical is only the shell of the spiritual man which he is and always has been.

Consider the lowly caterpillar. It is self-evident that the caterpillar and the butterfly live in entirely different worlds, and no one would ever say that a caterpillar is a butterfly or that a butterfly is a caterpillar. And yet we know that the caterpillar and the butterfly are simply different levels of expression of one entity. The caterpillar *can* fly, but not as a caterpillar—only as a butterfly. He has the potential, but something has to happen to him. You can do the things Jesus did, but not as the man you now are. Only when you are "born anew" into a higher state of consciousness.

A caterpillar looked up and saw a colorful butterfly flitting around. He shook his head ruefully and said, "They'll never get me up in one of those contraptions." And they never will, either! The caterpillar just cannot get up in flight. Yet, as the caterpillar changes its embodiment, it enters a new world. Suddenly, there is a whole new set of principles at work, and he releases a whole new potentiality.

In human consciousness, man is involved in all sorts of limitations: sin, disease, privation. And in this consciousness, all the things that Jesus did were absolutely miraculous! Looking as a "lowly worm of the dust" would see, just imagine turning water into wine; feeding five thousand hungry people with a few loaves and fishes; healing people lame and blind since birth. Impossible! Or at least miraculous and beyond duplication. Yet Jesus dealt continuously with the higher nature of man. He healed and helped and transformed people by the power of *their own* higher nature, and not by any special power of His own.

Jesus knew that everyone had within him the divine level of being, and that in the Divinity of Man is the limitless potential of healing. It is because of the divine potential within you that it can be said, regardless of any medical prognosis, "You can be healed." Regardless of what evaluation we may make of our lives from the human level, there is that in us that transcends the human.

Now you can't make a butterfly out of a caterpillar and you can't make an egg spread its wings and float lazily over a canyon. More than this—you can't make a good man out of a bad man. This is logical on the human level of evaluation. But in a way beyond knowing, the caterpillar becomes a cocoon and then breaks loose into a winged creature of the air, and the eggshell breaks and the bird steps forth, and the evil man suddenly sees a new potential in himself and begins to act upon that potential.

When we know the Truth of this great spiritual potential within us which Jesus called the Kingdom of God within, we are free to become our unlimited self, free to do unlimited things. We see things in a different light, we react to a different set of principles, we draw upon a higher potential, a potential that has always been within us, which has always really *been* us.

Thoreau talks about this in one of his most lucid moments:

If one advances confidently in the direction of his dreams, and endeavors to live the life which he has imagined, he will meet with a success unexpected in common hours. He will put something behind, will pass an invisible boundary; new, universal, and more liberal laws will begin to establish themselves around and within him, or the old laws be expanded and interpreted in his favor in a more liberal sense; and he will live with the license of a higher order of beings![2]

To return to the question, "Must I make a decision for Christ?" The answer is "yes," but with a more deeply mystical meaning, shorn of the emotionalism which relates to the personality of Jesus.

Many people find comfort and strength and inspiration in the emotional acceptance of Jesus as their "personal saviour." And this is good. There is much to be gained by a deep inner feeling of fellowship with the Master. For we do not want to infer here that the Fundamentalist or evangelical Christian is wrong. He is laying hold of Jesus at a very vital and helpful point. But our thesis here is that *this is not the high level of consciousness that Jesus had in mind when He said, "Follow me."*

We must begin to see Jesus as the great discoverer of the innate Divinity of Man, the supreme revealer of the truth about man, the pioneer and way-shower in the quest for self-realization and self-unfoldment. We must see Him turning to His fellow beings, including you and me, and saying, "Come and sit with me for a while and let me help you to see as I see, to feel the depth of the Spirit in you as I have felt it within me. Let me show you the way, the highroad to your own Mt. Olympus. Let me lead you into the wonderful world of the Christ within you, where you will know, and know that you know, that you are a limitless expression of the Infinite. And I can assure you that when you realize the Truth as I have realized it, you will be able to do all the things I have done and even greater things will you do."

But you must still make that great decision to affirm your unity with the Infinite. You must still believe that I AM, and then work tirelessly to act the part. You must claim your freedom, realizing that it does not mean doing what you like, but becoming what you should.

Emilie Cady says, "Oh, how in our ignorance we have mistaken and misunderstood God, in consequence of which we are today pygmies when He wanted to make us giants in love and health and power by manifesting more of Himself through us! We would not let Him, because we have been afraid to say, 'Have thy way in me; manifest Thyself through me as thou wilt.' "[3]

We may use the phrase "let go and let God." Actually, this is little more than a platitude until we make a conscious decision to let God really take over in every area of our lives. We may be slow to make this decision because we do not realize that it *is* a decision. In other words, there is a lot more involved than simply saying to ourselves, "Maybe God can handle this better than I can. If He has any good ideas on the subject, I will be glad to consider them."

It is a matter of earnest resolve to see ourselves in a new light, the light of the Christ and of our own unique unity with God. And then it is the determination to "act as if I were and I shall know that I am." This is the "great decision."

I am confident that there are non-Christian students on the quest who may be reading these lines. To you, may I say, "Don't fight the words 'Jesus' or 'Christ.' It is the idea, the spiritual Truth, the divine relationship that counts. You can lay hold of the Christian dynamic even if you mentally substitute the words "force," "genius," "potential" or any concepts that are meaningful to you.

Startling as it may sound, a man may hug Jesus to his breast in emotional adoration and still miss the dynamic that Jesus came to reveal, while another man may deny that Jesus ever lived and still catch the essence of His great Truth. As for me, fellowship with Jesus is invaluable in helping me to "learn of Him," to know the Truth as He knew it. But I am convinced that "accepting Jesus" is not indispensable to the student on the quest. The important goal for all is to find our unity with God. Achieve that unity and we will be doing as He did, even if we are not believing in Jesus.

Don't confuse the concept of affirming the Christ within you with the traditional acceptance of Jesus Christ. Jesus is the man who became divine through discovery of the dynamic that is innate within all men. But Christ is the self-livingness of God at the point of man. This is the unitive relationship between God and man. Jesus became so conscious of this Christ relationship that eventually we could not tell where one began and the other left off. Thus He became Jesus Christ, a legend, but more than this, a state of consciousness.

You and I can enter that state of consciousness. In the end we must do so—perhaps through following the stream of consciousness created by Jesus, perhaps through intuitively finding the way as He found the way. But we must all make the great decision to reach for the highest and to claim the divinity within us.

4 Jesus' Unique Concept of God

> The starting point in spiritual realization is a right understanding
> of that One designated as the Almighty.
>
> *Charles Fillmore*

JESUS had a unique concept of God. To Him, God was not an object of worship but a Presence dwelling in us, a force surrounding us, and a Principle by which we live. It is not too much to say that anyone who catches the idea of Jesus' concept will find himself caught up in a new consciousness that will change his whole life. He will never be the same again.

Ask the average individual if he believes in God and he will very probably say, "Why yes, of course I do!" However, it is unlikely that he has ever asked himself what he means by God. In a recent survey, some 90 per cent of the people who were asked the question, "Do you believe in God?" answered, "Yes!" But when asked further, "What is your conception of God, and what do you think God has to do with your everyday life?" only a few had any comment to make.

Everyone has some sort of concept of God—even an atheist. God may not have become a part of his personal philosophy, but even if he spends his time denouncing God, he reveals a concept of a being capricious and unjust, which he has intellectually rejected but which forever hounds his life. One avowed atheist told a reporter, "Thank God, I am an atheist!"

The atheist has at least engaged in some deep thinking about God.

27

Many people have not. To them, any references to God are invariably in clichés, such as: "the man upstairs" or "someone up there loves me." Parents compound their own lack of the consciousness of God in their lives by threatening their children, "You had better be good or God will punish you." And unthinking friends will often try to comfort someone in bereavement by saying, "God has taken your dear one home."

The thing that makes Jesus' concept of God so unique is that His gospel is set against the backdrop of the Old Testament deity who wiped out whole cities, who was jealous, angry, vengeful—who both loved and hated, created and destroyed, blessed and cursed.

A few years ago there was an item in the papers about the desecration of the cemetery of a little church in England. The minister, understandably infuriated by this act of vandalism, stood before his congregation on Sunday and, not so understandably, invoked a curse "in the name of God" upon whoever had desecrated the cemetery. One thing we know, this curse may have been in the name of his own concept of God, but it most certainly was not in the name of the God of Jesus.

Little wonder that some of our progressive theologians are proclaiming, "God is dead." Bishop John Robinson (in his book, *Honest to God*) says:

The idea of a God spiritually or metaphysically "out there" dies very hard. Most people would be seriously disturbed by the thought that it should need to die at all. For it is their God, and they have nothing to put in its place. And for the words "they" and "their" it would be more honest to substitute "we" and "our." For it is the God of "our" upbringing and conversation, the God of our father and of our religion, who is under attack. Everyone of us lives with some mental picture of a God "out there," a God who exists above and beyond the world He made, a God "to" whom we pray and to whom we go, when we die.[1]

The problem has been that we have been conditioned to think of the God concept of the Old Testament. It has not been properly explained to us that the Old Testament is the story of the unfoldment of the God-idea and of the relationship of man with God.

In pre-Mosaic Israel, God was conceived of as being attached to places, altars, trees, pillars, wells, and other natural objects. And Moses popularized the Ark, which was supposed to house God. They carried Him around with them in the Ark. If the Ark was captured they simply couldn't win the battle. In later times, the Ark was given a fixed place in the Temple. Thus, the Temple became the "house of the Lord." Today the idea still persists. Great throngs of people stream into churches, temples and synagogues because this is the way to get close to God.

Most of us have grown up with a primitive concept of God—a big Man, big and good, but still a big man, managing the world from the outside, a kind of absentee landlord. The attitudes of the little child toward God are not substantially different from the conceptions of primitive man, who found it difficult to conceive of God except as attached to something he could see—hence idols and fetishes.

A little child was tearfully objecting to being put to bed in a dark room. The mother attempted to soothe her with the reminder that she was never alone, that God was always with her wherever she was. The little child cried, "But I want someone with skin on." We may laugh at this, but many of us are influenced by this desire to clothe God in human form.

Too, we have been greatly influenced by the artist's visualization of divinity. A good example is Michelangelo's classic frescoes on the ceiling of the Sistine Chapel in Vatican City. As I stand looking at this tremendous work of art, I find myself saying, "Beautiful—but hideous." It is beautiful because as art it is breathtaking in design, in depth, in form and proportion. And yet it is a hideous demonstration of man's attempt to define the indefinable—to visualize the infinite in terms of himself.

Unfortunately, the God concept that dominates most Christian theology is the primitive concept of pre-Mosaic Israel. And Jesus, with His unique concept of God, has never really had His say in many Christian churches.

Oh, there have been modifications. For instance, consider the doctrine of the Holy Trinity. God in three persons. But what does this mean? And how did such a concept evolve? This is one of the "great historic creeds." It doesn't seem to disturb many that these doctrines were created during an age of speculation—when the bishops of the church gathered in great conclaves and argued about the nature of God and of Jesus.

It was in such meetings that most of the doctrines of the church were formulated. This was the evolution of the religion *about* Jesus. But what about the religion *of* Jesus?

The Council of Nicaea was called by Constantine in A.D. 325 to secure unity in the Christian fold for his own political support. The council was called for the purpose of hammering out a concept of God that would be acceptable to all factions—almost like a modern union-management negotiation. History records that there was a bitterly-contested struggle, during which Arius got up to speak and Nicholas of Myra punched him in the nose. Finally, the votes were taken, and with a narrow majority what came to be known as the Doctrine of the Holy Trinity emerged.

So, a group of men in debate determined for all time the nature of God. Now God became three persons: Father, Son, and Holy Ghost. No one has ever really understood it and it has been the source of endless wranglings and schisms. Oh, we can and often do make an interesting metaphysical case out of it. But strangely, Jesus, who should be the central figure in any Christian theology, had nothing whatever to say about the Trinity. Thus, it becomes obvious that Jesus was relegated to a secondary role in the Church that had sprung up around Him. He was important only as a fixture, sitting by the opaque window through which no one could see anymore.

It is much like a society wedding for which I officiated a few years ago. It was a sad spectacle, though it was a thing of beauty. It was beautiful because they hired an expensive wedding counselor who knew his job. He had everything beautifully organized and staged: lovely gowns, inspiring music, and a well-rehearsed pageant—for that is what it was. It was a sad spectacle because the poor young people who were being married were reduced to cogs in a machine. They were made to move on cue, to rehearse every little action, even their postnuptial embrace. Certainly, they could not feel the spiritual impact of this time of consecration. After the ceremony was over, I had a strong inclination to take them out into the woods so they could feel together the presence of God and experience a true union in communion. That wouldn't have been possible, though, because the party had to be seen (and photographed) leaving the church in a glamorous parade.

How often the worship service becomes a pageant, and even simple prayers become a performance, in spite of sincerity and good intentions! Probably, the weakest aspect of Christianity today is that there is seldom heard a clear articulation of Jesus' concept of God. For the most part, the church teaches the Old Testament concept of a God of the skies, a God of vengeance and wrath.

It is interesting to contrast the God of the Old Testament with the unique concept revealed by Jesus:

And while the children of Israel were in the wilderness, they found a man that gathered sticks upon the Sabbath Day. And they that found him gathering sticks brought him unto Moses and Aaron, and unto all the congregation. And they put him inward, because it was not declared what should be done to him. And the Lord said unto Moses, The man shall surely be put to death: all the congregation shall stone him with stones without the camp. And all the congregation brought him without the camp, and stoned him with stones, and he died; *as the Lord commanded Moses* [Num. 15:32–36].

Contrast this with an event of fifteen hundred years later:

And it came to pass, that he went through the cornfields on the sabbath day; and his disciples began, as they went, to pluck the ears of corn. And the Pharisees said unto him, Behold, why do they on the Sabbath Day that which is not lawful? . . . And he said unto them, The sabbath was made for man, and not man for the sabbath [Mark 2:23, 24, 27, av].

Or hear the prayer of David, "the man after God's own heart," asking vengeance upon his enemies:

Let his children be fatherless,
   And his wife a widow.
Let his children be vagabonds, and beg;
   And let them seek their bread out of their desolate places.
Let the extortioner catch all that he hath;
   And let strangers make spoil of his labor.
Let there be none to extend kindness unto him;
   Neither let there be any to have pity on his fatherless children.

And then listen to Jesus: "But I say unto you, Love your enemies, bless them that curse you, do good to them that hate you, and pray for them which despitefully use you, and persecute you" (Matt. 5:44, av).

A little boy, after having many weeks of Sunday School lessons devoted to the Old Testament, and then coming to the first lesson in the New Testament, remarked to one of his classmates after Sunday school: "Boy, God sure got better as He got older, didn't He?"

Certainly, man's understanding of the Infinite evolved over the centuries. This is not too unusual. From a scientific standpoint, we have a far different knowledge of the earth than people had in Old Testament times. Genesis reveals an earth that is the center of the Universe, with sun and stars that hang in the sky, and with the firmament overarching the earth and God somewhere up there behind the canopy. We have come a long way in science. And Jesus' unique concept of God was a long way from the concept of Moses' day.

In His discourse to the woman at the well of Samaria, Jesus said, "God is Spirit and they that worship Him must worship in spirit and truth." The Latin word *spiritus* from which we get our word "spirit" comes from a root that means "to breathe, to blow, to live." Spirit, then, is the *Life Principle*, the divine breath which God is breathing out *as* man and the Universe. The word "spirit" implies—unformed, unspecialized, unrestricted, limitless. When Jesus said, "God is Spirit," He was not giving a definition. You cannot define God. Jesus was simply giving a guide to direct our thoughts away from finite form, or from thinking of God as a superman.

When we think of God as a person, He is always "up there" or "out there." We are forever trying to find Him, to reach Him, to influence Him. When the first Russian cosmonaut orbited the earth, he came back saying, "There is no God, for I didn't see him out there." He *was* looking, so maybe he, too, says, "Thank God I am an atheist." He may not have *found* God, but with every breath he drew and with every thought he formed, he expressed Him. Maybe he didn't see God, but then he didn't see gravity either. Yet, if gravity hadn't been there, Ivan might still be following an inertial pattern to oblivion.

Paul Tillich, a catalyst for progressive theological thinking in modern times, referred to God as the "Ground of our very being." In his book, *The Shaking of the Foundations*, he says:

The name of this infinite and inexhaustible depth and ground of all being is GOD. That depth is what the word God means. And if that word has not much meaning for you, translate it, and speak of the depths of your life, of the source of your being, of your ultimate concern, of what you take seriously without reservation. Perhaps, in order to do so, you must forget everything traditional that you have learned about God, perhaps even that word itself. For if you know that God means depth, you know much about Him. You cannot then call yourself an atheist or unbeliever. For you cannot think or say: Life has no depth! Life is shallow. Being itself is surface only. If you could say this in complete seriousness, you would be an atheist; but otherwise you are not. He who knows about depth knows about God.[2]

You do not have to look "out there" to find the *Life Principle*. "Closer is he than breathing and nearer than hands and feet."[3] The principle is personalized in what Jesus referred to as "The Father within me." This *Life Principle* at work in you, and *as* you, is all-knowingness; "Your Father knoweth what things ye have need of even before ye ask him" (Matt. 6:8). It seeks ever to express and fulfill itself in and through you: "It is your Father's good pleasure to give you the kingdom" (Luke 12:32). And it is the source of any creative power you may seem to have: "I do nothing of myself . . ." (John 8:28). "The words I say unto you I speak not from myself: but the Father abiding in me doeth his works" (John 14:10).

You can never be separated from God because you are an expression of God, the very self-livingness of God. God cannot forsake you any more than gravity can forsake you. As an expression of God, you are God expressing Himself *as* you. And your greatest desire should be to let Him have His way. Meister Eckhart had this feeling when he said that God expects only one thing of you, and that is that you should stop thinking of yourself as a created being and let God be God in you.

Take a sheet of paper and tear it into little pieces. Now you have a divided, fragmented paper. The whole paper is the sum of all the fragments. That is division. But Spirit can be individualized. This means it may be manifest in many parts, in an infinite number of people, with each containing the essence of the whole. Each is *spiritus*, and the whole is no less for having been divided.

The true self of you, the Christ, spiritual man, is the individualization of God. You are the Presence of God at the point where you are. Thus, it is true of you as it was of Jesus, "I and the Father are one." You are an individualized part, but the whole is always in the part;

thus God is within you. However, God is not in you in the same sense that a raisin is in a bun. That is not unity. God is in you as the ocean is in a wave. The wave is nothing more nor less than the ocean expressing as a wave.

Sometimes in the study of metaphysics, we are so zealous to erase the idea of a personal God that we talk of God as Mind, God as Principle, God as Substance—but we do not emphasize God *as me*. Even when we refer to God as Mind, it is mind somewhere. We may use affirmations in place of the old form of supplicatory prayer, but we may still be reaching out and straining up to God "out there."

Though God is not a person, yet God *is* personal. There is nothing impersonal about God-Mind in me. It is my mind at the point of God-Mind, but it *is* my mind. I am sustained by the *Life Principle*, but that principle is expressing as me. It *is* my life. It is me. This is the great unitive idea that Jesus taught. "I and the Father are one"— not two, but one. The Father in me *is me* on a higher dimension of living.

Jesus' unique concept of God reveals a new concept of prayer. Prayer has usually been directed *at* God. Thus the typical prayer begs and pleads, is couched in pious language, is carefully intoned, and uses "vain repetitions." Jesus says, "Your Father knoweth what things you have need of, even before you ask him" (Matt. 6:8). In Jesus' concept, prayer is not for God, but for you. You pray, not to change something in God-Mind, but in your own.

Jesus' prayers were unlike anything that had ever been heard before His time. Obviously, they were disturbing to the conservative Pharisees. Jesus seemed to have an inflated ego. He was so confident of the results of His prayers that His efforts seemed almost brazen. Standing before the tomb of his friend who had been dead three days, He prayed, "Father, I thank thee that thou heardest me. And I knew that thou hearest me always." And then He spoke the word, "Lazarous, come forth" with complete confidence. (John 11:41, 43.)

How could He be so sure? Why is the mathematician so sure of his computations? Why does he have such confidence that the principle will support his conclusion? Simply because he knows it *is* principle. He never thinks of accusing the principle of mathematics for any error that he may make. It never occurs to him to trace the errors of his ledger to the principle of mathematics. To him, it is the most unerring thing in the world. And so prayer was with Jesus.

It never occurred to Jesus to trace the death of Lazarus to God. Other men might have thought that it was God's will, and that for some wise and inscrutable purpose of His own, God had taken this fine youth from his two sisters in the healthy prime of his life. Men might think that, but not Jesus.

The one thing fixed in the mind of Jesus was that "It is not the will of your Father . . . that one of these little ones should perish" (Matt. 18:14). Jesus interpreted the will of God according to Divine Principle and not in line with the old Jehovistic concept of God. It never occurred to Jesus that God would cause victory to perch upon the banner of one army over against the contending army.

Scientifically speaking, in order to have One God we must have divine principle which knows no change, which does not send evil or sickness or poverty or pain or perplexity. In James 1:17 we read: "Every good endowment and every perfect gift is from above, coming down from the Father of lights, with whom there is no variation or shadow due to change" (RSV).

Recently, I read a prayer by a sincere, intelligent man. He was talking to God: "O Lord, we ask Thee in all Thy clemency and tenderness and affection to intercede with those conflicting nations to bring peace instead of war; to change the hearts of men so that love will take the place of hate and anger and malice." Now, this is a perfectly marvelous prayer under the old concept; and one most typical in our day of followers of the religion *about* Jesus. But it is not scientific. It relates to a God who is variable, who can guide one person and restrain the other, who can say "yes" to some and "no" to others.

When Jesus says, "God is spirit, and those who worship him must worship in spirit and truth," He is saying, "If we want peace, we must get into the spirit of peace and affirm the Truth about it." In God "with whom there is no variation," peace is constant.

The question is often asked, "Why doesn't God stop the war?" There is no war in God. Why doesn't the principle of mathematics answer your problem or keep you from getting wrong answers? There are no wrong answers in the principle. If God knew war, or if the principle of mathematics knew wrong answers, then the world would be in a state of chaos. Water would run uphill and the earth would fly off into space to be lost in a wild ride to nowhere. Prayer can never influence God to be less than God or more than God. God is light and peace and love and wisdom. It does not matter who is praying or what the cause, the answer must be light and peace and love and wisdom.

That is why Jesus used the sun as a symbol for God. "He maketh his sun to rise on the evil and the good, and sendeth rain on the just and the unjust" (Matt. 5:45). The rays of the sun glint into the hospital cot, into the prison cell, into the palace and the hovel. The sun radiates anywhere men will permit. So it is with the great essence which is God. There is no place where God is not. He is not selective. He is there where anyone opens his mind to accept the within of himself. And even if the mind be closed, He is there anyway—for there is always a reality beyond every appearance, there is always a within to every man.

At the root of Jesus' unique concept of God was an awarenesss of oneness, or a spiritual unity with God and with all of God's creation. Paul refers to this unique awareness: "God in whom we live and move and have our being." In other words we live and move and have our being in an infinite ocean of intelligence and life and substance, and we are a wave within that ocean in which intelligence and life and substance are projected into livingness *as* the person we are. When we become aware of this unity, we are transformed from personality to individuality. In a sense, this places the entire Universe at our disposal and it says, "Son, thou art ever with me, and all that is mine is thine" (Luke 15:31).

Jesus gave an evidence of the cosmic vision of unity, where all men are one in God. While He was speaking to the multitudes on one occasion (Matt. 12:46), someone came to Him and said, "Your mother and your brothers stand without seeking to speak to thee." And He said, "Who is my mother? and who are my brethren?" And He stretched forth His hand toward His disciples, and said, "Behold, my mother and my brethren!" Jesus was simply explaining that in the cosmic awareness of unity with the whole, you are just as close to the man in the far corner of the world as you are to the person next to you, and you are just as much a part of the divine family of a person you have never seen before as of one who is your closest blood relative.

If you fly above the coast of the New York area, you see many islands: Manhattan Island, Bedloe Island, Staten Island, Long Island, Fire Island. And what are these? They are simply portions of the earth that have been projected above the water's surface. Beneath the water, they are all part of the common earth. In the same sense, all men are projections of God into conscious expression. As Paul puts it, "one body in which we are all members" (Rom. 12:4, 5).

This is the vision that runs all through the works of Walt Whitman, one of the great American poets. He says, "In all men I see myself. Not one barley corn more, not one barley corn less. And the good or bad I say of them I say of myself."[4] People did not understand him and still don't. But then neither do people understand Jesus' words: "Inasmuch as ye have done it to one of the least of these my brethren, ye have done it unto me" (Matt. 25:40, AV).

When the theologians cry, "God is dead," if this is disturbing to you, why should it be? If you have found yourself in the Presence, no intellectual debate about God can alter your inward feeling of unity. The theist who begins to sound like an atheist has a problem—but it is *his* problem. Why make it yours?

Perhaps you are disturbed because you have been leaning on a God of the intellect, a God preached about interminably, but a God whose presence you have never really felt. Thus, disturbing as the idea may seem, God is dead to you, if you are asleep to the activity of the Presence in you. If, like the Prodigal Son, you are living in the "far country" of superficial and materialistic living, then to all intent and purpose there is no power beyond the human in you, there is no infinite potential, and prayer is ridiculous. If you are not aware of the greater dimension of your nature, then it doesn't exist as far as you are concerned.

But when you come to yourself, when you wake up, when suddenly you come alive to the within of you, the depths of you, then God is very real to you—not as a person separate from you, but as an added dimension *of* you, as a living presence ever with you.

Now, when I said that if you are spiritually asleep there is no power beyond the human in you, this is not exactly true—for a very special reason, namely, the activity of what has been called *the Grace of God*. This aspect of the divine makeup of man has unfortunately been made either too theologically dogmatic or too metaphysically mystical. We must understand "grace," for it is an important facet of Jesus' unique concept of God.

You are beloved of God—simply because you are the activity of God living itself out into expression *as* you. God loves you because God is love and thus love is your true nature. Meister Eckhart put it bluntly when he said that he never thanked God for loving him, because God can't help Himself because it is His nature to love. "Yea, I have loved thee with an everlasting love" (Jer. 31:3). His love is changeless and without variation. There can be nothing less than love in God.

Why is your hand favored as a part of your body? Because it *is* your body expressing as a hand. Thus, the hand not only has the strength and creativity that is required in a given activity, but it also has feeling and tenderness. It is a hand, but it is also *you!*

God's will is the ceaseless longing of the creator to fulfill Himself in and through and as that which *He* has created. God's will for you is perfect life, perfect wisdom, perfect love. This will or divine desire is so great that it even seeps through our willfully closed minds. A person could continually declare, "I want to die—I don't want to live." By the action of the law of mental causation thoughts always tend to manifest themselves in experience. Yet this person thinks death and still goes right on living. Why? Because God's will for life transcends even man's desire for death. This is Grace.

Grace reveals a higher overtone of the idea of karma, the endless cycle of cause and effect. It is true, "As a man thinketh, so is he," and "As ye sow so shall ye reap." But God's desire in you to express perfectly through you is so great that you never completely reap the harvest of error, and always reap more than you sow of good. Isn't that wonderful? It might seem to negate the "principle" aspect of God, but it doesn't do this at all. It simply evidences the fact that we are all much more a part of this principle than we have realized.

There is a law of consciousness. Jesus makes it very clear, and we will deal with this in detail later in the book. But we are all better than we know. We have higher thoughts than we have realized. And none of us is as low or base as he thinks he is. Something of the depths of us is always filtering through and becoming part of our total consciousness. Thus, the most evil thought is modified by God's love in us, simply because we are really better than that thought.

Grace, the divine favor, the activity of God's love, works for us constantly. It is not dependent apon any special faith or prayer on our part. If we achieve greater power through faith or prayer, we achieve it by the law of causation. We lift up our consciousness and receive the corresponding action of divine law. But grace works beyond and in addition to law. It does not break law, but it fulfills it in terms of sustaining man in spite of himself. Like the buoyancy of water that holds a man afloat if he tries to force himself under.

Grace comes to all: by the grace of God the criminal who has broken the law is still loved of God, and he can find forgiveness and transformation through an activity of love that transcends law. Grace is an explanation of a wonderful facet of the activity of God. It is not something you have to work for. You can't stop it or start it. It simply *is*. It is an explanation of why things are never quite hopeless, why no condition is ever really incurable, and "All things are possible to them that believe."

Charles Fillmore says:

We must get rid of the idea that God punishes man in any way, or that He has made saints of some and withheld His grace from others, or that He will accede to our wishes and change laws in order to accommodate us, or that we are unjustly used because our poverty or sickness has not been removed after much beseeching. The whole order of our thinking must in this respect be reversed. God is more willing to give than we are to receive, and has actually placed every desire right at our hand waiting for us to get into the proper mental attitude to have them fulfilled, for God is not matter, nor do His gifts consist of things made; God is Spirit, and they who receive His gifts do so in Spirit; and through the spiritual wisdom and understanding which is poured into the consciousness they create through mental action the fulfillment.[5]

To Jesus, God was not simply an object to worship, but the very principle by which we live. Dwell much on the idea of your unity with God. It is the basis of Jesus' teaching, and the very foundation of the Abundant Life which He promises.

Remember God is in you as the ocean is in the wave. There is no possible way in which the wave can be separated from the ocean, and there is no way in which you can be separated from God. Because you *are* the activity of God in manifestation, there is no place in all the world where you can get closer to God than where you are right now. You may become more aware of God, but you can never change this closeness which is the Presence of God in you. This is the great Truth that Jesus came to teach.

5. From Miserable Sinners to Masters

I say no man has ever yet been half devout enough, none has
ever yet adored or worship'd half enough, none has begun to
think how divine he himself is, and how certain the future is.[1]
Walt Whitman

CHRISTIANITY HAS BEEN exclusive and sectarian, but if Jesus' concept
of the Divinity of Man could be clearly understood and widely
disseminated, His teaching would sweep the world and create a
great spiritual revolution. He taught, "Ye shall know the Truth and
the Truth shall make you free" (John 8:32). Man hungers for freedom from want, from sickness, from oppression, and most of all from
his own fears. The religion *about* Jesus has failed to open the way to
this freedom. However, in the simple but dynamic teachings *of* Jesus,
we have a message that is universal and practical. It contains the keys
to the kingdom of health and prosperity and peace and freedom.

The central theme of Christianity has been sin and evil. We have
heard more about Hell than Heaven, more about the Devil than
about God. And though we have been presented the picture of Jesus'
mastery, man has always been pictured as a poor miserable sinner.
There has been a kind of hopelessness in Christianity's attitude
toward man. It is as if we were taught that man is a sinner, the same
yesterday, today, and forever; and that all we have to look forward to
is to becoming a good sinner.

Recently, a man was confiding in me about his feelings for religion

41

and the church. He said, "I gave up on the church years ago and I'll tell you why. I used to go to church faithfully every week; and Sunday after Sunday I heard the same old broken record about the sinfulness of man, how we were all miserable sinners, unfit to darken the doorstep of God. I finally faced myself with the question, 'Why should I go to church week after week to have the preacher tell me how awful I am. I already know that. I need somebody to tell me about the goodness that is in me and help me to reach it. And if there isn't any goodness in me, then I might as well forget the whole thing!' "

How did all this come about in Christianity? Jesus discovered a divine dimension in man, and He proved that man can live in it and find fulfillment through it. More than this, He believed in a repeatable Christ for He said, "Ye therefore shall be perfect, as your heavenly Father is perfect" (Matt. 5:48). Would He have made such a statement if He had the slightest question of man's potential? And why would He say that man could do all that He did and more, unless He was absolutely convinced of the essential Divinity of Man?

A historical study of the evolution of the "historic creeds" of the Christian church is amazingly revealing—perhaps even startling and disturbing. The doctrine of "original sin" did not come out of Jesus' teachings. It was the deliberate creation of theologians in the early stage of Christianity. It was sincerely formulated to offset a trend toward rationalization among Christian scholars. In the "age of speculation" there crept into the Christian movement the so-called heresy of Gnosticism. *Gnosis* means knowledge. The Gnostics felt that they had a superior knowledge from an inner illumination, so they felt themselves to be superior to Christians, and equal or superior to Jesus.

This was a heresy to Christian leaders, and in order to offset this movement among liberal theologians, the leaders of the church met and drew up decrees stating that Jesus was "very God," that He was God who had come down from "out there," had put on clothes as a man and walked among men. Yet He was in no way human.

To make the distinction between Jesus and other men unmistakable, the doctrine was formulated of the degradation of man, the original sin by which man would be forever cursed with the stigma of humanity. Elevated to a central position was the statement of Psalm 51: "I was shapen in iniquity; and in sin did my mother conceive me" (AV). How this point has been labored in Christian pulpits: "Shapen in iniquity and in sin conceived."

Actually, this statement is taken out of the context of the inspirational nature of the Psalms. Without a doubt, some of the Psalms reach high-water marks in man's eternal song of the soul. But a few of the Psalms are songs of pain and despair. Such is the nature of Psalm 51.

Nathan, the prophet, has just reprimanded David for his dastardly act of sending the husband of Bathsheba to his death in battle so he could have her for his own. David is remorseful and, in Psalm 51, he is soliloquizing over his sins. In your lowest moments have you never said, "Oh, I am no good. I wish I had never been born." David is imagining that he certainly must have been born in sin and in sin conceived, or else he could not have done such a foul deed.

Here is one of many paradoxes we can find in the theological application of the Bible. We would not hold up David's act of stealing another man's wife as law for all men for all time. Certainly not! And yet we take his emotionally-prompted words of remorse and despair and give them a central place in our theology. It just doesn't make sense, but that is exactly what has happened.

It makes even less sense when we remember another soliloquy of David's expressed at a time when he was in a high state of consciousness. In Psalm 8, we find a complete contradiction of Psalm 51 and a wonderful tribute to the Divinity of Man:

When I consider thy heavens, the work of thy fingers, the moon and stars, which thou hast ordained; what is man, that thou art mindful of him? And the son of man, that thou visitest him? For thou has made him but little lower than God, and crownest him with glory and honor. Thou makest him to have dominion over the works of thy hands; thou hast put all things under his feet. . . .

The question, "What is man" is probably best answered in the most majestic statement of the entire Bible: "God created man in His own image, in the image of God created He him; male and female created He them" (Gen. 1:27). The "image" is man as God sees Him. The "likeness" is that which must be worked out in man's own mind and made manifest in his body and affairs. It is man's destiny to produce a likeness in the without of the image within himself. This is precisely what Jesus did.

The theologians declared that Jesus was God become man. But Jesus knew that God had already become man when He first breathed the breath of life into His own image and that image became a living soul. Jesus' idea of Himself was not that of God suddenly become man; but of man, already God's image, becoming like unto God. Did He not pray, "Father, glorify thou me with thine own self with the glory which I had with thee before the world was" (John 17:5).

The aim of the spiritual evolutionary process in you is to produce a man who completely manifests the inner life of the spirit. And Jesus' teachings deal with techniques that you can use to fulfill this process in and through you.

We see then that the heart and core of Jesus' teachings concerned not *His* divinity, but the Divinity of Man—the principle of divine sonship. He discovered this principle in general, and the divine potential in Himself in particular. He demonstrated the Christ-Spirit in action in His own life. But His ministry was devoted to teaching the universality of the principle, and to helping people rise from their sins to self-mastery. "And nothing shall be impossible unto you." Nothing!

We need to get this idea into our consciousness—that man, made in the image and likeness of God, is no mere figure of speech. It is a practical fact, a dynamic Truth. When the people sought to stone Jesus for saying that God was His Father (John 10:34), He replied by quoting Psalm 82: "I have said ye are gods; and all of you are children of the most High." And He added, "The scripture cannot be broken" (AV). He was saying in effect, "I am only saying of myself what your own law says of you. I don't set myself forth as an exception, but as an example of what the nature of man really is."

Charles Fillmore, who had one of the keenest insights into the Divinity of Man, writes:

What Jesus did we all can do, and it is fair to say that His is the normal standard for every individual and that every other expression of life is abnormal, the result of insufficient Christ elements. . . . We need not look for another in whom to witness the Christ, as did John, the Baptist, but we must look for Christ in ourselves, precisely as the man, Jesus, found the Christ in Himself.[2]

The word "Christ" is a problem in semantics. Because of a lifelong conditioning, most of us think of "Christ" and "Jesus" as synonymous. Lest it be thought that we are making a big issue out of a small matter, we must emphasize that this distinction is the hinge upon which the whole Gospel message turns. Unless we are secure on this important point, the whole structure of the Divinity of Man breaks down for us.

Get this point clear in your mind! Drill yourself on it. You will become aware of the frequency with which the distinction is either clouded or completely confused. You will hear people referring to "When Christ was alive. . . . When Christ walked the earth, etc."

Christ is not a person, but a principle. Christ is a level of the particularization of God into man, the focal point through which all the attributes of God are projected into livingness. When Paul says, "Christ in you, your hope of glory," he isn't referring to Jesus. Jesus discovered the Christ principle within Himself. But He revealed it as a principle that involved all humanity by revealing the new dimension of divinity. Christ in you is your hope of glory, for it is that of you that is of God and *is* God being projected into visibility as you. Christ in you is your own spiritual unity with the Infinite, the key to your health and success.

Christ in you is "the true light which lighteth every man, coming into the world" (John 1:9). In other words, this point of light in the heart of man which Paul called the Christ, was also in Lao-tze, in Confucius, in Zoroaster, in Buddha, in Plato, in Emerson, and (in a very real sense) in you and me.

The difference between Jesus and each of us is not one of inherent spiritual capacity, but a difference in the demonstration of it. Pontius Pilate and Jesus Christ were one as regards *being,* but they were poles apart as regards manifestation. However, we must realize that the principle of the Divinity of Man must extend to Pilate and Judas and a modern Hitler and Eichmann, or else it is not really a principle at all. Every man is a spiritual being. Every man is innately good. Every man is a potential Christ. But only a few know this, and an even fewer number succeed in expressing any marked degree of the perfection of the Christ indwelling.

It is not that we want to depreciate Jesus. We couldn't do that if we wanted to. We are not pulling Him down to our level, but show-

ing that we can be lifted up to His level. Low and base as man's
actions may at times be, he is still a child of God. He still has the
potential of the Christ within him. And this is the hope without
which the whole Christian religion doesn't make much sense.

It is not hard to find where Jesus stood on this issue. He said
(though there are those who would like us to forget it) that every
single one of us can do and be all that He revealed if we stand where
He stood and see as He saw and lay hold of the Truth as He laid hold
of it. Jesus did not ignore nor deny man's weakness and his outright
sinfulness. But neither did He insist that man was bound to weakness
nor that He was an incurable sinner. He implied very strongly that
sin is simply the frustration of the divine potential in man and that
what we call evil is simply the concealment of the good.

Jesus' heart went out to people because He could see that they
were not living up to the best within them. So He urged them to pick
up their bed and walk and to go and sin no more. He didn't enter
into any debate considering the worthiness of the individual to be
healed. This is one of the things that disturbed the Pharisees. They
felt He was usurping God's power of forgiveness of sin.

But you see, Jesus believed in the divinity of each individual, in
each person's innate right to health and fulfillment. He insisted that
the power that supported Him can also inspire and support each of
us to a beneficial expression of the creative urge within us. This does
not mean that we can all become a Michelangelo, an Einstein, or a
Schweitzer. We wouldn't really want to, for this would be imitation,
and Emerson was probably right when He said that imitation is
suicide. But there is a divinely inspired potentiality for creative
expression within each one of us that the world needs and is awaiting.

Jesus saw the divinity in people, and He challenged all men to see
the good, the God-self, in all people with whom they associated. This
is obviously what Henrik Ibsen, the Norwegian playwright, has in
mind when he talks about seeing a clerk behind the counter or a
common laborer in the mines and looking upon him as a Lincoln or a
Beethoven in the making. He feels that the man may possess the
potentialities of a transfigured genius or saint, a martyr or a hero, a
poet or a statesman.

This is what Jesus had in mind. Thus, He wasn't working magic or
committing blasphemy in His teachings and ministry. He was saying,

"You can be free from sin, you can overcome, you can be healed, not because I am something special, but because *you are* something special—because you are, after all, a child of God."

A light bulb, the simple ordinary light bulb that we have in our homes, has the potential to radiate the light energy to illuminate a room. If the filament is in order and if the connections are made, and if the electric current is properly plugged in, the light bulb will have light—whether the bulb is big or little, round or square, yellow or white, and no matter how it has been used in the past. It will light, simply because it is, after all, a light bulb.

You can be healed, no matter who you are or what you have been or done, if you make the contact with the "same light that lighteth every man coming into the world"—simply because you are, after all, a child of God. It is as simple as that. And this is the key to the potential dynamics of Christianity.

Yes, the great Truth that Jesus taught and demonstrated is amazingly simple. It is simple, but not easy. It is not really complicated, though it is true that we often do complicate its simplicities. Maybe our problem is that we lose our perspective in an intellectual quest in a maze of complicated metaphysics. The great depths of cosmic law taught or implied by Jesus reduce themselves to the simplest of concepts. But when we have them in this form there is nothing left for us to do except to live them—and this is not easy!

Not one person in a million is living up to the best within him. The great wisdom of the ages still lies locked in the depths of man's mental capacity, the great possibility of health and healing and eternal life still lies undiscovered in the depths of man's inner life, and the great key to success and opulence still lies within man's undiscovered potential. Oliver Wendell Holmes obviously had this in mind when he wrote:

> A few can touch the magic string,
>   And noisy Fame is proud to win them:—
> Alas for those that never sing,
>   But die with all their music in them![3]

When we measure man from the viewpoint of the human, we come up with a table of limitations. When we measure him from the criterion of the Divinity of Man, we must conclude with Jesus that "all things are possible." How are you measuring yourself? Whatever challenges you are facing, whatever desires you may harbor, even where fulfillment seems to be a human impossibility—remember the principle of divinity. See yourself in terms of what you *can* be. Look about you. Has anyone fulfilled what you desire? Then remember *what God has done, God can do*. Ask yourself, "Could Jesus have done this?" If the answer would seem to be "yes," then recall that He insisted that all that He did you can do, too! Such thinking may seem strange to you. It might even seem sacrilegious. Challenge yourself to keep thinking such thoughts until they become second nature to you, for that is exactly what the Christ within you is.

Jesus once asked His disciples (Matt. 16:13–17), "Who do men say that the Son of man is?" They replied, "Some say John the Baptist; some, Elijah; and others Jeremiah, or one of the prophets." Then He asked, "But who say ye that I am?" You can just image the embarrassed silence as the disciples puzzled over His meaning and searched themselves for an answer. It was Peter who braved a reply: "Thou art the Christ, the Son of the living God." And Jesus said, "Blessed art thou, Simon Bar-Jonah: for flesh and blood hath not revealed it unto thee, but my Father who is in heaven."

The point that is being made here is that no matter who it is we are appraising, we cannot really know the man by means of our knowledge of his background or by our intellectual analysis of his character. The only correct evaluation of any man is in terms of what he can be, his potential. Jesus is saying to Peter, "You did not arrive at this answer by reason of my personality, my physical stature, or by anything that has come by sense observation. You have had an inner revelation of the divinity within me. You have seen the Christ, not by sight, but by insight."

Let us be careful at this point, lest we lose sight of the principle of the Divinity of Man. This has often been used to prove that Jesus was the Christ of God, that He was God coming down from "out there" to live as a man for a while. Look again at this incident and you will note that it is Peter and not Jesus who is being lauded. Jesus had proved His divine capacities many times over by seeing into the heart of people and drawing out their innate greatness. But now it is Peter who has a flash of spiritual perception and who sees beyond the person to the real, to the divine, in Jesus. Peter reveals his own divinity just by the fact that he sees Jesus' divinity.

Jesus is delighted with this evidence of spiritual insight. He says, "Thou art Peter, and upon this rock I will build my church; and the gates of Hades shall not prevail against it. I will give unto thee the keys of the Kingdom of Heaven; and whatsoever thou shalt loose on earth shall be loosed in heaven" (Matt. 16:18, 19).

It is unfortunate that confusion at this point has been responsible for the particular development of the Christian church. It has un-equivocally been accepted that Jesus is saying, "Peter, I am so proud of you that I am going to build my ecclesiastical organization upon you." So literally has this been accepted that St. Peter's church in Rome is reputed to have been built on the interred bones of Peter.

What did Jesus really have in mind? First of all, we must remember that the man we call Peter was really named Simon. "Peter" was a nickname that was used only after this incident. The very first time it was used was when Jesus said, "Thou art Peter and upon this rock I will build my church." He was not naming the man but praising a quality displayed by the man. The quality was *petros*, which is a term similar to our word "faith"—it means rocklike steadfastness.

Jesus is praising Simon (Peter) for being stable and perceptive. And He is saying that it is upon this kind of perception that the church must be built. We read into the word "church" all that it has come to mean through the centuries since that time. But at that time, there was no precedent. The word "church" meant "called-out ones." Knowing that Jesus always dealt with thoughts rather than things, we can see that He was dealing with the aggregation of ideas in spiritual consciousness. Paul must have caught this meaning, for he said, "Know ye not that ye are a temple of God, and that the Spirit of God dwelleth in you?" (I Cor. 3:16).

The "church" Jesus talks about building is the inner life of man. He is saying that to build this inner life we must develop the perception to see ourselves and others in the context of the Divinity of Man. Actually, it seems evident that Jesus is giving Simon (Peter) something to live up to. He was anything but rocklike in character. He was the most impetuous and unstable of all the disciples. Jesus probably had been troubled about him. But in this flash of insight, "Peter" had given evidence of his inner potential. Jesus was delighted, and He gave him a prayer treatment to build up his consciousness of faith and stability. Later events show that this high trust took some doing for Peter, but eventually he did demonstrate all that Jesus had claimed for him and more. When we see it in this light, it gives hope for you and me, doesn't it?

Consider the question, "What is man?" Not what is this man or that man, in which cases we might be influenced by "flesh-and-blood" considerations; but what is man in general? This is not easy to say, because we have seen so many different levels of expression of men. Even considering one man specifically, we see a whole performance of his possibilities in various degrees of manifestation. It is like trying to answer the question, "What is a dandelion?" It is a tiny seed. It is a small green shoot coming out of the ground. It is like a miniature golden sunflower. And it is a puffball that disintegrates into a shower of tiny silver jewels with a gust of wind. But what is a dandelion? *It is the whole performance.*

What is an acorn? It is an oak tree in the making. What is an egg? It is the first stage of a performance that will lead to a bird. What is man? A man is what he can be. And what is that? Only spiritual perception can tell. Answer the question from the "flesh-and-blood" level, and you will define man as being limited to only one part of the eternal performance. But spiritual insight reveals man to be "The Christ, the son of the living God."

In all experience, life asks the question of you, "Who do you think you are?" The challenge is to get still and quietly reflect upon the whole man that you are. Humanly you may be terribly sick, discouraged, insufficient. But this is only one glimpse of the eternal performance of the soul on its journey to mastery. Is the dandelion only the tiny shoot? Are you only the limited person you appear to be or think you are? No! You are what you can be. And what can you be? From the standpoint of your divinity, you can be a perfect, healthy, confident, radiant expression of the living God.

Thus, when life demands of you, "Who do you think you are?" speak the word of Truth. Affirm for yourself, "I am a spiritual being. I am whole and free. I am confident and capable. I am the master of my life."

Today science is on the verge of a discovery that is called "the field theory of life." This is based upon the assumption that as the dandelion moves on through its performance or its little symphony of life, there is an electromagnetic pattern which surrounds the process and becomes the conductor and the musical score. Science may well be giving proof of the Kingdom of Heaven, which Jesus describes as located "within you." It may well be the force field which is the divine activity that is being specialized *as* you. It is what you can be. It is the wholeness that is in you even when you are experiencing limitation. Paul may well have had this in mind when he said, "Not discerning the Lord's body . . . many are weak and sickly among you" (I Cor. 11:29, 30, AV).

Adolf Portmann, the distinguished zoologist at the University of Basel, gives an exciting example of evidence of an electrodynamic body, in his book, *New Paths in Biology.* He asks us to consider the Planaria. This is a genus of flatworms which is found in river gravel. It is about as low a creature as you can find. If we are inclined to hark back to the reference to man as a "worm of the dust," consider the Planaria.

If you cut one of the Planaria in half, you find that each part, each half, develops into a whole worm. The front part acquires a new body, and the back part organizes itself a new head, complete with brain. Let us reflect on this astounding statement, "the back organizes itself a new head." What is this "self" which creates a new brain—a brain that must guide the regenerated organism as a whole? How can it create a brain without a brain to guide the process? This process of regeneration helps us to explain the healing process on which our own healing and well-being depend every day of our lives, and it brings us face-to-face with the secret of the self within us, the divinity within us.

When you are facing some limiting challenge or tragedy, when you are sorely tempted to answer life's question, "Who do you think you are?" with the lowest possible appraisal of "flesh and blood"— consider the Planaria. The whole is in the part. Even when you "lose your head," there is a directive force within you. The whole is always in the part. What you can be is what you now are even if you do not know it and are not experiencing it. There is help for you, there is healing for you, there is guidance for you. And this help and healing and guidance is in you, in the Kingdom of Heaven in you, in the Lord's body in you, in the Christ in you. But it *is* you. Claim it. Affirm the Truth of your wholeness now.

Obviously, we do not see this potentiality in the life of many people. It is not easy to see in any person, even in ourselves. That is why Jesus says, "Judge not according to appearance, but judge righteous judgment" (John 7:24). He is saying, "Don't be misled by the façade, by the personality or superficiality of yourself or others. There is always that of you that is greater than your littleness. There is that of you that is stronger than your weaknesses, wiser than your follies, better than your deeds."

Even the criminal is far better than he thinks he is. He, too, is a performance, but he is misreading the notes and creating a dissonance. The Great Teacher would see Him with spiritual perception, and would call forth the divinity in him as He called Lazarus from the tomb. He would say to the man, "You are a child of God but you haven't known it. You have been acting the part of weakness, but you are really strong. Accept this God-self of you *as* you, and go and sin no more." Criminologists must know and work with the metaphysics of man if they are to be successful in solving the problems of crime in our day. Prisons must be converted into institutions of *higher* learning, where we condition the criminal to know himself as a whole person, where we teach him to know and release the higher levels of his nature.

We have been chained to an unfortunate belief in "good people" and "bad people," and of "strong people" and "weak people." We assume that the world's problems are caused by the "bad" and the "weak." This concept must be changed. Perhaps it is one of the most important break-throughs to be made in our time. In the concept of the Divinity of Man, there are no bad or weak people. There are only good people expressing themselves incompletely, and strong people frustrating their potential of strength.

Many will object to this by saying, "Don't be ridiculous! Isn't it a fact that this man who committed the crime recorded on the front page of today's newspaper is a criminal?" It is true that the man is a criminal at the human level of his being. His performance is antisocial, and he evidences a depravity of moral or spiritual values. Yes, all this is a fact about the man. But what is the Truth about him? Again, what is man? Man is what he can be. What is this man? He is a good man, ignorant of his innate goodness, expressing himself incompletely, frustrating his divine potential. Granted, he has acted the role of a vicious criminal. But what are we going to do with him? Lock him up? Chain him? Punish him? But does this really correct him? Does it change his view of himself?

Do we really want to separate the bad from the good, the chaff from the wheat, so that the good can enjoy life in freedom? If so, who is to decide what is bad? Is it all black and white? Hitler made a decision to separate the "Aryan" race from that which was "impure." He even thought of the aged and infirm as "bad" in terms of a perfect race. Even with our criminal element, is it all crime or honesty? And what do we do with the criminal? Hitler's "final solution" was appalling, but what solution can we find?

The fact is that our whole program of dealing with delinquency and crime has been based upon an immature and unrealistic attempt to remove the aberration from sight. The unruly child reminds the parent of weaknesses in himself, so "make him stay in his room, till he learns his lesson." What lesson? That he is bad and weak? If a parent doesn't believe that all children are innately good and strong, what hope is there for society?

If we really want to help people in their discordant "performance," we will have to develop the insight that Jesus praised in Peter, so that we will look beyond the "flesh-and-blood" appearance and see the Christ, the son of the living God. We will have to develop the perception to sense the spiritual dimension of their lives, to see them as whole, to salute the divinity within them. A child comes running into the house after he has been playing in the coal chute. His mother exclaims, "You dirty little boy." But he is not a dirty boy at all. He is a boy with dirty hands and face. Bathe him and dress him and we find revealed the nice little boy that he has always been beneath the surface. There are a lot of people with dirty hands and faces, but there are no dirty people.

The German poet-philosopher, Goethe, holds that when we take a man as he is, we make him worse; but when we take a man as if he were already what he should be, we make him what he can be. The child who is taken only as he is—whose potentiality is ignored or slighted—remains where he is, or even slides backward. But the child who is treated as if he is already what he should be, often begins to make the most startling progress to what he can be.

Jesus sums up His teaching of the Divinity of Man in the parable of the Prodigal Son. The story says, very simply, that man is a spiritual being, but he must be "plugged in." If he is detached from his source, he "comes to know want." The young man took his inheritance and went off into the "far country," where he lived riotously. Living at the circumference of experience, he could only identify himself from "flesh-and-blood observation." Thus he came to know want, as we always do when we forget who we are.

The son and the father in the story are really one person. They represent: (1) the wholeness of you or Christ of you, and (2) the present level of performance of you (that is, the human and divine of you). The human consciousness comes to believe, with Yeats, that the key to life and living is not in the center but somewhere out in the whirling circumference. This is the first stage of what eventuates in sickness, failure, unhappiness, and inner and outer turmoil.

Eventually, "he came to himself." Suddenly, after much suffering, he saw his experience for what it was and he saw himself for what he was. It was as if he had been dreaming and he woke up. He said, "I will arise and go unto the Father." This indicated the firm resolve to return in consciousness to the whole person that he really was. And when he did in fact make this return, he was greatly blessed. The dirty boy was only a boy with dirty hands and face.

Regardless of the sinfulness of man, the depravity, the sickness, the weakness, the despair, he can "come to himself" at any time and find healing, because man is a spiritual being. There is no unforgivable sin, there is no incorrigible criminal, there is no incurable condition. This is the obvious conclusion that we must draw from the parable of the Prodigal Son, and from the principle of the Divinity of Man that it articulates. Jesus is saying that any man may come to himself and release his innate divinity. This is the goal of everyone, and every experience in life, hard as it may seem to be, is an opportunity to take the step that leads to the "glorious possibility" that you are.

Ernest Holmes has said:

There is hidden within the mind of man a Divinity; there is incarnated in you and me that which is an incarnation of God. This Divine Sonship is not a projection of that which is unlike our nature; it is not a projection of the Divine into the human. God cannot project Himself outside Himself; God can only express Himself within Himself. There is and can be no such thing as a distinct or separate individual that would be separate from the Universe. . . . Man is not an individual *in* God, for this would presuppose isolation and separation and disunion. Man is an individualization *of* God. . . . There is no God beyond Truth, and no revelation higher than the realization of the Divinity within us.[4]

There is a lovely Hindustani word of greeting or salutation, "Namaskar" (pronounced *nummusKAR*). It literally means, "I salute the divinity in you." The use of such a form of greeting could build the perception that Jesus was praising in Peter. How wonderful if we could always approach every person with whom we must find a relationship in the consciousness, "Thou art the Christ, the son of the living God." Namaskar!

Use of this salutation could help us to express the very best within us, and it could help us to remember to deal with other people as souls and not as personalities. It could be a fine affirmation to use when we find ourselves getting irritated or angry with someone. Much quicker than counting to ten, we could say, "Namaskar!" I salute the divinity in you!

We could use it for ourselves on awakening in the morning: Namaskar! "I salute the divinity in myself. I am strong and able. I can do all that I need to do this day. My mind is alert, my body vital and healthy, and my way will be strewn with golden opportunities. No matter what this day will bring to me, there is that in me that is great enough to meet it, overcome it, and be blessed by it. Namaskar!"

No matter where you are or what you may be, no matter how much you have lost or how little you have gained, no matter how far you may think yourself to be from the heights you have set for yourself or feel that God has set for you, the power to become is your divine inheritance. You can overcome, you can succeed, you can be healed—if you believe in your divinity, bless it, act as if it were the real and true of you and keep on in the effort to "open out a way whence the imprisoned splendor may escape."

> He whose heart is full of tenderness, and truth;
> Who loves mankind more than he loves himself,
> And cannot find room in his heart to hate,
> May be another Christ. We all may be
> The Saviours of the world, if we believe
> In the Divinity which dwells in us
> And worship it, and nail our grosser selves,

Our tempers, greeds, and our unworthy aims,
Upon the cross. Who giveth love to all,
Pays kindness for unkindness, smiles for frowns,
Lends new courage to each fainting heart,
And strengthens hope and scatters joy abroad,
He, too, is a Redeemer, Son of God.

Ella Wheeler Wilcox[5]

6. The Amazing *BE* Attitudes

IF WE WANT TO KNOW the basic philosophy of a scientist or politician or scholar, it is logical to study his speeches—especially those which are made to fellow members of his own profession. Thus it would seem equally logical, if we want to discover what Jesus really taught, to lay aside for a while the tomes upon tomes of sermons and essays *about* Jesus, and study the only sermon that Jesus gave that is completely recorded: His immortal "Sermon on the Mount."

The Sermon on the Mount is a well-detailed, well-organized piece of masterful writing (Matthew, chapters 5 through 7). Dr. George Lamsa says that he believes Jesus actually had a carefully prepared manuscript for this particular sermon, and this quite likely fell into the hands of Matthew. It is an interesting point, since Matthew is the only writer who records this sermon in its unabridged form. A shorter version appears in Luke (6:17–49), which appears to have been copied from the Matthew version.

The sermon proper is introduced by an eight-verse prose poem that has been called "The Beatitudes," which is a general summation of the whole religion *of* Jesus. He does not commence by saying, "You must do this" or "Thou shalt not do that." This was the style of the "law and the prophets" which underlined conformity to external practices such as keeping the Sabbath and observing the Passover.

Jesus speaks not of conforming, but of transforming. Paul reflects this ideal when he says, "Be not conformed to this world, but be ye transformed by the renewing of your mind" (Rom. 12:2, AV). The old order taught men what to do, but Jesus showed them what to be, how to think. Thus, the outline of His ideals is actually a series of attitudes of being, states of mind, clearly promising definite results that follow certain inner changes.

Jesus taught no theology or doctrine. His teaching is simple, direct, and practical. All the complexities, the forms, the ceremonies, the ritual, the customs and the costumes have been added through the long years of the evolution of the religion *about* Jesus. Jesus did not authorize such things.

Emmet Fox says:

Perfectly sincere men, for example, have appointed themselves Christian leaders, with the most imposing and pretentious titles, and then clothed themselves in elaborate and gorgeous vestments the better to impress the people, in spite of the fact that their Master, in the plainest language, strictly charged his followers that they must do nothing of the kind. "But be ye not called Rabbi: for one is your master, even Christ; and all ye are brethren."[1]

The Beatitudes (*BE attitudes*) begin with the word "blessed." It is an important word. To bless is "to confer prosperity upon, to enrich." Thus "blessed" makes a wonderful promise, telling you what will happen to you if you condition your mind to the full acceptance of these attitudes. In each case through the eight *BE attitudes*, the "blessed" is a one-word definition of all the good that will come to you if you understand and live by these amazing attitudes of BEING.

Blessed are the poor in spirit:
    for theirs is the kingdom of heaven.

We have been a long time outgrowing the misunderstanding that has stigmatized this Beatitude. Throughout the ages of Christianity it has been a virtue to be poor. "Suffer patiently through your poverty today, for in some future heaven you will have your reward." This theme has prevailed throughout the teachings *about* Jesus. But it is a misunderstanding of the meaning implicit in these significant words.

The root word that is translated "spirit" is more accurately and meaningfully translated "pride"—"poor in pride." Jesus says, "theirs is the kingdom of heaven." But keep in mind that "heaven," as Jesus uses the term, is not a place in the sky or a reward for after life. The word "heaven" comes from a Greek root that means "expanding." Thus, Jesus is talking about the expanding potential within the individual—within you. Heaven is the potential of the Spirit in you that is wrapped in your human nature.

To be poor in spirit or pride means to empty yourself of the desire to exercise personal will in the quest for self-realization. You cannot storm the gates of heaven. You cannot achieve an understanding of God through the intellect alone. Scholars of all ages have spent innumerable hours trying to rationalize or intellectually define God. No one has ever succeeded. History records that a group of theologians debated once for days about how many angels could dance on the head of a pin. This was an earnest though misguided attempt to find God through reason.

"Blessed are the poor in pride." Blessed are they who can let go of the attempt to understand intellectually, who accept the deep things of spirit as a little child. Blessed are they who are teachable, openminded, receptive to the Truth, willing to renounce preconceived opinions and prejudices and entertain a new concept of life.

If you go to college today and you want to understand the new science of the Universe in the light of what has developed in the Atomic Age, you will have to relinquish a lot of ideas that you may have learned as facts in high school chemistry or physics twenty-five years ago. In other words, before you can actually understand what is being taught, you must be teachable, you must be "poor in pride," you must be willing to say, "I don't know the answer, but I am willing to learn."

This is not an easy attitude of mind. To really *know* the Truth means so much more than knowing *about* the Truth. You may read many books and take many courses of study. You may even acquire a fine intellectual grasp of metaphysical principles. But to *know* the Truth you must keep on, beyond the end of the book, beyond the conclusion of the course of lessons. You must keep on until you catch on. It is not something you come to, but something that comes to you. It is an inward revelation.

A Rich Young Man once came to Jesus wanting to be a disciple. Jesus told the young man that he must sell all his possessions and give to the poor and then come back and join the group. We are told that the man "turned sorrowfully away because he had great possessions." This is a sad story. The young fellow just didn't understand. Jesus didn't mean that one must be poor to be a follower of Truth.

Jesus referred to possessions of the mind—mental baggage. And the young man was "loaded" with them. His problem was not his possessions of intrinsic worth, but his mind full of false values, including the notion that riches were the key to his security. In a very real sense he did not have great possessions. Great possessions had him! Jesus was simply testing the young man to see if he was ready to walk the path of discipline of mind and spirit. If he could have renounced his wealth, he would not have had to do so. That he would not, indicated that he could not enter into the higher dimension of spirit. It is a sad and sobering story with deep personal implications.

"Blessed are the poor in spirit," who are receptive to the flow of good through them and who acknowledge God as the source. "Theirs is the kingdom of heaven"—they will actually release the imprisoned splendor of the depths within themselves.

So, here is the first *Attitude of Being* put in the form of an affirmative treatment:

I AM OPEN AND RECEPTIVE TO THE INFLOW
AND THE OUTPOURING OF ALL THERE IS IN GOD.

Blessed are they that mourn:
for they shall be comforted.

This has usually been interpreted to mean, "You are richly blessed to have the tragedy and sorrow now, because your reward will come in a future heaven." I always feel saddened when I read or hear words of "comfort" for people who are ill which say that "it is your business to be ill, your appointment from heaven" and that "there is no other way to heaven except suffering." And the sad part is that these thoughts are given in the name of Jesus Christ.

But this is not at all what Jesus had in mind in this *BE attitude*. Jesus is not saying that it is necessary for man to sorrow or to experience tragedies, for there can be no sorrow or sense of tragedy to one who understands the dynamics of his own innate divinity. One who truly knows himself will not fall victim to sadness or grief, for he will always be the master of himself in every circumstance.

Nevertheless, sorrow and trouble, brought about by wrong thinking, can be useful. Many people refuse to open their minds to the Truth until they are backed against the wall, until they are "driven to their knees." In this instance, the sorrow may be a good thing, for a blessing may well spring from the fact that in the desperation of their sorrow they are willing to let go.

Jesus is telling us that there are two ways by which we may come into a knowledge of the Truth and experience the releasement of our inner power: (1) We can be "poor in spirit," and simply let go instantly with the receptivity of a little child, and let our Christ self express, or (2) we can resist the Truth of our divinity until our life is devastated by the fruits of wrong thinking, such as sickness and sorrow and failure. Then in these experiences we may find our self-will broken down and replaced by a new desire to reach for the absolute Truth of God. So, Jesus is saying, "The man who sorrows is fortunate, for in his sorrow, he may come to experience God's presence in his life."

It is not true that God sends problems to man, nor that man cannot find the heaven of fulfillment without challenges. However, the human of us tends to settle into ruts and routines and to resist the growth demanded by the expanding potential of our own divinity. Thus, it may well be that when some great problem comes to us, it is a fortuitous blessing because it leads us to "stir up the gift of God" within.

So, the second attitude of being put in the form of a treatment is this:

> I AM GRATEFUL FOR CHALLENGES THAT LEAD ME
> BEYOND MY EXTREMITY TO GOD'S OPPORTUNITY.

Blessed are the meek:
*   for they shall inherit the earth.*

Considered from the human standpoint this statement, or promise, is ridiculous. It is most certainly the aggressive and not the meek who inherit and possess the earth. In fact, the average individual has many discouraging moments when he broods on the great injustices of life, because "they" always seem to get the breaks.

Some have thought that Jesus is talking about a future millennium when these things would come to pass, when the quiet and the timid will have the upper hand, and the aggressive and overbearing will be rendered impotent. However, Jesus insisted that "The kingdom of heaven is at hand." His teachings always dealt with the *now* of experience.

Actually, Jesus is not talking about "meekness" as an approach to people. He is referring to an attitude toward God. Jesus was meek toward God. He knew that "I of myself can do nothing." He recognized that He was just a simple carpenter's son, who had found His spiritual unity with God, and in this discovery He had tapped the secrets of the Universe. But He knew that the miracle-working power that was now His came not *to* Him but *through* Him. As long as He was in tune, He could do all things.

The great tenor, Roland Hayes, always used to pause for a moment of quiet with eyes closed when he faced his audience for the first time in a concert. He was once asked by a reporter what he was doing. A humble man, Hayes was hesitant to reveal his secret. But eventually he admitted that he was praying. When asked what he prayed about, he replied, "I just get quiet and receptive and say, 'O Lord, blot out Roland Hayes, that the people may hear only thee.'" That is the meekness that compels God.

The Greek word, *praeis*, which we translate "meek," has the connotation "tamed," from the standpoint of harnessing that which is wild and unrestrained. Niagara Falls is an example of raw and unrestrained power. Tremendous forces are involved as the Niagara River dashes madly over the Falls. This vast energy was wasted for millions of years until we built several large power plants to harness the power for electricity. Today the Falls have been "tamed" as the water turns great turbines to generate electricity for many Eastern cities. We have become very dependent upon electricity, as the power blackout of 1965 verified. So the meekness of Niagara Falls has inherited the earth.

Meekness is a sensitiveness or surrender of consciousness to the influence of something. When Jesus says "Blessed are the meek" He doesn't mean a surrender to people, but to God. The best conductor of electricity is the substance that is least resistant to the flow of the electric current. Likewise, the best conductor of divine power is the person who is nonresistant to the flow of divine power. This attitude comes from a conviction that God is always the answer to human needs, and a willingness to submit wholeheartedly to the flow of the Spirit in and through us.

The man who is "fighting for his rights" is working in the wrong way. The only way to be sure that we get our "rights" in life is to "plug in" and let the divine activity of light and love express through us to do things in the right and perfect way at the right and perfect time. The artist, the composer, the scientist, the researcher—all demonstrate this attitude of meekness toward the law, toward the inner source of ideas. Einstein said that great ideas came to him after he had relaxed and ceased from strenuous search for his objective. The meek or receptive mind invites God-ideas.

The meek consciousness is not self-centered. It is God-centered. It is humble in the recognition of human limitations but confident in the conviction of divine resources. And it is not afraid of public opinion or of resistance—not even of failure. Because success to this person is not a matter of public-acceptance but of God-acceptance.

However, true meekness is not a show of humility or arrogant self-abasement to attract attention. When Thomas Mann was visiting America for the first time, one of Hollywood's literati abased himself before the novelist, emphasizing that he was nothing, a mere hack, his work not to be mentioned in the same breath with that of the master. Mann listened with infinite patience and courtesy, but when the party was over, he turned to his host, an old friend, and said, "That man has no right to make himself so small. He is not that big."

Realize that the great source of wisdom is intuition, the great source of vision is insight, the great source of power is innate spiritual power. Work diligently to get this consciousness of meekness which is the "taming" or harnessing of your inner potential—and you will become a master in your field. You will "inherit the earth."

Now, let us reduce this beatitude into a BE attitude. Let us affirm:

I AM IN TUNE WITH GOD—THAT WHICH IS
GOD-INSPIRED AND GOD-DIRECTED SHALL PREVAIL

Blessed are they that hunger and thirst after righteousness:
   for they shall be filled.

It is important to remind ourselves over and over in our study of the Gospels that Jesus is dealing with but one thing: "states of mind." As used here the word "righteousness" simply means "right thinking."

We have held a lot of "fuzzy attitudes" about righteousness. We have thought this refers to living by a religious code, going to church, carrying a prayer book under our arm, doing all the things that pertain to a formal acceptance of religious beliefs. It is unfortunate that religion for many is one grand cliché, and its practice is the repetition of pompous platitudes. This is a far cry from Jesus' concept of righteousness.

Jesus deals with attitudes and not platitudes. It is right attitudes that make the successful man. It is right attitudes that make and sustain good health. It is right attitudes that enable a person to overcome alcohol or smoking or overeating. No matter what your need, you can be "transformed by the renewing of your mind." A right attitude is the key to any desired good.

"But," Jesus is saying, "you must be hungry." You may desire healing and you may be affirming life and wholeness for yourself. But you must "hunger and thirst" for health, want it to the exclusion of all else, want it enough to let go of your feelings of self-pity and the satisfaction that comes through the sympathy and attention of others.

Often it is said of an athlete, "He is not hungry enough." By this it is meant that he is not living up to his best, not giving peak performances because he has become satisfied, complacent, and indifferent. It is not always the strongest or fastest or best that wins in athletics, but the one who has the greatest desire.

To "hunger and thirst for righteousness" is to want to be helped and healed to the extent of renewing the mind. If a person is in the gutter, the only way he can get out of the gutter is to look up and reach for something higher. He can be helped. He can rise out of the gutter of life, but first he must begin thinking "out-of-the-gutter" thoughts. This is true at every level of human experience. If a person is ill in mind or body, before he can get out of the experience of sickness, he must begin to think out of it. He must look up. He must entertain the possibility of something different in his life. He must desire it enough to reach for it—and reaching is actually accepting.

The story is told of a mystic teacher of India who used an interesting technique to impress his students with the importance of the "hunger and thirst for righteousness." He would take a student into the river, plunge his head under the water and forcibly hold it there until his lungs were fairly bursting. Finally, after letting him up, the teacher would ask, "What were you thinking about? What did you want more than anything?" The student would always reply, "Air! I wanted air!" "Ah," the teacher would say, "and when you want God as much as you just wanted air, you will be filled."

The fundamental idea of Jesus' teaching is that man is essentially a divine creature. The potential for wholeness is forever with him and within him. Thus help and healing are not dependent upon some special act or will of God. They are a matter only of man's faith and vision, his desire and acceptance, his "hunger and thirst after righteousness." If men fulfill their part, the promise is "they shall be filled."

So, here is another vital attitude of being to be built into our consciousness:

> I SEEK WITH ALL MY MIND AND HEART,
> AND I SHALL FIND.

Blessed are the merciful:
   for they shall obtain mercy.

This attitude reveals the law of consciousness. If you want to be loved you must love; if you want friends you must be friendly; if you want just treatment, be just. Life is lived from within out. You may not always be able to change the world about you, but you can change your thoughts about the world; and when you do this, you change *your* world, which is a world of your thought.

This is a hard lesson for most of us, for we are not conditioned to believe that we can solve our problems with people and with the world by an inner adjustment. We are inclined to think "If my wife would just stop nagging . . .; if my boss would just give me a break . . .; if the weather were not as bad as it usually is . . .; if this or that or the other would happen, then I would be happy."

Jesus is emphasizing that what comes to you is what your consciousness has drawn to you. You may not like what you see in your world, but it is your attitudes and reactions that have been the attracting force. You can change the pattern of attraction and change your world. This is why Jesus later says, "Love your enemies and pray for those that despitefully use you"—not because they deserve it, but because you must take a step up in consciousness to evoke the higher working of the law. As long as you have an enemy, you also have enmity. We may debate whether the enemy caused the enmity or the enmity drew the enemy. But that all becomes academic, if you want freedom enough to take the first step—neutralize the mental pattern of enmity within yourself. When you have no enmity, you have no enemies—as far as you are concerned.

Often, through a sense of insufficiency as a person, we form our attitudes after we have appraised our world. Thus we say, "There is danger before me, so I am afraid; people are staring at me, so I am self-conscious; people seem to be slighting me, so I am hurt; they say we are in for an economic recession, so I am worried." This is a common but completely unrealistic approach to life.

Decide the kind of world you want to experience, the kind of friends you want to have, the success you want to achieve, and the kind of conditions you would like to see manifest in your home, your neighborhood, your office—and begin to think the kind of thoughts that will draw them to you by the irresistible force of consciousness.

And the wonderful corollary to this law is that when you build a consciousness of love and justice and friendliness and peace, you no longer look for or identify with any apparent enmity or injustice in others. You actually walk in a magic circle of protection. You draw the best kind of people to you, and you draw the very best from all the people with whom you associate.

Let us build this attitude into our consciousness:

I KEEP MY THOUGHTS CENTERED UPON ONLY THOSE THINGS THAT I WANT TO SEE MANIFEST IN MY LIFE.

Blessed are the pure in heart:
  for they shall see God.

On the human level man's contact with the world about him is through the senses, predominantly through sight. On this level, he sees good and he sees evil, and life is a precarious experience. But life is whole, even though man sees only part. Thus, Jesus says, "Judge not according to appearance, but judge righteous judgment" (John 7:24). Don't let the apparent block the real, He is saying.

The human man will defend his appraisal of the facts of life. "Things are as they are and there is nothing I can do about them," he will say. However, what the eyes report is determined by what the mind believes. Shakespeare reflects this concept when he says that there is nothing either good or bad but thinking makes it so.

This *BE attitude* suggests the tremendous insight that will be yours when you develop an inward purity of thought. "Lift up your eyes" and get your thought centered on the good, the true, and the beautiful, and you will see God. This requires discipline of thought, for one does not easily see beauty in ugliness, life in sickness, or abundance in poverty. To "lift up your eyes" means to turn from the part to the whole, from the faulty projection to the image being projected, from the incorrect addition to the mathematical principle.

We have a paradox. We are told, "No man hath seen God at any time" (John 1:18), and yet here we are promised that the "pure in heart shall see God." The answer is really quite simple, but we should not take it lightly because an error is quite common. You cannot *see* God with the human eyes in the sense of locating Him in a place, manifesting as a form. God is not to be seen with the physical eyes, for God is a whole of which man is a part. Every part is a manifestation of God, an expression of Infinite Mind, an animation of God-life, an activity of Divine Substance. So every part contains the essence, and thus the potential of the whole. If man is conscious of the whole within himself, then he *is* whole. It was in this consciousness that Jesus declared, "He that hath seen me hath seen the Father."

When man learns to see in God-consciousness, then he sees beyond appearances to the innate potential of all that appears. "Righteous judgment" is seeing *from* God-consciousness. And this is the meaning of "Blessed are the pure in heart: for they shall see God." When you are pure in heart, when you are unalterably convinced that "There is only one presence and one power, God, the good, omnipotent," then you see God everywhere, you see good everywhere. However, you are seeing things, not as they are, but as you are.

This "seeing" is an insight which influences the outlook. The physical eyes are no longer organs of sense impression. They become channels for the expression of inner power. Seeing becomes an actual projection of God-power—a power of blessing. When you are "pure in heart," when you are established in spiritual principle, you view all things from God-consciousness. Jesus saw God, or good, in all men. He refused to settle for the belief in the partial man of sin or weakness or affliction. From God-consciousness, He saw the whole man within the part, and this seeing was the key to His healing power.

Man is not in the world to set it right but to see it rightly, and right seeing is the passport from illusion to the heaven of accomplishment. If you want to change the world, or to be an influence for such a change, you must begin within yourself by changing the way you see the world. Get back to the principle—a whole Universe, a whole man. See in this purity of consciousness, and you will project a healing or wholesome power.

Many preachers focus their vision upon, and week after week preach their sermons about, sin and evil. The Church would do well to embark upon a "new evangelism" based upon the omnipresence of God, the good, and the practice of viewing life from the highest rather than the lowest point of view. People need to be trained to develop a spiritually oriented insight that will lead to the positive, creative, and loving outlook. When enough people get this training, and develop the ability to see from God-consciousness and to project this consciousness by seeing the depth in every experience and dealing with the highest in every man, then we will soon begin to progressively unfold the millennium of Heaven on earth.

This is a tremendously important BE attitude. Let us put it into a usable affirmation for self-treatment:

I SEE THE WORLD, NOT AS IT IS, BUT AS I AM,
AND I AM IN SPIRITUAL UNITY WITH GOD.

Blessed are the peacemakers:
   for they shall be called sons of God.

This is an important key to the potential God-power in man. Man is a spiritual being, a true child of God in spirit—but he only becomes this in fact and expression when he is attuned to the Infinite and expresses his God-potential of love and peace. This calls for much meditation and scientific prayer, the diligent conditioning of the mind to the accepting and releasement of the dynamic God-potential within.

Man has so long functioned on the level of his humanity, it is difficult for him to acknowledge anything greater in himself. He may say he believes in God, but it is a God "out there," to whom he gives prayerful obeisance. He really doesn't expect any divine intervention in human needs, because he has not really believed in God in himself.

This is why there is such an urgent need for Jesus' revelation of the Divinity of Man. Man needs to know that he can resolve his deep frustrations over prolonged pleading to the unresponsive heavens for help. There is help for him beyond "the end of the rope." This help comes not to him, but through him. In other words, as a scientist recently put it, "Maybe God will work a miracle for us if we don't make it too hard for him." There is a miracle-working power within every man, but we must condition the mind to receive and express it.

The peace that we desire and need in the world is that which "passeth understanding." It cannot come by treaties or agreements, or by wars and boundary lines. Peace can only come when men become receptive to it and become peacemakers in the process of expressing it from within.

Now there is an important key in this BE *attitude* that must not go unnoticed: The peacemakers are not only called sons of God. That is the result that comes later. The first step is—they must call themselves sons of God. This is the action step: call yourself a child of God. Affirm for yourself that you are divine in potential. Declare for yourself: "I am a spiritual being with the potential for peace and harmony and overcoming within me at all times. I am a radiating center of divine light, life and wisdom." In this way we keep the light turned on.

Call yourself a child of God—and believe it—and you become a true peacemaker. It is not a thing you have to do in the world around you. In the most dramatic way, the world around you will be changed "in the twinkling of an eye" as you change. An electric light doesn't have to go out into the room and try to sweep away the darkness. When the light is turned on, the light radiates and the darkness disappears. It is as simple as that—but it is not easy.

So, let us work to build this *BE attitude* into our consciousness so that we may take our place in the world as bringers of light rather than as purveyors of darkness:

> I AM A CHILD OF GOD AND I ACT LIKE ONE.
> I AM A RADIATING CENTER OF PEACE AND LOVE.

Blessed are they that have been persecuted for righteousness' sake: for theirs is the kingdom of heaven. Blessed are ye when men shall reproach you, and persecute you, and say all manner of evil against you falsely, for my sake. Rejoice, and be exceeding glad: for great is your reward in heaven: for so persecuted they the prophets that were before you.

At first reading this would seem to be completely inconsistent with Jesus' *BE attitudes* up to this point. And certainly a literal acceptance of this has led thousands of people down through the Christian centuries to accept martyrdom with a kind of stoic passivity. Fortunately, this is not at all what Jesus had in mind.

Now we might as well face it, there are challenges to living the right or righteous way. A youngster who is ridiculed by his less principled friends because he will not engage in petty thievery is being persecuted for righteousness' sake. A woman is required to engage in certain practices by an unscrupulous employer. She refuses and is summarily dismissed. She is being persecuted for righteousness' sake.

However, there is a deeper and more meaningful application of this *BE attitude*. The emphasis is on attitudes. It deals with our thinking. The persecution takes place within our mind, and the persecutor is an errant thought of our own mind.

Whenever you set a course of righteousness, or right thinking, when you begin a program of discipline and self-restraint, you will invariably run into the crosscurrents of your own static thoughts. In physics, to move something that is still or to stop something that is in motion, you must overcome inertia. The inertial force holds a thing in rest or in motion until it is acted upon by an external force. There is a kind of mental inertia that resists any change. For even the effort to improve your life will necessitate coming to grips with the states of mind that have directed the kind of life you are now experiencing.

Paul undoubtedly was puzzled over this mental inertia when he said: "For the good that I would I do not, but the evil which I would not, that I do. . . . For I delight in the law of God after the inward man; but I see another law in my members, warring against the law of my mind, and bringing me into captivity . . ." (Rom. 7:19, 22, 23, AV).

And Jesus experienced the challenge of mental inertia in the account of His struggle with "Satan" in the wilderness. What is temptation but the inertial pull of limited states of consciousness resisting the upward reach of man's higher aspirations? Jesus had caught the ideal of the Divinity of Man, and He had set His course in the direction of personal fulfillment. But Satan, the human consciousness of Jesus, was saying, "Don't be foolish. You have fabulous powers by which you can control the world. You can be rich and powerful." But the "external force" of Jesus' unshakable faith and vision overcame the inertial pull of the human man. He said, "Get thee behind me Satan" (Matt. 4:10).

So now, when Jesus says, "Blessed are they that have been persecuted for righteousness' sake," He is saying, "there is nothing wrong with being tempted within yourself. It is a sign that you are growing, you are reaching for greater things even if the human man is pulling to keep you in lower things." The completely negative person is not tempted. There is no need for temptation, for he is constantly involved in negation. Wherever there is temptation, there is aspiration. Wherever there is a conscience over human weakness, there is an evidence of an awakening divinity.

The chances are very likely that when you take your stand in Truth, and launch into a program of self-improvement by self-realization and the disciplining of your thought, you will experience the "slings and arrows" of human consciousness pulling against you. Jesus is saying, "Don't worry about this, and by all means don't fight it. You are blessed because the persecution represents the first reaction to the 'external force,' and that force is of divine origin. 'Greater is he that is within you than he that is in your world' " (I John 4:4).

Jesus is saying in this *BE attitude*, "You have put your hand to the plow, so do not look back. You are on the way, and the inward persecution of the warring thoughts of human mind prove it. Press on past the inertial pull of your humanity to the releasement of your divinity."

This is a great and most important *BE attitude*. Let us give some serious thought in self-treatment to this affirmative restatement of this final preparatory attitude of being:

IN MY QUEST FOR TRUTH I PRESS ON PAST MY HUMANITY
TO A DEEPENING AWARENESS AND AN INCREASING RELEASEMENT
OF MY POTENTIAL DIVINITY.

7. Your Thought Is Your Life

God's greatest gift to man is the power of thought, through
which he can incorporate into his consciousness the mind of God.[1]
Charles Fillmore

WE ARE LIVING in an age of discovery. A day rarely passes when the
news media do not report the discovery of some new star or technique or cure or process. The pace of scientific and technological
discovery is almost unbelievable. Automation of production, com-
puterization of information, supersonic transportation, communication by satellite, the exploration of space, new uses for nuclear energy
—all developments of the last twenty-five years—are only the beginning. It is estimated that man's total body of knowledge doubled
between 1775 and 1900. It doubled again between 1900 and 1950,
again between 1950 and 1958, and it is now thought to be doubling
every five years.

This is a tribute to man's curiosity and his relentless quest for
understanding. But it is important to recognize that discoveries in the
world around us are really self-discoveries. We do not create the
growing body of knowledge. Man is simply gaining insights into that
which has always been. Nothing has really changed in the nature of
the Universe in the past two thousand years, but we have opened our
eyes to see things more completely.

Locked within the superconsciousness of man are the answers to all

73

the problems and the secret of all the mysteries that mankind will ever face. Man is a thinking being. The very word "man" comes from an ancient Sanskrit word which literally means "to think." Through thinking, man has the possibility of knowing God and expressing the wisdom of Divine Mind. Man is the greatest concentration of divine energies in the Universe. He is the greatest natural resource. And the world of possibilities within man is still the great frontier.

Jesus was the Christopher Columbus of the soul. He crossed the frontier of the mind and discovered a new world within Himself. He realized that man has the responsibility of keeping his mind stayed on God, so that the Heaven of innate possibilities can unfold into expression. He realized that the mind is the bridge between man and the Infinite, and that the important element in religion is not simply fervency and feeling, but man's thoughts and attitudes.

Jesus' Sermon on the Mount is the most articulate and practical outline of metaphysical Truth known to man. The object is not so much man in general as *you* in particular. The technique is not theology or symbolism, but the molding power of your own thought.

Ye are the salt of the earth: but if the salt have lost its savor, where-
     with shall it be salted? It is thenceforth good for nothing but
     to be cast out and trodden under foot of men [Matt. 5:13].

Jesus was a revolutionary at heart. He wanted to set the world on fire, to change the old order, and to establish the kingdom of right-eousness on earth. However, His was a spiritual revolution. He had no desire to overthrow governments. His object was to change thoughts. He was talking here to disciples and followers, telling them that great numbers were not needed to change the world order. Even as it takes only a pinch of salt to change the taste of a pot of stew, so a handful of dedicated disciples can change the consciousness of the world.

In Leviticus we read (26:7, 8): "And ye shall chase your enemies, and they shall fall before you by the sword. And five of you shall chase a hundred, and a hundred of you shall chase ten thousand; and your enemies shall fall before you by the sword." The enemies are the adverse attitudes and beliefs in the world and the sword is the word of Truth.

"You are radiating centers of the Truth in the world," Jesus is saying, "but be mighty sure that your awareness of the Truth is dynamic and not static." Your knowledge of the Truth must first of all lead to self-knowledge. In your study of the Truth, remember: "With all thy getting get understanding." If we collect Truth like we collect facts, fill our notebooks with pages of notes, fill our library with books, cover our walls with certificates of courses of study we have taken, then certainly the salt will lose its savor.

The reference to salt without savor being cast under foot is to the flat and lifeless salt that was gathered at Lake Asphaltites and put on the floor of the Temple to prevent slipping in wet weather. Salt of itself is a useless food. Its value is in seasoning nourishing food and in whetting the appetite. Many otherwise sincere students of "the way" *are overread and underdone.*

Jesus challenges you, the student, to accept the responsibility of bringing the spiritual leaven of Truth to the world. As Chaucer says, with reference to the clergy, "If Gold ruste, what shoulde iren doo?"[2] If you, who believe in the divinity of man and the omnipresence of God, do not act as if you believe it, then what hope is there for the world?

When you are seasoned with the salt of Truth, your own body of knowledge suddenly reveals a new dimension. The principle of relativity is made practical in a new concept of *unitivity.* You will come to see that even as the subatomic particle has no existence outside of the electromagnetic field that holds the atom together, but *is* the field expressing as a particle, so man has no existence outside of God, but *is* the activity of God expressing as man. All your scientific facts suddenly come alive, they become dynamic potencies. And with this keener insight, you become a seasoning influence in the world. You become a peacemaker.

Ye are the light of the world. A city that is set on an hill cannot be hid. Neither do men light a candle and put it under a bushel, but on a candlestick: and it giveth light unto all that are in

> the house. *Let your light so shine before men, that they may see your good works, and glorify your father which is in heaven* [Matt. 5:14–16, av].

We really do not know much about light. Scientists say it is "an electromagnetic phenomenon," but then freely admit that they do not really know what it is. We know that light waves travel the 93 million miles from the sun to the earth in seven minutes, bringing light and life to all; that a piece of coal is but stored-up sunlight that shone down on the earth millions of years ago—and that this coal may be returned to light and energy by the process of combustion.

In the same sense, we do not know much about the God-potential in man, "the light that lighteth every man coming into the world." But we see that light in the love and joy and radiance in the faces of people, and we saw it in the life of Jesus. Within the very nature of man, every man, there is a stored up substance or divine energy, like the coal in the earth, which may be stirred up and released to illumine the lives and light the way of men.

Paul said, "Stir up the gift of God, which is in thee." (II Tim.:6) And really, wasn't that the true mission of Jesus—to help all people to discover the light-energy within themselves and to let it shine? There are reserves of light within you, but they must be discovered and released.

The house referred to above, according to Dr. George Lamsa, was a square building large enough to hold between forty or fifty people. The house had as many candles or lamps as the number of families dwelling in it. Some houses had three to seven families. The lamp was set on a lamp-holder fastened to a pillar. It gave light to the family and it could not help but throw some light on the other parts of the house.

Sometimes, poor families who had no butter for fuel could not light their lamps and depended upon the lamp of their neighbor. They sat in darkness waiting for another family to come in and light a lamp so they might see. In a peaceful house, the people gladly shared with their neighbors. However, there were some selfish people who would rather not burn a light and be in darkness themselves than let their light shine into the house of another. They might even go so far as to do their work literally under a basket so as not to let their light shine for another.

Jesus is telling us through this striking example that you cannot hide spirituality. Students of Truth are sometimes embarrassed to let their family or friends know about their preoccupation, and thus they hesitate to take a positive stand on Truth in a negative situation. Jesus is saying, "Hold to the Truth and let the chips fall where they may!"

On the other hand, the student is often constrained to bring the Truth to his family and loved ones. Often, through his overzealousness, the very ones he is trying to help or influence become antagonistic to everything pertaining to Truth.

In both cases, the answer is "Let your light shine." You don't really need to put the Truth into words. Emerson refers to the possibility that what you are speaks so loudly that one cannot hear what you say. This puts the emphasis where it should be—on being rather than talking.

For every spiritual concept that excites you, get still and reflect quietly upon it until something happens in you. When you read something that seems strangely familiar, something that is inspiring and unforgettable, it is because the words have stirred up an awareness of a depth of spirituality within yourself. It is the releasement of this innate potential that is the object of all study. The words of the teacher, the book, or the course of study—even the words of the Bible—are not the object of your search, but the means to the end of a personal revelation of Truth.

The person who has the compulsion to introduce Truth to other people may well be one who is having a difficult time making it work in his own life. He has a large supply of facts about Truth. And he has "seniority." He may tell you over and over that he has been a student of metaphysics for "thirty years." This may be a parallel to the Israelites who were forty years in the wilderness. They had set out to find their "Promised Land," but though they lived out their lives at the border, few of them could bring themselves to "enter in and possess the land."

Jesus is talking to you who are timid about speaking the word of Truth, and also you who talk too much *about* Truth. "Ye are the light of the world." Isn't that a wonderful thought? The light of the world is the very spirit of Truth. You are the very activity of God in expression, so there is no place where the light of God is any more present than where you are. And there is no one who is any more privileged to radiate that light than you. "Let your light shine."

Think not that I am come to destroy the law, or the prophets; I am not come to destroy, but to fulfill. For verily I say unto you, till heaven and earth pass, one jot or one tittle shall in no wise pass from the law, till all be fulfilled [Matt. 5:17, 18, AV].

A nonconformist, an individual thinker, is always dangerous. Obviously, the Temple rulers were concerned, for Jesus dared to bypass form and ritual and the temporal rules of worship, and to deal with pure Truth. They could not understand a man who "taught as one having authority, and not as their scribes" (Matt. 7:29). How could a man dare to assume that Truth came from within Him?

By whatever definition we hold, Jesus was a mystic of mystics. It has been said that a mystic is one who is no longer mystified—by religions, by theologies, by doctrines. The Temple rulers were mystified by Jesus' mysticism, and they were mystified by their own creeds. Now these men were sincere people. The Temple was the repository of the accumulated facts about God, and the body of this kind of knowledge was tremendous. The rulers were the keepers of the keys, as it were, the defender of a faith that they did not understand. How then could they understand one who did?

The "law and the prophets" refers to the Jewish Scriptures. Jesus says that the fundamental law can't be changed. He is saying, "I am not bent upon refuting the scriptures or destroying the Truth as taught by the prophets. I want to help you to understand spiritual law, that the promises of your own scriptures may be fulfilled—and now."

The laws of the universe cannot be destroyed, simply because they *are* law. Men thought Jesus destroyed the old law because He fulfilled it so easily, and He did such amazing things. Sight was restored to the blind, hungry multitudes were miraculously fed, even the dead were brought back to life. Everywhere He went, He left a trail of puzzling miracles in His wake.

But miracles are miracles only because we do not understand the processes involved. The dictionary defines the word "miracle" as: "an effect in the physical world which surpasses all known human or natural powers and is therefore ascribed to supernatural agency." In Jesus' day to have picked up a telephone and conversed with a loved one thousands of miles distant would have been a miracle. Yet, even the least among us today make frequent use of the telephone and simply take it for granted as a part of our modern way of life. The impossible has been made practicable through modern scientific research. When you use the telephone today, you do not break the law as man once understood it. But you fulfill the law by applying it with understanding of a deeper dimension.

Actually, Jesus did not do anything that had not been foretold by the prophets of old. However, He accepted the prophetic vision and declared, "Now is the time." He proclaimed that the Truth should set all men free from bondage to sickness or poverty. He knew that the reason people were not demonstrating the possibilities promised by their prophets was not that God was withholding, but because they were not keeping the spirit of the law.

Jesus knew that the Spirit in man is a miracle-working power. He knew that we do not experience this power because we make it too hard for the Spirit to express. We judge ourselves and the world by appearances. We measure man's possibilities by his past experience rather than by his innate potentiality. God can work a miracle for you, if you do not make it too hard for Him. This is what Jesus was saying over and over. Know the Truth about yourself, about the indwelling potential of your own divinity. Know the divine law and open your inner eye to see life from a higher dimension. "Ye shall know the Truth and the Truth shall make you free."

Jesus then teaches a great mystical Truth:

Whosoever therefore shall break one of these least commandments, and shall teach men so, he shall be called the least in the kingdom of heaven: but whosoever shall do and teach them, the same shall be called great in the kingdom of heaven [Matt. 5:19, AV].

This is a vital point that can be so easily misunderstood, and usually is. First of all, let us look at this little word "break." My dictionary

lists more than forty different meanings. To break the commandments could mean to violate, to dissolve or annul, to suspend
temporarily, or to penetrate or make one's way through. In the
general context of Jesus' teaching, it is obvious that He has the latter
meaning in mind here. He is talking about breaking the commandments down into understandable form. He is clarifying them. A
commandment is both a dogmatic assertion in a catechism and a
fundamental law of life. Before the law can be fulfilled, we must
break through the dogmatic shell and realize our spiritual unity with
the underlying principle.

Jesus was first of all a teacher, and it is the duty of any teacher to
break commandments and teach others to do so. Jesus taught men
how to break down the crystallized creeds of religion and know the
Truth inherent within them. He showed men how to break the law
of the Sabbath by fulfilling it. "The Sabbath was made for man, not
man for the Sabbath" (Mark 2:27). In this sense, it is the purpose of
this book to break all the commandments, to clarify them, to
simplify and make them usable and demonstrable.

Secondly, let us remember that "Heaven," as Jesus uses the term,
refers to a present potential rather than a future place. He said, "The
Kingdom of Heaven is at hand" (Matt. 3:2). The Kingdom of
Heaven is always within the creation as the oak tree is always in the
acorn. The whole is always in the part. The divine man that you can
be is always the depth-potential within the struggling human man
that you now are.

We might have a clearer insight into Jesus' intention here if we
think of "least in the Kingdom" as "*at least* in the Kingdom."
Heaven being the innate potential, the least in the potential would
mean the starting point of its releasement. Jesus is simply saying that
anyone who makes the break-through from dogma to consciousness,
in himself or for others through his teaching efforts, may not have
achieved all his goals in life, but he is "at least" on the right path.

The "great in the Kingdom of Heaven" refers to those who are
actively working with and applying the fundamental spiritual laws. In
the one case we "break the commandments" by breaking them down
into practical insights. In the other case we "do and teach them," or
actually work diligently with these insights in the direction of our
dreams.

For I say unto you, That except your righteousness shall exceed the righteousness of the scribes and pharisees, ye shall in no case enter into the kingdom of heaven [Matt. 5:20, AV].

The key word here is "righteousness." This has always meant keeping the commandments in their packaged form. It would mean going to church regularly, carrying a Bible under your arm, always having a head-covering when you enter a church and keeping the many sectarian observances.

Now this kind of righteousness is not bad. In fact, it is an excellent discipline. However, discipline is like a trellis whose main purpose is to support the growth of a rosebush. But if we do not plant and nurture the rose, the trellis becomes highly inconsequential. The Scribes and Pharisees were excellent trellis builders. Under their care, a trellis was well-preserved and even jewel-studded but there were no roses.

Jesus is saying that your righteousness must achieve a new dimension or else there will be no real growth of the flower of your own Christ-self. Righteousness to Jesus meant the actual practice in thought of one's essential spiritual unity with God. It is the *right-use-ness* of spiritual law. It is a trellis designed for the disciplined effort to keep the mind stayed on God, to think rightly, to "practice the presence of God" by "thinking His thoughts after Him."

We must be constantly on guard against the human tendency to create habit-patterns. Even a sincere affirmation of Truth, if voiced repeatedly over a period of time, can become an object rather than a means of worship. Perhaps we need, from time to time, to go out into our garden of accumulated knowledge of the Truth and to break down the trellises and to rebuild them only as and if they can give support to the growth of the flowers of spiritual insight.

Ye have heard that it was said to them of old time, thou shalt not kill; and whosoever shall kill shall be in danger of the judgment; but I say unto you, that every one who is angry with his brother shall be in danger of the judgment, and whosoever shall say to his brother, Raca, shall be in danger of the council, but whosoever shall say, Thou fool, shall be in danger of hell fire [Matt. 5:21, 22].

Jesus gives a good example of breaking the commandments. He gives the commandment, "Thou shalt not kill," a whole new scope of application, by upgrading it from the social and moral level of application into the mental and spiritual frame of experience. In no way could it be said that He violated or annulled the commandment, but He brought it grippingly into the experience of every man. It has been all too easy to say, "I keep the commandments; I have never killed anyone." But in their expanded form, this is no longer enough.

Jesus is saying that murder or stealing or even adultery are acts of thought. As far as the mental law is concerned, we break the law, or break ourselves upon it, every time we think in negative or destructive ways. Your thought is your life. One may keep all the commandments in his Bible, and still experience the judgment of hell fire in his experience. Sad as it is to see a "righteous" person suffer like this, the answer is very simple: It is not enough to "keep the commandments in the Bible." We must take them out of the Bible and break them one by one—break them down into workable rules for living *and thinking*.

When Jesus refers to "the judgment" and "hell fire," He is referring to states of consciousness. The judgment is in ourselves. Every act fulfills itself. Every day is a day of judgment. Man is not punished for his sins, but by them. And the punishment is the hell fire of inner conflict that leads to physical stress and pain and disease, and to the human problems of lack and failure.

Jesus is simply pointing to the fact that we all do a lot of killing that does not come under the restraint of the commandment as it has been traditionally accepted. Every destructive thought is a killing thought, and "there is the devil to pay." When we permit ourselves to go on emotional binges of anger, hatred, bitterness and fear, there is no dodging it—we must pay the "hidden luxury tax of negative thinking." In other words you can't have your pet peeves and have peace of mind too.

Interestingly enough, at one time the accepted version of Scripture read, "whosoever is angry with his brother *without cause*. . . ." Careful scholarship later revealed that the words "without cause" had been added by the translators for some reason known only to themselves. Obviously, they must have thought that something was missing. Jesus must have meant the person who is angry without cause, for surely there are many times when one has a perfect right to be upset and disturbed and angry. So the translator made a slight change in the Scripture, rationalizing the belief in righteous indignation.

Yes, you have a "perfect right" to be angry at some injury that has taken place in your life, but you also have a right to the nervous disorder or stomach ulcers that inevitably follow. For we are always dealing with law. Your responsibility to yourself as well as to the divine law, is to keep yourself inwardly poised and to keep your thoughts positive and loving, in spite of injustice or disorder around you.

This is a large order! But then we are dealing with a large and wonderful principle, the divinity of man. If you remember who you are, and keep your inward contact, you will not let yourself be drawn into experiences on another's level of thought. You will meet them on your level, for your thought is your life.

A Chinese proverb says: "A man may not be able to prevent birds from flying over his head, but he has a right to determine whether they shall make nests in his hair." If someone is getting in your hair or under your skin, it is because you are violating the spiritually upgraded commandment, "Thou shalt not kill." The person may be outwardly annoying, but when he becomes annoying to you, it is your thought about him that is the problem. Change this thought and you change the whole experience.

Therefore, if thou bring thy gift to the altar and there rememberest that thy brother hath ought against thee; leave there thy gift before the altar, and go thy way; first be reconciled to thy brother, and then come and offer thy gift [Matt. 5:23, 24, AV].

Prayer is of the spirit; it is not form. If we pray, "Forgive us our debts as we forgive our debtors" and do not forgive our debtors, who are we fooling? Jesus challenges us here to break through the shell of formal prayer and fulfill the law of spiritual consciousness.

Jesus says that the great gift we must offer at the altar of inner prayer is the pure heart—and not some material gift that is an appeasement for a state of mind that we have no desire to relinquish. In Truth we come to know that we can have either the demonstration of our desires or our indignation; but we can't have both.

We will be dealing at length with Jesus' concept of prayer in a later chapter. He is talking here about thought. He is emphasizing that even prayer is no sanctuary from the responsibility of right thinking. Prayer may and should help you to reestablish yourself in spiritual consciousness and in right attitude of mind. But, He is saying, if you are praying for harmony in a relationship in which you still are harboring feelings of bitterness toward those people involved, you had better get those thoughts right, or forget the whole thing. For prayer changes things only as it changes *you.*

Agree with thine adversary quickly, whilst thou are in the way with
him; lest at any time the adversary deliver thee to the judge, and
the judge deliver thee to the officer, and thou be cast into prison.
Verily I say unto thee, Thou shalt by no means come out thence,
till thou hast paid the uttermost farthing [Matt. 5:25, 26, av].

We must remind ourselves that Jesus is talking about thought and the laws of mind action. There are two key words here: (1) "agree," meaning to settle with, to dispose of; and (2) "adversary," meaning your adverse thoughts or reactions to people or situations.

His reference to the adversary delivering you to the judge and officer and prison is a good illustration. It means that when a negative thought or fear comes to mind, if you don't settle with it and dispose of it immediately, it can lead you to sickness or inharmony in many forms.

In every experience we face, there is always a time when ultimate problems exist merely as seed possibilities. In all bitter feuds between people, in all wars between nations, in all emotional problems of individuals, there was always a time when misunderstanding could have been turned to understanding, when envy could have been turned to respect, when resistance could have been resolved by love. Jesus is saying, "Don't procrastinate. Whenever you begin to experience adverse feelings within yourself about someone, deal with those feelings immediately. If you don't the fire will spread and you may ultimately be imprisoned in a difficult experience."

"Agree quickly"—get your mind into a state of love and understanding and nonresistance. The only way you can do this is to dispose of the adverse thought and agree with God, with Truth. One woman has a pet statement, "I agree with God only!" This is her way of "practicing the Presence." She begins her day knowing that "There is only one presence and one power in my life, God, the good, omnipotent." And she keeps this idea alive by meeting every changing, challenging experience by affirming, "I agree with God only."

When you find yourself getting resistant or hostile or envious or angry, when the seeds of conflict begin to reveal themselves in you, settle with them immediately by "agreeing with God." Affirm your unity with Infinite Mind and the inexhaustible resources of love and peace.

If someone is criticizing you, "agree quickly"—which means "get yourself in neutral." Deal quickly with the tendency to flare up and resent the critic, so that you can deal impersonally with the criticism. It may be a helpful comment that will mean blessings to you. If it is not justified, you can easily discard it without personal animosity.

However, if you do not make that quick agreement—if you do not dispose of the adversary of your own negative reaction right at the outset, you may well create a poison within you that will extract a tremendous price in terms of peace and well-being. You may carry this person on your back in hurt and anger for years. But it is completely in your mind, for your thought is your life.

Suppose you have a sudden thought of fear about catching cold, or about the security of your job. Jesus says, "Deal with and dispose of this thought immediately." Don't procrastinate, and don't give in to it.

All contagion begins in the mind. There is a moment when you can say "no" to every physical affliction that comes to you. Deal with the fear-thought quickly—affirm, "I am a spiritual being, and therefore I will not accept this thought of weakness."

All lack and financial difficulty begin in the mind. When the earliest experience of anxiety or concern or fear or worry about money or work comes to mind, right then say "no!" to the whole chain of negative thought. Then say "yes" to God, to good, to abundance, to your personal security. Affirm, "I agree with God only."

The danger is when we let these fear and worry thoughts simmer in our minds. We need to be stern with ourselves. We must take action immediately. Stand up and speak the word of "peace" to the storms of human thought.

This is portrayed in the story of Jesus with His disciples on the stormy sea of Galilee (Mark 4:37–41). Jesus was asleep in the bow of the boat when the storm came up. The disciples were fearful, so they awakened Jesus and said, "Master carest thou not that we perish?" Jesus arose and "rebuked the wind" and said unto the sea, "Peace, be still." And the wind ceased and there was a great calm. And He said unto them, "Why are ye so fearful? How is it ye have no faith?"

This dramatic story reveals the power of the law of agreement. Jesus was the Master of the situation because He was Master of His own thoughts. He agreed with God always. He kept Himself in tune, in a state of spiritual unity with God. This was accomplished by the discipline of frequent periods of meditation. Thus in a crisis He was prepared, because He was *pre-prayered*.

Note carefully that Jesus didn't say, "Well, now, boys, let's not get too excited. Things are never as bad as they seem. We'll pull through this thing somehow." He did not acquiesce in the thought of danger at all. He did not let the storm have place in His mind in any way as something to be worried about. In perfect agreement with God, He simply spoke the strong word of power, and the storm subsided.

Jesus always shows the highest and most absolute goal toward which we must reach. We are all on the path, but we may have a long way to go to reach this lofty goal. Possibly, some of us in the situation of the storm, even through faith, might be looking to the lifeboats as our means of escape. And, if that is our level of consciousness, then this same law of agreement will work for us too. We will be free from worry or fear as we make our careful preparations to abandon ship, or we may calmly bail the water out of the hold, or send our SOS on short-wave radio.

In the world today, there is much disagreement among people and among nations. There is often much talk about getting both parties to the bargaining table. Beyond this, unless there is at least an agreement to disagree agreeably, there is little hope for harmony.

The rules of all bargaining sessions or peace conferences should include the agreement that they will treat each other on the level of their innate divinity. This agreement would lead to the opening premise that would be in essence a prayer even if it were not prayerfully invoked—the thought that God is on both sides of the table. This would lead to an open-minded listening to one another's views.

It would lead us to deal with one another as real people rather than as capricious personalities. It would lead to love and understanding between the people regardless of the views they hold. And this would lead to a gradual convergence of views based on the awareness of unity of long-range goals.

"Agree with thine adversary quickly," remembering that the adversary is not the person or situation that stands before you, but your reaction to or feeling about it. It has been said, "Things may happen around you, and things may happen to you, but the only things that really count are the things that happen *in* you." We can't always control what happens to us. But we can control what we think about what happens—and what we are thinking *is* our life at any particular moment.

8. The Law of Nonresistance

In his *Outline of History*, H. G. Wells gives the names of those who he believes to be the six greatest men who ever lived, and the name of Jesus heads the list. He says Jesus is entitled to human leadership because of His doctrine of nonresistance, "the greatest truth ever uttered by man."

The others on his list are Buddha, Asoka, Aristotle, Roger Bacon, and Abraham Lincoln. An interesting list of people with a wide diversity of backgrounds—obviously picked because they took little from the world and left much.

Abraham Lincoln was a man of great meekness and great strength, of great nonresistance and great accomplishments. Lincoln was once asked why he did not replace one of his cabinet members who constantly opposed him on every move he made. Typically, Lincoln answered with a story:

"Some years ago, I was passing a field where a farmer was trying to plow with a very old and decrepit horse. I noticed on the flank of the animal a big horsefly, and I was about to brush it off when the farmer said, 'Don't you bother that fly, Abe! If it wasn't for that fly this old hoss wouldn't move an inch!' "

Lincoln is saying that the difficult people that he had to work with were providing the challenges that kept him digging in himself for greater strength. Thus he was accomplishing great feats, not in spite of, but because of his opponents. It takes a great man to see and admit to this. The "thorn in the side" that we resist so strenuously may be more important than we know in the accomplishments we do make or the success we achieve.

One of the saddest things in life is man's propensity to use force to get his way—to use the battering ram instead of the key to open doors. This tendency is the cause of most of our world conflict and most of man's inner conflicts, which in turn cause most of his physical ills.

Without a doubt, if Jesus' teachings of nonresistance were universally understood and practiced, we would see an end to all war, to all conflict between nations, between factions, classes, and races. And we would see the one giant step needed toward eliminating the root cause of all physical illness. This concept is found in Matthew 5:29–49—"The Law of Nonresistance."

And if thy right eye causeth thee to stumble, pluck it out, and cast it from thee: for it is profitable for thee that one of thy members should perish, and not thy whole body be cast into hell. And if thy right hand causeth thee to stumble, cut it off, and cast it from thee: for it is profitable for thee that one of thy members should perish, and not thy whole body go into hell [Matt. 5:29–30].

Jesus is a genius in the use of metaphor. He is pointing out here that the one true need in our lives is to get right, in consciousness, with God. And anything that is standing between us and our spiritual unity with God must go.

The "eye" is a symbol in the metaphorical language of the East. One often hears it said, "Cut your eye from my boy," which means "do not envy my boy." Or, "Do not cut your eye from my family while I am away," which means "look after their best interests in my absence." In our own idiom we say, "Keep an eye on him," which means to take care of him. We also say, "Keep your eye skinned," which means to be watchful.

Jesus wants us to root out thoughts of lust, covetousness, envy, and greed. He says it is better to lose the things we want than to acquire habits which would ultimately destroy our whole life.

To "cut off your hand" in Aramaic means much the same thing. People often say to each other, "Cut off your hand from my vineyard," which means "stop stealing my grapes." Or, "His hand is too long," which means "he is a thief."

Jesus refers to the "right eye" and the "right hand." This is a very important point. "Right" refers to what is good and right; and "left" refers to what is evil and wrong. If it had been the "left" eye or hand, it would mean an evil kind of envy or lust and a selfish or even dishonest act. But the "right" eye or hand refers to those situations where your intent has been misjudged and where you have been unjustly treated.

We may wonder why Jesus always uses these extreme cases as his illustrations. We can only assume that it was because He was a master psychologist. He knew human nature as no one has before or since. If He had talked about "anger without cause," or, in this instance, of actual lust or stealing, this would have opened the door to much hypocrisy. It would be easy to nod one's head and agree, thinking He was talking about someone else.

There is a story told of a simple woman in a backwoods region who sat in church every Sunday enthusiastically responding to every word of the sermon. One Sunday as the preacher talked about the evil of drinking and gambling and swearing and carousing, the woman was right with him with her responses of "Amen! Praise the Lord! That's the Truth, brother!" Then the minister launched into a tirade against smoking. This caught our pipe-smoking grandma by surprise. She said, in a voice audible through the entire church, "Thar' now, he's stopped preaching and gone to meddling!"

With the Gospels of Jesus, there is no escape. The emphasis is upon *you* in every circumstance. He deals, not with abstract commandments or vague religious ideals, but with basic thoughts and feelings. Everyone has had the experience of being unjustly treated for some act of good intention. Jesus is saying, "Even in these instances, if you are angry or upset, cut it out."

Suppose you are moving with a line of traffic in your automobile, and suddenly the traffic light changes and you are left out in the middle of the intersection. A harassed policeman comes over and proceeds to bawl you out for blocking traffic. But you are a victim of the traffic and cannot possibly avoid the tie-up. You could angrily scream back at the officer, at the price of a summons or an upset stomach, but it is not worth it. You should count the cost!

You may feel that you have a right to be upset and angry. And you may go on carrying this upset with you through the rest of the day, as you tell everyone about it. But to what avail? Why pay that price? The officer is having a bad day. Put yourself in his shoes for a while and you will realize what a nerve-racking role is his in a busy traffic period. His anger is *his* problem. But why make it your problem, too? "Cut off your hand" and say, "Sorry, officer. I will try not to let it happen again." Silently send him a blessing of love and understanding, and go on your way free.

It was said also, Whosoever shall put away his wife, let him give her a writing of divorcement: but I say unto you, that every one that putteth away his wife, saving for the cause of fornication, maketh her an adulteress; and whosoever shall marry her when she is put away committeth adultery [Matt. 5:31–32].

Jesus is concerned with the tendency to run away from problems. As long as we take the way of escapism, the problems we run away from will continually come up in a new guise at every turning of the road. Jesus uses the theme of marriage and divorce as an example.

Marriage is not a gateway through which two people in love enter into a land where they "live happily ever after." Happiness in marriage is a conquest and not a bequest. Marriage is the license by which two people, who have seen the greater possibilities in each other, may work together to bring forth those possibilities. It is a laboratory of individual unfoldment.

Marriage can only succeed when both parties see something of the divine in one another. If you cannot see beyond the appearances in another person, then you do not really love him. True love is spiritual perception, an insight sensitive to the innate divinity. Sometimes it is said, "I can't see what he sees in her." And, of course, you can't. For it is the perception of love that is a personal revelation. Marriage based on that perception is built on rock. It will lead to an adjustment of differences and a fulfillment of love. Without that perception, the house is built on shifting sands and, in storms and floods, it will surely fall.

Marriage is a phase of the over-all experience of human unfoldment. If it brings love and bliss, then this is the outworking of consciousness for both of the parties, and undoubtedly there will be challenges or tests for them in other areas of life. If the marriage brings seeming conflict between the parties, if it is a great challenge to either or both of them, then this is the next step in growth which the soul has drawn to each one. If we are mindful of this, instead of saying, "I don't have to stand for that," we will say, "This is the reason why we were drawn together—this is why we were married." If we run away and find escape in divorce, this may well be "putting off our salvation." If we "brush off the fly" we may very well take away the stimulus for growth.

One of Jesus' last words on the cross are recorded as "Eli, Eli, lama sabachthani" (Matt. 27:46), which Dr. Lamsa says translates from the Aramaic, "My God, My God, for this was I kept." Jesus certainly could have said, "I don't have to take this!" But, instead, He said, "This is a part of the great purpose of my quest to overcome death itself and prove the principle of the Divinity of Man."

Now Jesus did not change the Mosaic law which allows divorce on the grounds of adultery, but He was condemning the abandonment of wives by husbands on the most trifling of grounds. Some Christian groups hold that divorce for any reason is unthinkable and immoral. They cite Jesus' declaration that "What God hath joined together, let not man put asunder" (Matt. 19:6). But God is Spirit, Divine Law. What God joins together must be an energy field as relentless as gravity. How, then, can a marriage possibly fall asunder? The only conclusion is—if a marriage can be dissolved, then it was never divinely joined.

Any minister, priest, or rabbi would like to believe that the spiritual union takes place during the wedding ceremony and under his pastoral benediction. But most clergymen realize that the indissoluble marriage of souls is an ultimate that may take months and often years to reach in the relationship. The process of two becoming one flesh requires a lot of adjustment and a great deal of growing and maturing on the part of both parties.

It is doubtful if Jesus would have said that divorce should never take place. For if there is a strong adulteration of the original perception that enabled the parties to see something of the divinity in each other, then it may well be that what God would put asunder, let no man keep together. If there is a complete breakdown of communication, and a closed-minded refusal to repair the break, then a continuation of the marriage might work to the detriment of the mental health of both parties.

However, the tendency to escape from challenges is what Jesus has in mind. No matter what the relationship or experience, whether it is marriage or employment or environmental problems, if the person seeks divorce as his first recourse—quitting the job, running away—then he is putting off his salvation. He has the habit of flicking off the fly. His life is denied the spur of challenge—and there is no great life, no abundant living, without it.

Socrates was once asked by a young man if he should get married. The great sage replied: "Go ahead and marry. If you get a good wife, you will be happy. If you get a bad wife, you will become a philosopher and that is good for any man."

Life is a great and continuous process of growth. We move from classroom to classroom. And in school, we expect to be tested. School need not be an unhappy experience, but it is a happy time only if we are nonresistant to the process of growth and change. If we accept the "tests" as blessings to us, if we are nonresistant to life's demands upon us, we will forge happily ahead toward that ultimate graduation. And perhaps no man has the vision to know what or when that graduation will be, for "It is not yet manifest what man shall be" (I John 3:2).

Again, ye have heard that it was said to them of old time, Thou shalt not forswear thyself, but shalt perform unto the Lord thine oaths: But I say unto you, Swear not at all; neither by the heaven, for it is the throne of God; nor by the earth, for it is the footstool of His feet; nor by Jerusalem, for it is the city of the great King. Neither shalt thou swear by thy head, for thou canst not make one hair white or black. But let your speech be, Yea, yea; Nay, nay: and whatsoever is more than these is of the evil one [Matt. 5:33–37].

An understanding of the idiom is vital here if we are to know what Jesus has in mind. Hearing an Easterner doing business you can immediately see the pertinence of this illustration. Buying a pair of shoes, for instance, might be a day's work.

When the price cannot be settled by bargaining, merchants and their customers generally take oaths by temples and holy names in proof of their sincerity. They may say, "By God's name and his holy angels this pair of shoes cost me six dollars but you can have them for three." When this proves ineffective they might resort to swearing, "If I lie to you I am the son of a dog, the shoes cost me three dollars but I will let you have them for a dollar and a half."

The suspicious customer might reply, "By my only son's head, I will not pay you more than a dollar." Often, if this method fails, the merchant will spit in the face of his customer, saying "Raca"—which means, "I spit on you."

The Mosaic law forbade swearing by anything but God. Of course, it was done all the time any way. But the Master said, "Swear not at all." This means that we should not take or make vows. The main problem with the vow is that it is a mortgage on the future. For instance, if we impetuously proclaim, "I will never speak to him again as long as I live," we are limiting future experience to our present low state of consciousness. Usually, we come to regret such a vow. Either we break it with a sense of weakness of character or we hold to it stoically, feeling trapped by a regrettable decision.

How often the alcoholic vows never to take another drink. And how easily is the vow broken, each time reducing his already low self-respect. The fine organization of Alcoholics Anonymous wisely insists that such vows should never be taken for periods longer than one day—the theory being that anyone can restrain himself for twenty-four hours. And at the end of that time, he has the satisfaction of accomplishment. Then he can progress for another day.

There is only the eternal "now" in which we live. All that we resolve and affirm for ourselves should be for the present. Instead of saying, "I will never be critical of anyone ever again," how much better to affirm, "I am now free from criticism. I am loving and responsive to the divinity in everyone I meet." In this way we are free from any pressures of resolutions, free to become what we really want to be.

We may even wonder at the marriage vow, "till death do us part." Can we really predict our future consciousness without mortgaging our future experience? It may be that one of the problems in marriage is the feeling of being trapped by divine or civil law. Maybe there is a subconscious resistance against the implication that *you can never get out of marriage.* Perhaps rebelling against that trapped feeling has given rise to rationalizations of incompatibility. Maybe the religious and legal restraints on marriage have caused more divorces than they have prevented.

How much better it would be to replace the "vow" of marriage with a sincere consecration to behold the divinity in each other as a possibility and to work together to give releasement to the "imprisoned splendor" which love has perceived. An annual or even daily reconsecration to the spirit of marriage is by far preferable to a once-and-for-all vow to stay together, come what may.

T. S. Eliot characterizes the plight of so many marriages with devastating simplicity in this line from his *Cocktail Party:*

> They do not repine;
> Are contented with the morning that separates
> And with the evening that brings together
> For casual talks before the fire
> Two people who know they do not understand each other,
> Breeding children whom they do not understand
> And who will never understand them.[1]

Goethe says that marriage is not a goal in itself, but an opportunity to mature. I wonder what would happen to the people in Eliot's play if they would arise every morning with the dedication to seek for the greater insight of love to see one another in an entirely new light? In time, the morning would not separate, but would reveal joyous opportunities for a unity of goals and of efforts.

Many churches require members upon consecration of membership to solemnly promise that they will, for all their lives, continue to believe the doctrines of their particular sect. This is what Jesus wanted to prevent. Actually, if a person prays regularly and works to make his prayer experience real, he should grow in understanding. Certainly, he cannot go on holding exactly the same views as the years pass. Such a promise must surely mortgage his future of spiritual unfoldment, leading to the "unforgivable sin."

The unforgivable sin is simply the closed mind, the mind that is made up, that will not let the Spirit reveal new Truths. Of how many individuals could it be said:

I'm a Methodist born and a Methodist bred,
And when I die, there'll be a Methodist dead.

Jesus says, "Keep your mind open. Don't mortgage your future by making or taking vows. Be receptive to the continuous unfoldment of the Truth in and through you. Give thanks that life is lived one day at a time, and that every day is a glorious opportunity to be strong, to overcome, to achieve, and to be happy. Now is the time of salvation."

Ye have heard that it was said, An eye for an eye, and a tooth for a tooth: but I say unto you, Resist not him that is evil; but whosoever smiteth thee on thy right cheek, turn to him the other also. And if any man would go to law with thee, and take away thy coat, let him have thy cloak also. And whosoever shall compel thee to go one mile, go with him two. Give to him that asketh thee, and from him that would borrow of thee turn not thou away [Matt. 5:38–42].

This is one of the most profound messages of the entire Bible. It sets forth with unmistakable clarity the law of nonresistance. Unfortunately, it is not often taken seriously, for it would seem to make impossible demands upon the Christian.

The practical-minded person has said, "Oh, this is a beautiful ideal that is typical of religion, but it certainly is not common sense. If you do not resist evil, it will overcome you. And if you do more than you are supposed to do, more than you are paid to do, people will take advantage of you."

And he is right; it is not common sense. It is *uncommon sense.* Life has no meaning when it is motivated only by common sense, because there is nothing common about this thing called life. It requires uncommon perception and an uncommon approach to commonplace things.

The old law of an "eye for an eye" was designed to maintain some kind of order among a barbarous people. It was better than nothing. Actually, it has formed the foundation of a moral code which is still evident in modern civil and criminal law. The old law has been modified in our sophisticated modern sense of public justice. But human feelings are still sensitive to the old-law justice. We still reveal the tendency to want to "get even," to level things up somehow when we have been hurt. The killing of President Kennedy's alleged assassin was this kind of old-law justice in the eyes of one man.

Jesus is saying, in effect, "So you want to get even? That is a perfectly normal desire. However, you must know that there is only one way to get even with another who has wronged you: love him and bless him and forgive him." You may hold a person in enmity for the rest of your days, reminding yourself continually of what he did to you. But every time you display this enmity, you are holding up your manacles and saying, "See, I am making him pay the price." But you have become a slave in the process. The only way you can get even is to take off the manacles. Get rid of your enmity, and you can go free. This may be a bitter pill but it is one of the most important lessons of life.

The command to turn the other cheek has been grossly misunderstood. It certainly doesn't mean that we should become doormats, or invite further assault. It is strange—when Jesus says, "pluck out the eye," we know that He is using a metaphor that must be translated into modern idiom. When He says "cut off your hand," we know He doesn't mean it literally. Yet, we have missed a dynamic lesson because we have insisted on accepting the idea of turning the other cheek in a completely literal sense.

Remember, Jesus has made the great discovery of the Divinity of Man. He is trying to help us realize that there is always a depth-potential of strength within us even in times of weakness. He is telling us that if we find ourselves upset over something another person has said or done, our upset indicates that we have been in the wrong state of consciousness. To react to it in this same state of mind only compounds the problem within us. Jesus says, "Turn to the other side of your nature. You are both human and divine. There is that in you that can never be hurt, that is always poised and peaceful, that knows your spiritual unity with God and knows that no one can take your good from you. In this diviner state of consciousness, the hurt is healed, the influence of the other person on you is nullified and you become a healing influence upon him."

Sydney Harris, the distinguished news columnist, tells of visiting a Quaker friend for a weekend. Each evening, he would walk to the corner with the friend to buy the evening newspaper. The man would be cheerful and pleasant but the newsie would always reply with a grunt. Harris commented one night, "He is a mighty unpleasant fellow, isn't he?" The Quaker friend replied, "Oh, he is always that way." "But why are you so nice to him?" The answer is a classic that reflects a deep understanding of Jesus' law of nonresistance. The Quaker said, "But why should I let him determine how I am going to act?"

Here was a man who knew that his chief responsibility in life was to act the part of his divinity. Why should he let any man on the street cause him to lower his consciousness and thus reduce his whole experience of life? Here was a man who understood himself. We can be certain that if he were to find himself flaring up with anger at some irregularity in another person, instead of saying "What is the matter with that man?" he would say, "What is the matter with me?" He would "turn the other cheek," or quickly remember, "I am not going to let him determine how I think and act."

Remember, you may not be able to change or control the people around you, but you can determine the level of consciousness on which you meet them and react to them. This is one of the most significant discoveries that man can make. It will lead to a tremendous stability and confidence. You will come to know that no matter what happens in your world, you don't have to be afraid, you really do not need to worry or be anxious. You can determine your reaction and thus your course of action. Turn the other cheek and meet the experience on the level of your divinity, and you will achieve self-mastery.

The admonition to go the second mile relates to the right of the Roman soldiers in Jesus' time to compel subject peoples to carry their burdens for one mile. It was the imposition of despotism, but the subject people could do nothing about it. Jesus indicates an uncommon-sense way of doing something about it. They could break their bonds of enslavement by doing what was demanded of them as if they really enjoyed doing it. And that doesn't make sense, does it?

A man tells of going into a restaurant where they had a policy that if any waitress failed to give at least one smile to a customer she was automatically discharged—if caught. He says it was interesting to see the forced, mechanical smiles of the waitresses, who seemed the more unpleasant because of this imposition of the management. But one girl stood out. She smiled like the rest but she kept on smiling—not just the one required smirk. She seemed to enjoy smiling. She actually beamed and radiated a contagious spirit of joy.

He talked to the waitress about this. She said, "Well, at first I resented the order to smile and I almost quit my job. It was no fun smiling when you were compelled to. Then I began to realize that all the smiles except the first one were my own, free of orders. So I always went beyond that one forced smile to feel the reward of smiling. And the result is I find it is an essential key to making my job an enjoyable experience."

Jesus knew that when you do what is required of you and no more, you are a slave. This is true whether it is meeting the whim of a demanding employer or keeping the laws of the land. To travel the first mile brings the pay check, the forced smile, the formal "thank you," and the humdrum existence. It is all that is expected of anyone. But if you want routine living to become abundant living, you must give more.

When you go the second mile—give more to your work, are more than thoughtful and kind to people, become a joyous giver and a gracious receiver—suddenly life takes on new meaning. On the second mile you find happiness, true friends, real satisfaction in living—and probably a larger pay check, too. Someone has said, "If you want to get ahead in your work, start taking advantage of your employer by doing more than is asked of you."

"But I do all I am paid to do!" And that may be true. They don't pay you for the extra joy and enthusiasm you put into your work. But then your pay can't give you satisfaction and a sense of fulfillment either. The person who receives only a pay check for his work is underpaid—and this is true even if he is paid in six figures. The true compensation of joy and fulfillment in a job begins where duty leaves off.

When Jesus says, "Give to him that asketh thee, and from him that would borrow of thee turn not thou away"—He doesn't mean that you should go out and fill every beggar's cup or become a "soft touch" for everyone who comes seeking a loan. This injunction is given in the context of the law of nonresistance. Let's face it— humanly, we all resent the intrusion of "him that asketh."

There are two ways in which we can "turn him away." First, we can bluntly and unkindly reject the overture. But, in terms of the damage to our own stability of consciousness, the cost may be more than the money we have withheld. Secondly, we can give him the gift or make the loan "to get rid of him." But, in this case, we may have hurt him more than we have helped, for we have brushed the fly away, thus removing the one motivation that might ultimately lead him to overcome his problem.

When you see the beggar (or the friend) approaching, if you find resistance welling up in you, "turn the other cheek" immediately. Get your mind on the loving, nonresistant Christ-consciousness. You cannot really afford to do less. From the level of your divinity, you will respond to the requests with love and understanding. You will recognize that he has a problem which may go deeper than his need for financial help. You will "salute the divinity" within him and deal with him on this level.

Now, in this consciousness, you can deal with him from the standpoint of his highest good. You may give him the money in the faith that he will use it wisely and responsibly. Or you may be led to withhold the gift, but to give him the blessing of your wise and loving counsel. Your blessing may help him to create a new self-image, to find new self-respect, to rise to new faith in his ability to meet life.

Wouldn't it be wonderful if we could always meet people in this consciousness? The beggars and irresponsible borrowers of the world would soon disappear. Perhaps it is at this point that the "war on poverty" must begin. Maybe, we have been failing our needy by simply "flicking off the fly." In so doing, we have taken away both their incentive and their self-respect. Perhaps more important than taking people out of the slums is the task of taking the slums out of people. Money may not be able to solve the problem alone. Maybe we need to salute the divinity in these people, to help them by our prayer and praise to "be transformed by the renewing of the mind."

Ye have heard that it was said, Thou shalt love thy neighbor, and hate thine enemy: but I say unto you, Love your enemies, and pray for them that persecute you; that ye may be sons of your Father who is in Heaven: for He maketh his sun to rise on the evil and the good, and sendeth rain on the just and the unjust. For if ye love them that love you, what reward have ye? Do not even the publicans the same? And if ye salute your brethren only, what do ye more than others? Do not even the Gentiles the same? Ye therefore shall be perfect, as your heavenly Father is perfect [Matt. 5:43–48].

Socrates once said that the unexamined life is not worth living. Jesus is constantly challenging us to take a good look at ourselves in the context of the divine potential within us. We must recognize that the basic problem in life is the frustration of our own potentiality. When we are faced with inharmony in relationships, it is not so much a problem between ourself and another who seems to be fighting us, as it is a break in our own circuit of good from the Father within.

Life is consciousness. The problems we face indicate that our wires are down. We need to repair the break within ourselves. The only existence an error-condition has, as far as we are concerned, is that which we give it in our own thinking. Withdraw the thought about it and it fades into nothingness. What matters to us, in reality, is not people or things or conditions in themselves, but the thoughts and feelings we harbor concerning them. It is not the conduct of others but our reaction to it that makes or mars our life experience.

Jesus challenges us to get a good understanding of this thing called love. He says you do not really love simply because you love those who love you. What does that prove? It is easy to be nice and friendly to those who are nice to you. It is no problem to "love thy neighbor" as long as we have something to say about who that neighbor may be.

Love is not an emotion that begins in us and ends in the positive response of another. Love is a divine energy that begins in God and has no end. We tune in on this energy and are moved by it as it flows through us. Shakespeare says, "Love is not love which alters when it alteration finds."[2] The classic illustration of this is in the statement, "I loved him with all my heart, but after what he did to me I hate him with a passion."

On the level of his divinity, man has tremendous and limitless powers as his inheritance. However, they are his to use only when he

acts the part of his divinity. So Jesus is saying, "Love your enemy—
not because he is especially deserving of your love, but because when
he causes you resistance, you are not acting the part of your divinity.
And the power that goes with your divinity is only yours when you
act the part."

A light bulb is nothing more than that unless it is turned on.
When the connection is made with electrical energy, it becomes a
radiant source of light and warmth. Man is a spiritual being, a child
of God, heir to all the infinite potential that inheres in all God's
creation, including Love, the strongest single force in existence. But,
in reality, the fulfilling of the power of our divinity comes only when
we are attuned to the Father and are expressing His love, light, and
power.

At any time, under any circumstances, we can turn on the light,
and the infinite energy of love will dissolve darkness, heal broken
relationships and become a veritable protecting presence. Man is a
creature of light. When his light is shining brightly in all directions
and in all situations, he is imperturbable, indefatigable and un-
defeatable. "Nothing shall be impossible unto him."

How we frustrate this potential of light! Consider this practical
illustration. If you were to walk into a room full of people who were
being hampered in their work by lack of light, and if you had a bright
lamp in your hands, would you turn your lamp down in reaction to
the dim light of the room? No, you would bring as much light as you
possibly could. But if you walk into a room of hostile people, what is
your reaction? Normally, you meet their hostility with hostility of
your own and walk away saying, "What an unfriendly bunch of
people!"

You may say, "But I am only human." This is the understatement
of your life. You are not only human—you are also divine in
potential. The fulfillment of all your goals and aspirations in life
depends upon stirring up and releasing more of that divine potential.
And there is really nothing difficult about letting this inner light
shine. All we must do is correct the tendency to turn off our light
when we face darkness.

A woman was walking home from a meeting at her church. It was
very late at night and the streets were very dark. As she walked past
an alleyway, a thief put a gun to her back and said, "Give me your
purse or I'll kill you."

The normal human reaction to such an experience would be to turn off the light instantly, and then to experience fear, anger, bitterness, and outright hatred. All these qualities are the frustration of our potentiality of the healing and protecting power of love. It was of just such experiences as this that Jesus spoke, when he commanded, "Love thine enemies and pray for those who despitefully use you, . . . that you may be sons of your Father." In other words love them, not because they deserve it but because you deserve it and need to keep your love-energy flowing.

Anyway, this frail little woman turned and looked the thief right in the eyes and said, "You can't hurt me because you are God's child and I love you." He said, "Look, lady, this is a gun and I mean to kill you if you don't give me your purse." But she simply repeated softly without any evidence of fear or excitement, "But you can't hurt me because you are God's child and I love you." He stood for a moment puzzled, shocked, and disarmed. His hand shook, his face flushed, and he dropped his gun and ran. This man was completely overpowered by love and nonresistance.

Unfortunately, a person is often filled with fear and anger at such a moment, leading him to do unwise things. Perhaps he tries to run, or to overpower the assailant. But he has turned off his light, and thus he is meeting darkness with darkness, resistance with resistance—and he is now on the level of the thief. Now he is in great danger. He may blame the thief for what may ultimately happen—the loss of his purse, or the injury caused by the frightened culprit. But, from the standpoint of the law of consciousness, and of realizing the potential of the Divinity of Man, the real crisis resulted when the victim turned off his light and thus fearfully caused a break in his relationship with the Light of God within himself. So, no matter what the difficulty around you or the darkness before you, *turn on the light.* No matter what happens, *turn on the light and keep it on.*

"Ye shall therefore be perfect as your heavenly Father is perfect." This is another important evidence that Jesus taught the Divinity of Man, and that man is intended to continue in unfoldment until he expresses and experiences the dynamic life of God.

I once heard a preacher say, "Jesus challenged men with unattainable goals. The fact is, of course, these goals are impossible for weak, sinful humans to attain. He knew that we had better have goals that are beyond our grasp, or what's a heaven for?" And this is correct. It is impossible for weak, sinful humans to fulfill the absolute teachings of Jesus. *But why be a weak, sinful human?*

Jesus is saying, "Much is expected of you because you are well endowed. You are a child of God, created in His image-likeness, possessed of the potential of the Christ indwelling. You are a growing, expanding, evolving, dynamic life-idea in God-Mind. There can never be a limit to God, and thus there can never be a limit to you if you get into God-consciousness."

It is not that Jesus challenges us with unattainable goals, but that He is continually reminding us of unclaimed possibilities. "Come ye blessed of my Father, inherit the kingdom prepared for you from the foundation of the world" (Matt. 25:34).

9   The Forgotten Art of Prayer

THE "call to prayer" is heard in all languages, by innumerable religions the world over. "Pray about it" is common advice to the troubled heart. "Prayer changes things" and "the family that prays together stays together" are popular slogans stressing the importance of prayer. But what do we mean by prayer?

The word "prayer" has no absolute meaning in our day. It means one thing to the child who says, "Now I lay me down to sleep." It means something entirely different to the person who says his "Our Fathers" unthinkingly in a monotonous drone. It means one thing to the person who sits quietly under the trees in a wordless adoration of life and nature and with a receptivity to the "still small voice" of Spirit. It means another thing to the congregation of the preacher who gives a twenty-minute prayer that is eloquent and studied, and that touches every area of human need. (It is said that some ministers give their best sermons in prayer.)

In Clarence Day's delightful book, "*God and My Father,*" talking of his father's peculiar attitude toward God, he says, "In moments of prayer, when he and God tried to commune with each other, it wasn't his own shortcomings that were brought on the carpet, but God's. . . . He expected a great deal of God. . . . It seemed that God spoiled his plans. . . . This aroused his wrath. He would call God's attention to such things. . . . He didn't actually accuse God of gross inefficiency, but when he prayed his tone was loud and angry, like that of a dissatisfied guest in a carelessly managed hotel."[1]

105

A study of all the prayer practices within the Christian family of denominations is interesting and revealing. It is also a commentary on how far traditional Christianity has strayed from the teachings of Jesus. We find prayers of flattery, expecting a vain God to be moved by praise. There are prayers of pleading and supplication, for coaxing a miracle from a reluctant God. There are prayers of vain repetition, where the asker hopes that if he prays long and loudly enough, an apparently inattentive God may hear and respond.

It is amazing that so few have really understood or paid any heed to the new technique of prayer that Jesus brought to the world. He shows that prayer is susceptible of being reduced to intelligible postulates that may be unquestionably proved in practice. He indicated that the principles of prayer are universally applicable in all places, at all times, and for all persons.

It is significant that Albert Einstein, who ranks alongside Newton as a great master in the field of science, the empirical approach to the Universe, believed very definitely in prayer. He refers to one law which contains the sum of all that mathematics and physics have proved true about the Universe. He says that this law is a positive force for good and that we tune in on its infallibly perfect working by the power of thought and prayer.

This is the key to understanding prayer—and the prayer idea that Jesus outlines. Prayer does not deal with a capricious God. It is a technique for achieving unity with God and His limitless life, substance, and intelligence.

> Prayer is not something we do to God but to ourselves.
> It is not a position but a disposition.
> It is not flattery but a sense of oneness.
> It is not asking but knowing.
> It is not words but feeling.
> It is not will but willingness.

Jesus said, "God is a Spirit and they that worship Him must worship in spirit and truth" (John 4:24). This is not a definition. Jesus knew that to define a thing is to limit it, and He was bent on expanding our thought of God as well as giving us a deeper insight into ourselves. He was giving a guide to direct our thoughts away from finite form, from thinking of God as a superman.

Man's dilemma is that he has become trapped in a religion of propositional theology. His attitudes about God and life and prayer have been cut-and-dried and bound into neat little packages. But you can't cut-and-dry Truth without its ceasing to live as Truth. Prayer becomes a sacramental ritual that is performed by professionals, or it is the experience of reading "prayers" from a book. This simplifies the process. But it also leaves a sense of frustration and an absence of any real sense of communion.

Bishop John Robinson indicates that clergymen feel this sense of frustration also, along with an even greater feeling of guilt:

I believe the experts have induced in us a deep inferiority complex. They tell us that this is the way we ought to pray, and yet we find that we cannot maintain ourselves for any length of time even on the lowest rungs of the ladder, let alone climb it. . . . We are evidently not "the praying type." And so we carry on with an unacknowledged sense of failure and guilt. I can testify to this most strongly from the time I spent in a theological college, both as a student and as a teacher. Here was a laboratory for prayer. Here one ought to be able to pray, if ever one could. . . . If one failed in these circumstances, what hope was there later on—when one was surrounded and sucked down by "the world"? And, yet, I believe I am not alone in finding a theological college the most difficult rather than the easiest of places in which to pray. In fact, I know I am not. For I discovered there what I can only describe as a freemasonry of silent, profoundly discouraged, underground opposition, which felt that all that was said and written about prayer was doubtless unexceptionable but simply did not speak to "our" condition. . . . But nothing else was offered in its place, and to this day, we have an inferiority complex. We dare not admit to others or to ourselves what non-starters we are. . . .[2]

Jesus addressed Himself to this whole problem. It is obvious from His words that the situation in His day paralleled that about which Bishop Robinson talks. Now let us consider Jesus' outline of the art of prayer in the "Sermon on the Mount."

Take heed that ye do not your righteousness before men, to be seen of them: else ye have no reward with your Father who is in

Heaven. When therefore thou doest alms, sound not a trumpet before thee, as the hypocrites do in the synagogues and in the streets, that they may have glory of men. Verily I say unto you, They have received their reward. But when thou doest alms, let not thy left hand know what thy right hand doeth; that thine alms may be in secret: and thy Father who seeth in secret shall recompense thee. And when ye pray, ye shall not be as the hypocrites: for they love to stand and pray in the synagogues and in the corners of the streets, that they may be seen of men. Verily I say unto you, They have received their reward. But thou, when thou prayest, enter into thine inner chamber, and having shut thy door, pray to thy Father who is in secret, and thy Father who seeth in secret shall recompense thee [Matt. 6:1–6].

Man is a thinking being, and the mind is the connecting link between God and man. Jesus is saying that prayer is not a matter of words or of outer forms. It is a matter of consciousness, of concentrated, rightly directed, spiritually oriented positive thinking. The law is, "As he thinketh in himself so is he."

When Jesus says, "The Father who is in secret and who seeth in secret," He means that divine law is a nonmaterial force that cannot be seen. You cannot see the wind. But when you see the rustle of the leaves you know the wind is blowing. You cannot see God, but you see the life of God in that which is living. You see the love of God in him who is loving. You see the wisdom of God in the intelligence of man. It was in this sense that Jesus said, "He that hath seen me hath seen the Father" (though this statement has been misrepresented as referring to His unique divinity).

There is a secret to everything. The seed works underground, sometimes for long periods of time, before it puts forth its green leaf; and throughout its growth its laboratory is still most secret. In the works of men, the mechanism that produces the fair showing is invariably hidden: the works of a watch, the kitchen that produces the banquet, the long hours of practice that produce the virtuoso performance. There is always a secret region of causation.

There is no mystery about the illumination in a room that follows the pushing of the light switch, but there is a "secret." There is a power plant somewhere that is generating the electrical energy that flows into the filament when the circuit is made. A television picture or a flying airplane might be a miracle to an Australian aborigine, but when we know the "secret" of the process involved, we accept these things as commonplace.

Because we haven't understood the "secret place" of unity with God, and have not entered into the realm of causation, we have thought of prayer as the attempt to perform miracles, but that is not its purpose. The results of prayer may be humanly astounding, but they merely demonstrate the art of unifying ourselves with the creative source of all good, the divine law of fulfillment.

When we think that "only a miracle can save us" and turn to prayer in that consciousness, we limit the power of our prayer. No miracle is needed to bring health or guidance or prosperity into our frustrated lives, because they are the very nature of God and the plan for His ideal creation, man. And that is the great "secret."

The word "hypocrite" is from the Greek, meaning a stage actor or masked player. It was the custom in those days for performers to herald their coming into a community (like the circus of more modern times) with advertisement by trumpeting and pageantry or parade of some kind. In early times, the word "hypocrite" was not used in the completely critical sense as it is today. It could be an epithet of praise or blame according to the judgment of the hearer. Call someone a "good actor" today and it will depend on how it is used. Obviously, the meaning is different if you use it in reference to, say, Laurence Olivier after a masterful Shakespearean performance, than if you are describing a man in a witness box.

Jesus is applying the term "hypocrite" to the religious zealot who makes a show of his religion and his prayer. But He is not condemning the person, only the practice. It is not often that this practice is a conscious attempt to show off. Because his religion has been given to him "custom-made," the individual may know no other way.

Men of all times have deluded themselves with the belief that outward acts which seem to be easy can be made to take the place of interior changes in thought and feeling which seem to be more difficult. How easy it is to fall into the practice of buying and wearing ceremonial garments, repeating set prayers by rote, using stereotyped forms of devotion, attending religious services at prescribed times, and still leave the heart unchanged.

Jesus is saying, "Make no parade of your religion. The Father in you knows you better than you know yourself. He doesn't want a pretender, a play-actor. He wants you. Your prayer is not to impress Him or anyone else. Your prayer is to lift your consciousness to a point where you may be impressed by His Spirit."

The meaning of Jesus' reference to the "left" and "right" hand is obvious when we think of the spiritual import of cause and effect, giving and receiving. "Let not thy left hand know what thy right hand doeth." Do not pray only for the purpose of, or with your eyes upon, results.

In his classic essay, "Self-Reliance," Ralph Waldo Emerson brings the idea of prayer into the sharpest possible focus when he says:

Prayer looks abroad and asks for some foreign addition to come through some foreign virtue, and loses itself in endless mazes of natural and supernatural, and mediatorial and miraculous. Prayer that craves a particular commodity, anything less than all good, is vicious. Prayer is the contemplation of the facts of life from the highest point of view. It is the soliloquy of a beholding and jubilant soul. It is the spirit of God pronouncing His works good. But prayer as a means to effect a private end is meanness and theft. It supposes dualism and not *unity* in nature and consciousness. *As soon as the man is at one with God, he will not beg.* He will then see prayer in all action.[3]

When you pray or speak the word of Truth, you are working in the causative realm, in the "secret" region of spiritual consciouness. It is the "right" hand that is setting into operation a divine law. The "left" hand is the manifestation or answer, the "all things added." It may also symbolize the thought of lack or limitation and the desire to have it filled.

Jesus said, "Ye seek me, not because ye saw the miracles, but because ye did eat of the loaves, and were filled. Labor not for the meat which perisheth, but for the meat which endureth unto everlasting life" (John 6:26, 27). We must work to alter the concept of God as the "answer man," the "super-doctor," "the divine warehouse," and the concept of prayer as the great "spiritual slot machine." Remember, "God is Spirit and they that worship must worship in Spirit and in Truth."

Often someone may say, "I haven't prayed much lately, because I have had no problems to pray about." This person has missed the whole idea of prayer. Most certainly, problems may be solved through prayer; but that is only a secondary value. The most important purpose of prayer is lifting ourselves to a high level of consciousness where we can be conditioned in mind and body with the all-sufficient life, substance, and intelligence of God.

Jesus says, "Do not pray to be seen praying. Do not pray because you think you should pray. Do not pray only to heal your arthritis or to get a better job. You will get your reward, but you will not experience the "meat which endureth." That is the great need. Pray to reestablish your contact with divine power, and 'all these things shall be added unto you.' "

Unless we pray in "Spirit and in Truth," prayer is simply a cold business transaction: "God, if you will heal my condition, or get me that promotion, or stop the war, I will give my life to you all the rest of my days."

When a good result does not appear, sometimes a person complains, "I can't understand why my prayer hasn't been answered. I have tithed my income, I have gone to church regularly, I have prayed many times a day." Why have you done these things? Is the "left" hand too much aware of what you are doing?

A man was ticketed for parking in a "no standing at any time" zone across the street from his church. Usually the policemen are lenient on Sunday, but this morning a "rookie cop" was on the beat and he was more concerned with making a good impression on his first assignment. The man fumed and fretted: "Here a man gets up early on Sunday when he could easily have loafed through the day, and what does he get—a ticket!" The patrolman replied unsympathetically, "So you went to church! What do you expect, a medal?" Why was this man in church? Because he sincerely wanted the inner sense of communion that could be derived therefrom, or out of a sense of duty?

"The Father seeth in secret." This means that your inward thought is all that counts. When you get still and get your thought on the side of the law of causation, you will find "answers without ceasing." Until you do, you have your reward in a more superficial fulfillment that is not really satisfactory.

"And in praying use not vain repetitions." Notice that Jesus does not condemn repetition, but *vain* repetition. Jesus, Himself, used repetition, on one occasion He repeated the same prayer three times. Prayer is to lift consciousness—yours, not God's. If the repetition is the effort to condition your mind with the thoughts of God, then it is good. However, if you parrot a prayer or affirmation over and over with the idea of conditioning God to your needs, then it is vain. Nowhere in Christian practice has Jesus' clear instruction been so disregarded as in this matter of prayer repetition.

If you owned a mountain cabin and wanted to make it fresh and habitable after a long winter, would you have to induce the air to enter the doors or plead with the light to stream in the windows? No, the moment you opened the doors and windows, the wind and sunshine would surge in of their own accord.

This is a good picture of God's relation to our lives. Prayer is simply opening our lives that we may receive what God has always been trying to bestow—conditioning our lives with God. Kahlil Gibran says: "For what is prayer but the expansion of yourself into the living ether?"[4]

"Your Father knoweth what things ye have need of, before ye ask him" (Matt. 6:8). This statement should be the preamble to every prayer. It should be read in every Christian church every time the "call to prayer" is issued. It should be embossed on the front of every Bible and prayer book, and should be prominently displayed in every prayer room. Certainly if we really believed that the Father knew our needs even before we prayed, it would cause some rethinking about prayer in general, and it would be a tremendous influence on every prayer for specific needs.

The obvious question is—If the Father knows our needs before we ask His help, then why ask? We must remember that "God is spirit." It is not easy to overcome the thought of God as the Supreme Being "out there" who can help us in our times of need if we ask Him and if He is in the right mood. When we thus endow God with human qualities, our "asking" implies the possibility of a "yes" or "no" answer. We may very well receive an answer of "no." However, the "no" has come out of our own consciousness, the effect of our own inertia in negative thinking.

God doesn't have what you want or need. God *is* the substance of that need. You don't have to ask God for life, for God *is* life. You are the projection of that life into visibility. The key to healing is to lift up your thought to the consciousness of the wholeness of life in you. You need not ask for it. God is that wholeness, but you must accept it into your mind which has been seeing in part.

You don't have to ask God for wisdom, for God *is* wisdom. Your mind is an activity in the Infinite Mind of God. If there is any break in the flow of the inspiration of the Almighty in you, that break is in you—not in God. Your need is to reestablish yourself in the consciousness of the all-knowing Mind of God in you.

How do you ask the sun for sunlight? By getting out into the sun. How do you ask electricity for light for you lamp? By turning on the switch. How do you "ask" God for what you want? By getting into the Spirit. It is not something that God must do for you. It is what you must do for yourself to enable God to do for you that which it is His ceaseless longing to do. "It is the Father's good pleasure to give you the kingdom" (Luke 12:32).

The word "ask" has many different connotations. If you ask your boss for a raise in salary, it is not at all the same as when he asks you to do a piece of work for him. If you ask a neighbor to "baby-sit" with your child, you have a different thought than when the landlord comes to the door asking for the rent. It is the former in each case that is the context in which we have thought of Jesus' reference to asking God. But it is the latter in each case that gives insight into Jesus' thought. In the original Greek for this word "ask," there is a connotation of "demand" or "claim." The boss can demand that you do a job because that is what you are paid to do. The landlord claims his rent as his rightful payment. And when you "ask" God for help, you are claiming your inheritance as a spiritual being.

Jesus says, "All things whatsoever ye pray and ask for, believe that ye receive them, and ye shall have them" (Mark 11:24). How can you ask for anything believing that you already have it? You can when you realize that, as a spiritual being, God has endowed you with built-in capacities and with a Kingdom within you of all-sufficient resources. Sickness or lack or indecision have no place in the plan of the Infinite for man. You are the very expression of God and it is His ceaseless longing to fulfill you as a total person. You ask for your good in the sense of claiming your inheritance, drawing upon your spiritual reserves with the same confidence as drawing savings out of a bank.

A careless worker, who "fudges" on his time slip and calls in sick at every opportunity, is creating conditions that make his eventual dismissal inevitable. On the other hand, a good worker, who comes early and leaves late, who always tries to improve his performance and to help the company, is "asking" for a promotion. And it usually comes, because he has created conditions that make that result inevitable.

You ask for life by affirming life. You ask for success by getting into the consciousness of success. You ask for peace, by affirming peace and letting the spirit of peace permeate your mind and heart. Prayer is not a way to turn on the light in God, but to turn on the light in you—and God is that light.

The purpose of prayer, then, is to affirm in our consciousness that which is true of God and of our relationship with Him. "In God, I am now a perfect child. I am strong, confident, and capable. I have the ability to do all that needs to be done. I am one with all-sufficient substance, so I am secure and fearless." These things may be urgent needs in your experience. But the Father knows even before you ask—and it is the Father's good pleasure to give you the Kingdom. Thus, don't waste your time asking for help. It is already yours. Claim it. Call it forth into expression. Speak the word of Truth.

Jesus was a master at the use of affirmations, and it may well be that He achieved mastery because of this. Jesus affirmed such Truths as, "I am the bread of life. . . . I am the light of the world. . . . I am the resurrection and the life. . . . I am the Way, the Truth, and the Life." Thinking in terms of the Divinity of Jesus, we have seen these statements as evidence that He lived under a special dispensation. Actually, He was demonstrating the Divinity of Man. He was simply claiming His spiritual unity with the Infinite, affirming the Truth for and about Himself. We must affirm the same Truths for and about ourselves.

"But when thou prayest, enter into the inner chamber and shut thy door." This is Jesus' teaching of the silence, the dynamic concept of deep prayer. In a very real sense, much that we think of as prayer is but a preparation for prayer. It is the process of resolving the conflicts of the mind so that we can "Be still, and know that I am God" (Ps. 46:10). When we plug the battery into a charger, it does not chatter away about how much it needs the charging. It simply and quietly accepts the inflow of energy. And when we pray, Jesus is

THE FORGOTTEN ART OF PRAYER | 115

telling us, we should get into the depths of our being, and shut out the concerns of the world, and "pray to the Father in secret."

As we grow in understanding of the Truth of our relationship with God, as we begin to see ourselves in the light of our divinity, prayer becomes an experience in the silence. We put the words of entreaty, of supplication, even of adoration behind us. Our heart speaks in the language of the soul. We praise God through our feeling of gratitude. We worship through our spirit of reverence. We ask for help through our receptive mind and heart. We affirm the Truth of being by meditating quietly upon it.

Then Jesus says, "After this manner therefore pray ye . . .," and He follows with what we have called "The Lord's Prayer." Jesus had no thought of giving a prayer to end all prayers. Rather He was giving a pattern of prayer to begin all prayers, creating a "frame of reference." He was telling us "how" and not "what" to pray. He was giving a series of dynamic Truths to illustrate the consciousness in which to pray.

Charles Fillmore says, "Jesus was quite positive and very determined in all His affirmations. He made big claims for God, and demonstrated them. . . . His prayers were made of one strong affirmation after another. The Lord's Prayer is a series of determined affirmations."[5]

Unfortunately, the translators could not understand this affirmative mood of Jesus. Thus, through slight variations of meaning, the prayer was made to appear to be a supplication for help. It seems to be pleading: "please give me," "please forgive us," and "we beg you not to lead us into evil." Fortunately, today we have available many more accurate translations which tend to reveal that the Lord's Prayer was intended to be a series of affirmations. A synthesis of the best translations available today would render the prayer something like this:

Our Father in heaven. Hallowed is Thy name. Thy kingdom is come, Thy will is done, in earth as it is in heaven. Thou dost give us this day and every day our daily bread, Thou dost always forgive, even as we forgive. Thou would never leave us in temptation, but art the very power of deliverance from limitation. For thine is the kingdom and the power and the glory, forever.

One great and powerful affirmation!
Let us consider the great prayer in a line-by-line study:

Our Father: This is the orientation, the "true point of beginning." God is my Father, I am His child. This declares our unity with God at the outset, which is man's greatest, perhaps his only, need. The prayer begins on this note, not to attempt to get God's attention, but to direct our attention to that in us which neither slumbers nor sleeps, that which "loves us with an everlasting love."

Who art in heaven: This forever locates God: "Neither shall they say, Lo, here! or there! for lo, the Kingdom of God is within you." We have within us every moment of our lives the great potency which is God. We have ignored it, shut our eyes and ears and understanding to its glorious possibilities. But it is ever there. We often hear about "repressed emotions," but good can be and is most often repressed. The "frustration of potentiality" may well be the root of all men's mental, emotional, and even physical problems. No religion in the world can make a man good by putting goodness in him. The purpose of religion is to provide the climate and encouragement as well as the techniques for stirring up and releasing "the gift of God" that is within.

Hallowed be Thy name: This is an important realization of the wholeness and the omnipresence of God. "Hallowed" comes from the root word from which we get the words, "whole, hale, hearty, heal, healthy." This means, then, "wholeness and perfection is the nature of God." We have been conditioned in orthodox religion to think of a duality, of God and the devil, of good and evil. But Jesus is here affirming the unity of the Spirit, the integration or wholeness of God. He said, "Doth the fountain send forth from the same opening sweet water and bitter?" (Jas. 3:11). God cannot *be* life and at the same time send sickness. He cannot *be* love and at the same time do something in wrath or anger. He cannot *be* a protecting presence and at the same time will accidents. These things are completely unlike His nature, which is *whole.* "Hallowed (perfect, whole) be (is) Thy name (nature)."

Thy kingdom come, Thy will be done in earth as it is in heaven:
God's Kingdom is the perfect creation. Each individual is a perfect
idea in God Mind, a divine possibility of infinite capacity. Like the
pattern in the seed, there is a plan for every person in the Mind of
the Infinite, which gives rise also to a ceaseless urge within man
toward fulfillment. This might be called God's will. How important
it is that we understand this. The will of God is the ceaseless longing
of the Creator to express Himself and perfect Himself in the
creation. There cannot be even the slightest implication of restriction
or limitation in the will of God. In the prayer, this statement is
simply a decree: "Let that perfect idea, which I am in spirit, unfold
in me and through me. Let the divine will lead me into a manifestation in the outer, of that which I am within."

Give us this day our daily bread: The spirit of the original form is
more like this: "Thou art our supply and the daily, perpetual
manifestation of that supply." This is not asking God for supply, for
that would be like a fish asking the ocean for water. It is simply an
affirmation of the Truth that God *is* substance, and a claiming of
one's inheritance. In all creation, man alone is an individual, man
alone is free. And yet, man alone is sick, suffers, is unhappy, and
knows want. This is because in his freedom man fails to claim his
divine inheritance. Someone said, "There is a legitimate, royal abundance for every living thing." Jesus obviously believed this, and with
this statement in the Lord's Prayer, He is claiming it.

Forgive us our debts as we also have forgiven our debtors: This
indicates the working of the great Cosmic Law. Give and receive,
cause and effect, forgive and you are forgiven. This is dealt with at
great length in a later chapter. This does not ask God's forgiveness. It
simply reminds us of the forgiving action of divine law, of infinite
love. It stresses that the action is started by our effort—"forgive and
you are forgiven." We push the button and the divine activity moves
in to cleanse and release.

Leave us not in temptation but deliver us from evil: How important
it is that we get the right interpretation of this statement fixed in our
consciousness. It has always been made to imply that God could and

would lead man into temptation, into difficulties, into evil. Years ago
Charles Fillmore adapted the modern and more accurate translation
to the old prayer by changing "*lead* us not into" to the more correct
"*leave* us not in." God would never lead us into temptation. Can
light lead you into darkness? There can be no darkness in light at
all.

So, in this statement Jesus is simply affirming the Truth that the
urge for the expression of our potential is so great in us (that which
we call the will of God), that it will never leave us comfortless in our
time of trial. It will never abandon us in confusion or in temptation.
It will ever be the very power of help and healing and deliverance.

It appears quite clear that Jesus realized that temptation came, not
from some outer power or influence, but from the "demon" of
human consciousness, from selfishness, pride, ego, etc. And the resulting "evil" is simply the "confusion" that arises from the temptations.
Regardless of the forms it takes, what we call evil is simply the
concealment of good. We need not fight the evil person or the evil
condition. The need is to "let your light shine." Light erases darkness, good is revealed, evil (so-called) disappears as darkness before
the rising sun.

In the prayer Jesus is saying, "God will not fail you nor forsake
you, for there is a spirit in man and the inspiration of the Almighty
giveth him understanding."

*For Thine is the kingdom and the power and the glory, forever,
Amen:* This is not part of the original prayer. It was added at some
time down through the years for liturgical purposes. It is a suitable and
quite effective closing, especially when we get into the consciousness
of the affirmative mood of the whole prayer. It is a very important
statement of humility and faith. It declares with Kahlil Gibran, "It is
thy will in us that willeth. . . . it is thy desire in us that desireth."[6]
It affirms that in God is the goal, the means to achieve the goal, and
the glory of its achievement.

The prayer ends with "Amen." This does not mean "so it *will* be,"
and certainly not, "I do *hope* it will be." In the ancient Hebrew, it
means, "Verily, it is established; it is true; this is the truth." Going
back to the first chapter of Genesis, we find that after each of the
steps of the Creation, it reads, "and God (did so and so). . . . *and it*

was so." In the original Hebrew this statement, "it was so" was written "Amen." Thus the word "Amen" is one of the most powerful words in the entire Bible. It is not just a formal way to close a prayer. And, when the prayer is in the affirmative, a summing up of vital Truths, the "Amen" is of extra special importance. For it reaffirms in the most forceful possible way, *"This is the truth. . . . and it is now* done."

It is certain that we have missed the whole idea in the traditional use of the Lord's Prayer. What should we do about it? Should we continue to voice the "Lord's Prayer" as in the past? Can't we formulate the intended positive sense into a new version?

It is doubtful if we could make much of a dent in the traditional use of the prayer. More than this, it is an important common denominator among Christian organizations. The sacraments and the variety of ritual have tended to divide the Christian family, but the Lord's Prayer has been a force for unity. Even students of metaphysics use the Lord's Prayer, so that they may stand with and for the Christian "way."

However, we can and should formulate a simple interpretation to fix in our consciousness, so that when we speak the traditional words they automatically take on a new connotation for us. Here is such an interpretation, a new version that has been helpful to many people. Perhaps it will help you. It is intended as a frame of reference in which to think about and pray the Lord's Prayer. Many people use it on its own merit as a kind of daily treatment:

Our Father who art in heaven: I am now conscious of the infinite and eternal Presence in whom I live and by which I think and create.

Hallowed be Thy name: This Presence in me is whole and complete. It is the activity of health that heals, of intelligence that inspires, of substance that prospers, and of love that harmonizes.

Thy kingdom come, Thy will be done, in earth as it is in heaven: I am God's glorious possibility. I now let His perfect idea of me unfold in me and through me. My desire for betterment is God's desire to perfect that which He is expressing *as* me, and I let Him have His way. I see myself doing that which He sees me as being.

Give us this day our daily bread: I have no existence outside of God's Presence, for I am that Presence expressing as me. Therefore, I can never be separated from the all-sufficient substance of the opulent Universe. I claim my divine inheritance and I daily, perpetually, manifest abundant supply.

Forgive us our debts as we forgive our debtors: The Presence in me is my potential for dissolving all conflicts or transgression. The Presence is Love, and it loves in me and through me as I forgive. It releases me as I loose and let go of all my limited thoughts about myself or others.

Leave us not in temptation but deliver us from evil: The Presence in me is my light and my deliverance. There is no darkness in the light, and there can be no darkness in me when I am established in spiritual unity with the Presence within me—which is "better than light and safer than a known way."

For Thine is the kingdom and the power and the glory, forever, Amen: In all that I seek to be or do or have, I humbly realize that in the Presence is my power to think, my very thought of aspiration, my will to commence, my strength to keep on, my power to achieve, and the glory of all my accomplishments. This is the Truth, and it is now done.

10 Sufficient Unto Today

THE GOSPEL of Jesus is not an outline of divine edicts which God has set down to be obeyed by man for some inscrutable reason of His own. It is a compendium of Jesus' treatment of the laws of living, the laws of our own being. These laws had been discovered and fully tested by Jesus in His own life. He taught the knowledge and application of these spiritual laws as the way to self-realization and self-fulfillment. "Ye shall know the truth and the truth shall make you free" (John 8:32).

This chapter deals with a section of the Sermon on the Mount (Matt. 6:19-34) that is vitally needed in the world today, especially in the market place. As a matter of fact, every man or woman who daily "goes to business" should read this portion of the "sermon" at least once a week.

Lay not up for yourselves treasures upon the earth, where moth and rust consume, and where thieves break through and steal: but lay up for yourselves treasures in heaven, where neither moth nor rust doth consume, and where thieves do not break through nor steal: for where thy treasure is, there will thy heart be also.

Many have rejected this teaching of Jesus, for it would appear that He is against thrift, or the making and saving of money. In Jesus' day, they didn't have banks or building and loan societies. Any accumulation had to be hidden in the walls of the homes—and usually valuables were in the form of useful items, such as silks or woolens or metal objects. They were always in danger of rusting out, wearing out, being destroyed by moths, or being stolen.

Jesus says, "Lay up treasures in heaven." He is referring here to a metaphysical principle—that material wealth is objectified thought. When we think of money as a thing in itself, and when we think of the accumulation of possessions as a goal in life, we are building life upon shifting sands. Jesus is telling us to put first emphasis upon building a mental bank account of faith, building an awareness of the opulent substance of Spirit. This consciousness will always attract to us experiences that reflect the mental pattern, "as within, so without."

Charles Fillmore says: "Watch your thoughts when you are handling money, because your money is attached through your mind to the one source of all substance and all money. When you think of your money, which is visible, as something directly attached to an invisible source that is giving or withholding according to your thought, you have the key to all riches and the reason for all lack."[1]

Let's get one thing straight: Nowhere in the Bible does it say, "Money is the root of all evil." This is one of the most misquoted and distorted statements in the entire Bible. What the Bible does say is, "The *love* of money is a root of all kinds of evil" (I Tim. 6:10). The problem is not with money but with our attitudes about it. Money is innocent.

Money supported Albert Schweitzer in the steaming jungles where he labored unselfishly for the natives for fifty years. Gandhi, in his extreme poverty and simplicity of life, was supported by money. One of his followers once jokingly remarked that it cost a great deal of money to keep Gandhi living in poverty.

Even Jesus and His disciples were supported by money during His ministry throughout Palestine. The Bible records that certain women "ministered unto Him of their substance." In other words, they helped pay the bills. They "picked up the tab"—and thus it has always been!

Money is a medium of exchange, a symbol of all-sufficient substance, an evidence of ideas in currency. Money can enable great things to be done, it can enable love to flow, service to be rendered, faith to be backed up by works. But when money becomes an object in life, it frustrates the creativity of man, it inhibits his spiritual life, and it becomes a kind of evil force, giving rise to greed, dishonesty, and graft.

So Jesus is telling us that if our evaluation of the important things of life is centered only in materiality, then the moths and rust of selfishness, covetousness, competition, fear, and tension will surely consume our possessions and even us—and the thieves of inflation and depression, both mental and economic, will steal our good from us.

In our day we have come to an almost universal worship of the false gods of security. We have health insurance, job insurance, social security, Medicare, old-age pensions, etc., all designed to shield our lives from the tyranny of change and misfortune. However, the kind of insurance that could make our lives perfectly secure would come at a price few of us would willingly pay. It has been said that the only truly secure person is a convict in a penitentiary. He has no worries over a place to live, food to eat, clothes to wear. He has true security, but how great is the cost?

When Jesus says that we should "lay up treasures in heaven," He is saying that we should become more conscious of what we have going for us in the depths of us, the divine of us. This is what we often refer to as "building a prosperity consciousness"—the realization that God is the source of our supply, that all supply comes from an inner resource and that our greatest need is not so much to build great reserves of wealth "out here," as to build up great faith that there will always be a flow of substance—through us as ideas, and into our experience as money—to meet every legitimate need.

Human values fluctuate like a cork bobbing on the water. When money and things become the treasure of life, then "Where thy treasure is, there will thy heart be also." We become slaves to our possessions. A woman watching a parking attendant handle her car carelessly, remarks, "If he scratches my new car, I will just die!" A man responds to the question, "How are you?" with the statement, "I don't know, I haven't read the stock market report yet." In both cases, the individual has lost sight of the real center of life within himself and has come to assume that life's center is somewhere in the "whirling circumference."

Take time every day, preferably in the morning before you start off to work, to get your thoughts properly attuned to Infinite Mind.

Affirm that you are rich and secure because you are a spiritual being and the Kingdom of God is within you. Determine that you will see money and all material wealth in the proper context—as symbols of a diviner substance. Occasionally read the statement on your bills, "In God we trust." And then determine that you will trust in God in all transactions and experiences.

The lamp of the body is the eye: if therefore thine eye be single, thy whole body shall be full of light. But if thine eye be evil, thy whole body shall be full of darkness. If therefore the light that is in thee be darkness, how great is the darkness.

The physical act of seeing is one of the great miracles of life. Our optical structure, with its marvelous retinal system of rods and cones, and its adjustable lens, is well fitted for the perception of colors and shapes of objects in the world around us. However, the more we understand about the working of the mind, the more we realize that true sight is insight.

A dozen people could carefully study a panoramic view and then draw or paint a picture of it, and the result would reveal a dozen different pictures with striking differences of detail. Each person is seeing the scene with eyes that are basically the same in structure. But each person brings a preconditioning of consciousness that is unique to him. He sees the same picture but, because his frame of reference is different, his artistic representation is completely unique.

A person who is unhappy sees things that tend to justify his unhappiness. The pessimist sees discouraging signs. Jesus says, "If thine eye be evil, thy whole body shall be full of darkness." Evil is not a power. There is only One Power, and it is wholly good. If your perception of the potential goodness of life has been obscured by your fears, your cynicism, and your negative habits of thought, then the "whole body" of life's experiences will reflect that concealment of goodness.

When we realize that evil is simply the concealment of good, then any person who is unloving, vicious, or unjust is actually a person who is good but doesn't know it. In a very real way, we can change him—at least as far as we are concerned. We can see him with the "single eye" that relates only to the good and the true. We can salute the divinity in him. For us he will be different. And if we expose him frequently to this kind of seeing, we will be a strong influence for his actual change.

This leads to a point that is interestingly made in a story that comes out of the lore of the Island of Java. A young man spied a beautiful girl on the highroad and followed her for a mile. Finally she turned and demanded, "Why do you dog my footsteps?" He declared feverishly, "Because you are the loveliest thing I have ever seen and I have fallen madly in love with you at sight. Be mine!" The girl replied, "But you have merely to look behind you to see my young sister who is ten times more beautiful than I am." The gallant swain wheeled about and his gaze fell on as homely a girl as could be found in Java. "What mockery is this?" he demanded of the girl. "You lied to me!" "So did you," she replied. "If you were so madly in love with me, why did you turn around?"

This is what Jesus is talking about. We think we know the Truth and are working with it. We think we believe that God is the only presence and power in our lives. But we "turn around" in fear that our bank account will not hold out, in resistance to the person who seems to be a threat to our position, and in apprehension over the dark road that looms before us.

Man is essentially a spiritual being, this world is essentially a spiritual world, and the underlying controlling force is spiritual law. When we really "fall in love" with this spiritual essence, or establish our spiritual unity with it, when we recognize that this is a good world and that all people are innately good people—then we will see with the single eye. We will see that goodness in all people and we will draw goodness from them.

There are many incidences in the Gospel of the actual healing influence of Jesus' single-eyed beholding of an individual. But it is most effectively described by Lloyd C. Douglas in his classic novel, The Robe.[2] Miriam is telling Marcellus of the experience of Zacchaeus, who had become a completely changed individual after spending one hour with Jesus in his home.

Marcellus asks, "But what had happened? What had Jesus said to him?" Miriam shook her head, "Nobody knows." And then, with reminiscent eyes, she added, half to herself: "Maybe He didn't say anything at all. Perhaps He looked Zacchaeus squarely in the eyes until the man saw—reflected there—the image of the person he was meant to be."

Jesus said, "Judge not according to appearances but judge righteous judgment." Righteous judgment is seeing with the single eye. It is seeing with a spiritual perception that reflects a spiritual unity with God-Mind. It sees people, not as they are, but as they can be. Zacchaeus was a typically materialistic man who had fought his way to the top of a "dog-eat-dog" world. He had money, position, prestige, and possessions, but he had no security, no inner peace. His eye was evil (centered in materiality) and so his whole experience was full of darkness.

Jesus looked right through the façade of the sophisticated and self-centered man of the world. He probably said to Zacchaeus, "My friend, you are a better man than you know. The very fact that you made the effort to see me indicates that you have the capacity and the readiness to see the Truth in yourself and in life. I salute the divinity in you. You are now free from your past illusions about yourself. Go forth and be what you can be." And Zacchaeus suddenly saw himself in the mirror of Truth and he was healed.

One of the greatest lessons we can learn from the concept of the Divinity of Man is that we can determine the level on which we are going to do business with men. If we make contact with another on the level upon which the appearances seem to indicate he is functioning, then our relationship will be completely in the framework of that level of consciousness. We may grumble and complain, "You just can't trust people these days," and "Why do people have to act that way?" Perhaps this individual *had* to act "that way" because that was the level of his total character that we made contact with. We drew it out of him. He might even say to himself, "What is the matter with me? Why am I acting in this way?"

On the other hand, if we precondition the relationship or transaction with the affirmative declaration, "I am established in spiritual unity with God and with all people—I express the divinity in me and I salute the divinity in everyone I meet," then we will find ourselves expressing more love, understanding, patience and trust. And the other person will correspondingly express himself on that level of consciousness.

When we know this process, we must be constantly on the alert to keep our vision "single-eyed" to the Truth. We should prepare our-selves for every foray into the world of human relationships. Don't let the world around you turn on the lights in you. You turn the focused spotlight of your spiritual insight onto the world. Don't let anyone determine how you are going to act (or react). You determine that you will "let your light shine," that you will think and act from the highest level of consciousness of which you are presently capable. And be quick to dispel all hostility or resistance in another by expos-ing him to a spiritual treatment arising out of your insight into his essential divinity. "Be not overcome of evil, but overcome evil with good" (Rom. 12:21).

No man can serve two masters; for either he will hate the one, and love the other; or else he will hold to one and despise the other. Ye cannot serve God and mammon.

The girl said, "You do not really love me as you say or else you would not have turned around to see if my sister was more beautiful." He thought he loved her "with all his heart, soul, mind and strength," but he couldn't pass the test. But don't be too hard on him. We all do the same in one way or another many times over. You cannot "salute the divinity" in yourself or in someone else and then im-patiently declare, "what a stupid thing that was for me to do," or "I can't understand how people can be so thoughtless," etc.

What you acknowledge to be your master, to that you are a servant. This is a fundamental metaphysical law and there is no escape from it. If you insist that "there is a lot of evil in the world today—you can't trust people any more," then you become a slave to the fluctuations of human consciousness, to all that is sordid and mean. And people will always seem to express the very worst that is in them when they are with you.

And if you make a god of your material interests—your work, your investments, your possessions—you become a slave to these things. You forget that all money, all creative work, all wealth are the objec-tification of divine ideas. Thus, your peace of mind and your sense of security is completely tied to locked doors, bank vaults, the "perfor-mance" of investments, and the stability of the stock market.

When the rich young man came to Jesus (Luke 18) expressing the desire to be a disciple, Jesus told him to go and sell all he had and give to the poor. The young man "turned sorrowfully away, for he had great possessions." Now Jesus had nothing against wealth. He was simply testing the young man in the same way the Javanese beauty tested her impetuous suitor. In both cases, the young man failed the test. They turned around.

There is a story that is told about Antoinette Bourignon, the spiritual leader who made such a stir in the religious world of the seventeenth century. As a young girl, she had a great vision of her spiritual unity with God, coupled with a great desire to communicate[17] to the people of her day who were walking in such great darkness. Her parents were on the verge of forcing her into an unwelcome marriage, so she decided to leave home. One morning, at daybreak, she started on her way, taking with her one penny for bread for that day. As she was leaving the house, she felt a presence within her saying, "Where is your faith, in a penny?" Without a moment's hesitation, she threw the penny aside and replied, "No, Lord, my faith is in thee and in thee alone."

William James comments on this in his *Varieites of Religious Experience*: "The penny was a small financial safeguard, but an effective spiritual obstacle."[3] Obviously, if she had turned around at that moment, she would have evidenced a state of consciousness that was completely lacking in the stability and faith she would need to do the great work that she had set herself to do. She had to prove to herself that she could go all the way.

When you really have faith in God, when you really believe that God is your supply, your security, your help in every need, then you will do the wise and discerning thing about your job, your possessions, your investments—but you will think of them only as channels through which your good comes. Wisdom will dictate an orderly handling of your financial affairs, but faith will keep you free from worry and fear. And when conditions change, as they always have and always will, you will hold fast to the declaration of the Psalmist, "Though the earth do change, I shall not be moved."

Mankind has yet to learn the lesson that legislation has never brought equality and freedom to people, that treaties have never secured peace, that padlocks have never prevented robberies and prisons have never deterred crime. If man wants peace on earth, he must get into the consciousness of peace and never look back. Health will become universal when we teach people to build a health-consciousness. The war on poverty will be won only by education in the art of thinking prosperously. It is the Truth that will make men free and there is no other way. This is what Jesus really taught.

Therefore, I say unto you, be not anxious for your life, what ye shall eat, or what ye shall drink; nor yet for your body, what ye shall put on. Is not the life more than the food, and the body than the raiment? Behold the birds of the heaven, that they sow not, neither do they reap, nor gather into barns; and your heavenly father feedeth them. Are not ye of much more value than they? And which of you by being anxious can add one cubit unto the measure of his life? And why are ye anxious concerning raiment? Consider the lilies of the field, how they grow; they toil not, neither do they spin: yet I say unto you, that even Solomon in all his glory was not arrayed like one of these. But if God doth so clothe the grass of the field, which today is, and tomorrow is cast into the oven, shall He not much more clothe you, O ye of little faith?

This should cause many of us to blush just a little. How much of our waking thought is devoted to such details as what we shall eat and drink and wear? And if Jesus were giving this sermon today, he perhaps would add a reference to mass anxiety neurosis about gaining weight and dieting to lose weight.

Jesus is saying, "Can you by worrying about yourself, change the person you really are? Does your anxious thought help to pay bills, does it make your work succeed, does it reap the harvest or fill the barn? You are a spiritual being, and your life is lived from within out. Relax and let go, and let life fulfill itself in you and *as* you."

Thoreau, who spent many a season in a continuing romance with nature, writes: "I saw a delicate flower had grown up two feet high between the horse's feet and the wheel track. An inch more to the right or left had sealed its fate, or an inch higher. Yet it lived to flourish and never knew the danger it incurred. It did not borrow trouble, nor invite an evil fate by apprehending it."[4]

Like that flower in the wheel track, it may sometimes seem that you are living on the edge of doom. However, though the earth is a sphere and we live on its outer edge with nothing but gravity to keep us from falling into oblivion, man has learned to live confidently in this precarious position because of the constancy and stability of gravity. The energy field that we know as gravity is an excellent illustration of the nonmaterial force that Jesus refers to simply as "The Father."

Lesser forms of life are bound by their place in nature to support by the life force. Man, because of the freedom implicit in his divinity, must acknowledge and consciously respond to this life force or divine presence. The bird or flower must simply be still and grow—it has no other choice. But man must "Be still and know that I am God." If he knows this—really knows it—he can rise to the very heights of abundant living, life without care.

Be not therefore anxious, saying, What shall we eat? or, What shall We drink? or, Wherewithal shall we be clothed? For . . . your heavenly Father knoweth that we have need of all these things. But seek ye first his kingdom, and his righteousness; and all these things shall be added unto you.

The important key to understanding man is that he is an identity in the Infinite Mind of God. He is actually an activity of God projecting Himself into visibility *as* man. In other words, the same force that creates man is a perpetual potency to sustain him. Every discovery that man has made in the world about him has come out of an inner discovery of the world within him. Man is a bundle of possibilities, and his only business in life is the "express business"—or the business of expressing his inner self.

That fabulous character, Mike Todd, is reputed to have said, "Many times I have been broke, but I have never been poor." Why? Because he had that intangible but very real spirit or consciousness that always acted as a magnet to attract his good to him. People called him "lucky." But it is only the immature who talk of luck. The spiritual realist knows that there is a law of cause and effect involved. Mike Todd obviously had an unshakable faith in his stored-up "treasure in heaven," faith that in the bank of the universe, his credit was always good.

Seek first to be, and you will have, Jesus is saying. To have more you must *be* more. Success cannot be measured by what you have amassed. It can only be known by the level of consciousness you have achieved. When you have a need for "these things," the first step should be to get still, acknowledge your spiritual unity with Infinite Mind, and rest quietly in the Truth of what you are. This is like instructing the electromagnet, "Don't worry about how you are going to lift the weights. Just plug into the current and let it create the magnetic field. You will easily attract (and lift) the load."

In the Divinity of Man, there is a changeless relationship with the principle in which every problem has an answer. "Before they call, I will answer" (Isa. 65:24), and the "I" here is that Father Presence in you that has nothing whatever to do but to work for your highest good. When there is a decision to be made, there is a right choice even before we begin to analyze the situation. "The Father knows"— the God-self of you knows. When there is a need for employment, there is a right and perfect job even before we set out to look for it. If you have a problem in addition—say four plus three—the answer is seven even before we put the figures down on paper. So you confidently put them on paper and add them up, and the right answer comes forth.

Jesus is saying, "When you have a problem—no matter what it is or how serious it seems—don't worry about it. Pray about it. Don't try to work it out with human resources alone. Get still and acknowledge the guiding principle and the all-sufficient substance of the Universe. Have faith in God, in an opulent, orderly Universe. And have faith in yourself and your innate divinity, by which you can do what you need to do and have what you desire to have."

Be not therefore anxious for the morrow: for the morrow will be anxious for itself. Sufficient unto the day is the evil thereof.

Very simply this says: Don't be worried about tomorrow, for tomorrow can take care of itself. Every day has its own challenges. The word "evil" here means the unrevealed potential for good. Every day is a new experience in growth and the potentialities for great things are always present, but often they are mighty well hidden. Ours is the privilege of uncovering the good and discovering the blessings intended for us—but we can only do this one day at a time.

Even in Jesus' day, the great cause of worry was tomorrow. Even as we become trapped in the emphasis upon things in life, the constant concern about "what we shall eat or what we shall drink or where-withal we shall be clothed," so do we become prisoners of time. We feel that we are chained to a relentlessly moving treadmill: "Time marches on. It is later than you think. With every passing moment the supply is depleted, and what will we do tomorrow?"

Jesus challenges us to consider a new concept. We must stop thinking of life as a journey between two points on an endless high-way. It is this subconscious feeling that leads to hurry and rush and tension. Life is eternal, and we are alive in eternity now.

Most of us are willing to admit that immortality is a fact that will be proved after we die. But this was not the teaching of Jesus. We are told that Jesus "brought life and immortality to light through the gospel." To bring a thing to light, you make it manifest. Jesus revealed that immortality is not a post-mortem experience but a present reality. "Now is the acceptable time; behold, now is the day of salvation" (II Cor. 6:2). "Sufficient unto today. . . ."

Immortality and eternity, then, are actually a higher dimension of life. In this "eternity" domain, or in Divine Mind, concurrent with his manifest experience, man is perfect beyond his imperfection, whole beyond his sickness, intelligent beyond his poverty and lack. In the Kingdom of Heaven within us, health, wealth, harmony and peace are constant, and they are always "sufficient unto today." Thus when we "seek first the kingdom," we get into a higher level of thinking where there is no tomorrow. We claim our good today. And there is no anxiety or fear for the future. Our "daily bread" for every day is part of the unfolding possibility which that day is.

Most of our thoughts about "what we shall eat and drink and wear" are related to tomorrow. We scrimp and save and provide for the "rainy day." We develop a kind of neurosis based on subtle fears for the future. We save our best linen for special occasions. Certain items of clothes are "too good to wear for every day." Often they deteriorate before we ever put them to use. Today, insurance is a protection against the unknown of the future. Many people carry so much insurance against future discomforts that they may go hungry today in order to pay their premiums. They make themselves unhappy now, in trying to keep from being unhappy in the future.

When you know your own divinity, you know it is not for just a day but for always. As a child of God, you are richly endowed with an all-sufficiency in all things. You know that God is your instant, constant, and abundant supply. When you "seek first the kingdom," you meditate deeply on the Truth of your oneness with God. You enter a higher dimension in thought, and you come to live "with the license of a higher order of beings." There is no concern for tomorrow, for tomorrow only exists when it becomes today. And when it becomes today, it brings its own challenges and its own blessings.

11 The Law of Compensation

IN THE RELIGION about Jesus, God is often portrayed as capricious
and changeable. Good people suffer for some "inscrutable reason of
His own," but they are to be rewarded in some future heaven. Bad
people go unpunished now, but their reward will come in a future day
of judgment with relegation to a roaring, roasting hell of eternal fire.
It is likely that the whole Christian concept of "Judgment Day" has
arisen out of man's feelings of self-pity in the face of the inequities of
life and his subconscious desire to even things up in some later time.

The word "judgment" is from the Latin *jus*, right, and *dico*, I
declare. It is a declaration of what is right or just, and it is only in its
secondary sense that it has acquired the meaning of "condemnation"
and has come to be associated more with guilt than with innocence.
Whenever we discriminate between good and evil and range ourselves on the side of good, we have made a declaration of justice (a
judgment). This is for us a "judgment day."

Every day is a day of judgment. We are told "choose you this day
whom ye will serve" (Josh. 24:15). And we make our choice constantly. We decide to dwell on the right side of divine law, or we
break the law. In either case, it is our day of judgment and we reap
the results of the inexorable law of compensation. There is no caprice
involved at all. We are not punished for our sins but by them.

Judge not that ye be not judged. For with what judgment ye judge,
ye shall be judged: and with what measure ye mete, it shall be
measured unto you [Matt. 7:1, 2].

THE LAW OF COMPENSATION | 135

This is the GREAT LAW! It is a universal principle that is operative constantly for saint and sinner alike, for rich and poor, for young and old, for Easterner and Westerner! Until one understands this basic Truth he will follow human reasoning in thinking that "some people get all the breaks" or "why should this happen to me?" etc. The great "misconception" of the law leads people on the endless round of trying to get something for nothing, of hoping for the lucky break. It is this limited view of life that motivates the thief, the gambler, and even the speculator in the business world.

We cannot get something for nothing. We cannot break the law and go unpunished. This is what Jesus taught. This concept is also found in the Hindu doctrine of karma. A man is what he is, in respect to his fortune or place in life, because of his karma. Karma fixes consequences of one's acts. All mistakes, failures, and sins must be atoned for in some way at some time. They become a karmic debt that must ultimately, from lifetime to lifetime, be paid. For another fundamental of Hinduism is the law of reincarnation.

The Hindu explains everything in his world by karma; suffering, blessing, sorrow, joy, low caste, high caste, pauper and prince, poor man and rich man, the pitifully sick and the radiantly healthy. Nothing a man does is ever lost, nothing is unaccounted for, nothing is forgotten, discarded, or irrelevant.

On the surface the doctrine of karma would appear to be the equivalent of Jesus' teaching of "the law of compensation"—but there is a vast and irreconcilable difference. The Hindu concept centers its attention chiefly on man's past and ultimate destiny. There is little or no hope or promise of freedom today. Karma becomes a cycle of penalty and retribution that continues on from one incarnation to the next. The individual is chained to a relentlessly moving wheel by the accumulated sins of past lives.

The Hindu has a resulting sense of hopelessness and futility. There is no healing, no way to overcoming, no way out. He evidences amazing qualities of patience and nonresistance. The sick man does not try to get well, for he is uncomplainingly bearing the burden of past karma. The "untouchable" makes no attempt to better his appalling condition, nor does he harbor envy for Indians of higher caste. He bears his lot stoically, for it is karma.

The essential difference between Jesus' teachings and the Hindu concepts is the Divinity of Man. The Hindu is working toward the same goal as that which Jesus taught—oneness with God, self-realization, and purification of the soul. However, the Hindu is working to *reach* the divine while Jesus taught that man is already divine. Thus, while Jesus taught us to pray believing that help and healing are already ours because of our unity with God, the Hindu seeks only to control his karma by thinking, speaking, and acting today in a manner that will bring good consequence in some future life.

The dynamic of Jesus' teaching is found in the words, "Ye shall know the truth, and the truth shall make you free" (John 8:32). He accepted the fundamental underlying the karmic law, and much of His teaching reflects this acceptance. But He taught that sequence and consequence, cause and effect, are law for matter and mind only; they are not law for the Spirit. There is no law of retribution in God. "Yea, I have loved thee with an everlasting love" (Jer. 31:3).

Both the causes and the effects function in a realm outside the kingdom of God-consciousness. Thus, no matter what the causes or the karmic debt, the effects can be dissolved by "knowing the Truth," by raising our consciousness above the level of sin and its atonement.

Paul refers to this: "There is therefore now no condemnation to them that are in Christ Jesus (in the consciousness of the Christ, their innate divinity). For the law of the Spirit of life in Christ Jesus made me free from the law of sin and of death" (Rom. 8:1).

When we enter into the Spirit, we are free from bondage to the flesh, our debt is canceled, and we begin to know and experience life and wholeness. This is the basis of prayer. It is the key to healing, the principle of demonstrating prosperity, the way to overcoming of any kind. "Know the truth, and the truth shall make you free." This was Jesus' great contribution to man's eternal quest for Truth. And, strangely enough, it has been seldom emphasized in Christian theology, if it has been emphasized at all.

In Jesus' concept of prayer, it is not a matter of bribing God for release from some karmic burden of debt, or from the effects of the law of compensation. It is simply that the higher law of Spirit overrides or supersedes the lower laws of the mental and physical planes.

This is not so strange when we see it in the light of progress in science. One hundred years ago it was thought to be a scientific fact that nothing heavier than air could fly. Observing the birds breaking the law, however, the dreamer dreamed his dreams. Today mammoth air-cargo planes easily carry many tons through the air. All this has come about not at all by breaking the law of gravity, but by the discovery of other laws through which the limitations of gravity can be transcended.

Jesus was a great way-shower. We might say that man was earth-bound by the law of karma. His karmic burden was so great that his plight on earth was little short of hopeless. Then Jesus made his great discovery of the Divinity of Man. He discovered that man was one with the transcendent Spirit of God and thus, by knowing the Truth of his spiritual unity, man could remove the mountains of human suffering and find abundant life here and now.

At this point, you may object, "Ah, now you have a contradiction. First you insisted that you can't get something for nothing, that all sin is punished, that consequence always follows cause. Now you say that there is a way to be free from the punishment, that you don't really have to pay your debt."

The answer to the apparent contradiction is this: Every sin must be atoned for, all karmic debt must be paid. However, the choice is ours whether we work it out in the cycle of retribution, through prolonged suffering in "the furnace of affliction," or whether our payment of debt is through the discipline of rising above the consciousness from which the act was committed into the freedom of spiritual understanding where we go forth and "sin no more." This is what Jesus called "forgiveness." It was the key to His tremendous ability to be instrumental in changing the lives of people. It is the key to healing and overcoming for us.

All this notwithstanding, we cannot overlook the underlying truth of the law of karma, the law of compensation. For it is basic in your life and in mine. As we think, speak, and act toward others, so will others think, speak, and act toward us. As we give we receive. What we do to others comes back to us in some way at some time.

The reason this does not seem to be true is that we are looking for the "comeback" from the same people. A worker may say, "After all that I have given to this organization, they fire me." A parent may complain, "I have slaved and sacrificed for my children and what thanks do I get? They go off and live their own lives with no concern for me." This frustration comes because of the common mistake of thinking the recipient is obligated to return what he has received. In human relations, we may be motivated by such a sense of obligation. But, under the law of compensation, the return need not, and probably will not, come from the recipient, but it *will* come.

When we understand the working of divine law, we begin to see how very practical are Jesus' teachings. For instance, when He talks about giving and serving and loving one's neighbor (even loving an enemy) it would seem that His ideals were completely impractical and unsuited for life in our times. But Jesus is not instructing us to do these things simply to fulfill a divine edict for some reason that only God knows. These ideas are the very practical means of setting up causes that will have good effects in our life. They simply stress the importance of making positive deposits in the cosmic bank, to insure the flow of good. "Lay up for yourselves treasures in heaven . . ." (Matt. 6:19).

And why beholdest thou the mote that is in thy brother's eye, but considerest not the beam that is in thine own eye? Or how wilt thou say to thy brother, Let me cast out the mote out of thine eye; and lo, the beam is in thine own eye? Thou hypocrite, cast out first the beam out of thine own eye; and then shalt thou see clearly to cast out the mote out of thy brother's eye [Matt. 7:3–5].

The word "mote" means a splinter of wood or a speck of sawdust; the word "beam" means a log or a large plank. This is a figure of speech that is purposely grotesque, like the camel and the needle's eye. Nothing is more absurd than for a man to try to pin the blame for his problems on the slight misdeeds of others, when there are glaring limitations in his own consciousness.

Jesus was a master psychologist. He knew that people have a tendency to attempt to justify their own weaknesses by looking for weaknesses in others and also to rise above their own sense of insufficiency by cutting people down to their size. Quite often the "reformer" in life is trying to change the world and the people in it because he has a secret sense of injustice in the way the world has treated him.

He who would save the world must first of all save himself. He who would enlighten his brother must first of all be enlightened himself. What we see in others is an evidence of the level of our own consciousness. Everyone is a spectrum of many levels of consciousness —ranging from the very good to the very bad, from the very strong to the very weak. If we include the spiritual dimension along with the human level, it might be said that we can find anything in another that we want to look for. Thus, it must follow that what we find in him is more a judgment of the beholder. The shortcoming we find ourselves harping on in another is an evidence of a state of consciousness in us. More than this, it may well be the key to the cause of certain "unjust" experiences we are facing—for which we are unconsciously trying to dodge responsibility by engaging in criticism of others.

So Jesus advises, "Forget about that speck of weakness or limitation you can find in the other fellow. Get busy changing your own level of consciousness." This might help us to understand his declaration: "I, if be lifted up from the earth, will draw all men unto me" (John 12:32).

There is a tendency that prevails in human consciousness that we all must come to grips with. Man harbors a kind of subconscious sense of self-pity for the inequities of life. He secretly feels that "other people get all the breaks," and that his lot in life has not been fair and just. So, when he gets hold of a spiritual concept that seems practical and livable, he can hardly contain his desire to pass it on to other people. "It is just what my husband (or boss or next door neighbor) needs." And this reveals that he secretly feels that these people are the cause of his problems.

Unless this tendency is faced and corrected, our religious study can lead to a completely hypercritical attitude. A story of unknown authorship tells of a Persian family in which a pious son rose early to read the Koran each morning and to meditate and pray. One morning his father awoke while his son was performing his devotions. The son said, "Your other children are lost in irreligious slumber, while I alone am awake to praise God." The wise father answered, "Son of my soul! It is better to sleep than to awake to notice the faults of others."

There would be a world-sweeping renaissance throughout all religions if people would become aware that religion deals with but one thing: the relationship of the individual with God. Every individual has a built-in capacity for divinity, but he must discover his depths and activate the process of his own spiritual growth. This is a full-time job. When he is busily engaged in removing the "beam" from his own eye, he has no time or inclination to try to remove the "mote" from his brother's eye.

The amazing part of all this is that when you get the "beam" out of your own eye and see things and people from the standpoint of Truth, lo and behold, the mote in your brother's eye has disappeared. Either it only had existence in your mind, or the influence of your vision was a healing treatment that dissolved the limitation in him. Or, perhaps, you have become so loving and understanding that the speck of sawdust that once loomed so important to you has faded into insignificance. You have found so much good in the person that his slight imperfection has become irrelevant.

Give not that which is holy unto dogs, neither cast your pearls before the swine, lest haply they trample them under their feet and turn and rend you [Matt. 7:6].

The word "cynic" comes from the Greek word that means *dog*. We can see that Jesus is again using a classic figure of speech. He is not calling narrow people swine or canines. He is simply saying, "Don't waste your time trying to present the Truth to the cynical person. He won't understand it and he will only tear your arguments to pieces."

It is vitally important to you to keep your thought stayed on the good and thus to see the good in people. But, much as you love someone, don't try to make him over. See the good in him, but don't try to put words in his mouth. Lift your thought to a level where you can see him in the light of his innate divinity, but don't try to convert him to your way of thinking.

Every religion in the world has its religious zealots. They paint signs on mountainsides, they distribute pamphlets on the street corners, and they try to impose their views and favorite prayers and affirmations on their loved ones and associates. This individual is forever being hurt, simply because he is scattering the jewels of Truth before the cynical and they turn and rend him. They discredit his faith and tear his metaphysical arguments to shreds.

If you find yourself being hurt by the resistance of the cynic, ask yourself, "Why am I so obsessed with the need to give him the light of Truth?" Perhaps it is because you are attempting to escape the responsibility of meeting problems in yourself. See the good in other people and then leave them alone. Get the log out of your own eye. Work to eliminate from your mind the thought that this other person desperately needs the Truth. As long as you are concerned about his problems, you are seeing limitation, you are "impure in heart." Heal your concern by using your "pearls" of Truth on yourself.

Ask, and it shall be given you; seek, and ye shall find; knock, and it shall be opened unto you: for every one that asketh receiveth; and he that seeketh findeth; and to him that knocketh it shall be opened [Matt. 7:7, 8].

This clearly implies divine law and not caprice in God's response to prayer or human effort. In prayer we are working with the law of compensation. We may have thought that prayer was a way to overcome karmic law or to dissolve the bad debts we have accumulated, a way of getting God to interfere. But God doesn't interefere. There is no possible way we can get something for nothing, not even through prayer. Prayer works with and through the law of compensation, not in opposition to it. The law is exact and, so Jesus says, "Ask and it *shall* be given you" (Matt. 7:7). He does not say "Ask and maybe it will work out," or "Keep looking and some day, if you are fortunate, you will find it." No, he says, ". . . it *shall* be given," ". . . ye *shall* find," ". . . it *shall* be opened."

As we have previously pointed out, the word "ask" has a much broader meaning than is usually realized. A study of the root meaning of the word in the original Greek reveals a connotation of "claim" or "demand." To ask for something in prayer is to accept it in consciousness, to lay hold of it. Isaiah says (45:11), "Concerning the work of my hands, command ye me." As a child of God you not only have the right but the distinct responsibility to command the law— because it *is* law. There is nothing capricious about law. It works for you as you work with it.

When you pray you are fulfilling divine law. It is another way of

giving that you may receive. You are giving receptivity. If you go to a
water faucet for water, you take an empty cup. You give the receptivity of the cup to the faucet, and the water fills the cup to over-
flowing. There is no question about it—an empty cup under an open
tap means it "shall" be filled. If you have a need in your life, you give
that need to divine law. You give it in the faith and assurance that it
will be filled under divine law. And it is filled.

Asking, seeking, knocking are all claiming your good, commanding
the unfoldment of inner power. "Ye *shall* receive." You give the
receptivity, the faith, the self-contol, and the law will do the rest—
because it *is* law.

Jesus then gives the illustration of an earthly Father to give us an
analogy that might help the finite to understand the Infinite:

> What man is there of you, who, if his son shall ask him for a loaf, will
> give him a stone; or if he shall ask for a fish, will give him a ser-
> pent? If ye then, being evil, know how to give good gifts unto
> your children, how much more shall your Father who is in
> heaven give good things to them that ask him? [Matt. 7:9–11].

Jesus realized that one of man's greatest problems is that when he
thinks of the Infinite he is forever clothing Him in human form. He
is forever creating God in his own image likeness. We may well be
relating to a personal God whom we talk to, reason with, plead with,
supplicate, and influence—a God who changes His mind, holds
grudges, takes revenge and becomes angry. Jesus knew that this image
of God is forever standing in our way.

Now, when He says, "If ye, then, being evil," we must be careful
not to lose the thread of the Divinity of Man. Evil is not some force
that emanates from part of a supposed duality of the Universe. Evil is
simply the concealment of good—like darkness is the abscnce of
light. "Ye, being evil" means—you who do not realize your innate
goodness and haven't been acting the part of your divinity. Even in
the concealment of your divinity, He is saying, you would not take
revenge on your children or consign them to a hell of fire. How much
more would your Father in Heaven deal lovingly with you?

The "Father in heaven" is the divine level of your own self, the
potential for your fulfillment which is forever with you and within

you. How much more shall this divine side of your nature reveal itself in you and fulfill itself through you in the form of your desired good. You see, Jesus is relating to the Divinity of Man rather than to a far-off God.

One of the commonest causes of weakness in man's pursuit of the good in life is the plaguing doubt, "perhaps it is not God's will." The term "God's will" has so long been considered in the light of a capricious and whimsical God of the skies who pulls strings to direct our lives like robots. We might be immeasurably blessed if we could eliminate the term from our vocabulary. Even a person who has gained a new vision of Truth may well be following an old concept by saying or inferring in his prayers, "if it be God's will."

Jesus actually ridicules such a thought. He says, "Even in your human consciousness, far from the awareness of the depth potential within you, you would want only the very best for your children, so how much more would the divinity within you want to express through and as you."

There is absolutely no place in this picture for a hell of everlasting torment or for a person or force that would or could attempt to put you there. Nor is there any place for the thought that sickness or deformity or death or poverty or limitation of any kind is the will of God. The will of God is the ceaseless longing of the Spirit in you to completely fulfill in the outer the potential within you. The will of God in you is the pent-up energy of your own divinity that is seeking releasement and fulfillment in your manifest life. It is God seeking to express Himself as you—as radiant health, as eternal youth, as an all-sufficiency of supply, as freedom from limitation of any kind.

"But how can we know that our desire is good," we might be asking? A wise criterion is to work for or claim only that which we are willing that all humanity should receive equally with us. When you are yearning for something, and you wonder, "How do I know this is right for me?" or "How do I know it is God's will for me?" then it is well to upgrade the desire into a more universal form. Ask yourself, "Am I willing to have this desire be fulfilled in the life of every person on earth?"

This may force you to change your emphasis. You may object, "But I am praying that this man marry me. I want *this* man." Actually, your true desire is for companionship and love and fulfillment. It is on the human level of consciousness that you think "this man." Upgrade your desire and put it in spiritual terms in the form of an affirmation: "I am God's child and it is right for me to have love and companionship and fulfillment. I claim it, I give thanks for it." Now you become an attractive force. And if "this man" is the person attracted to you, then so be it.

It is not God's will that interferes with the right answer to our desires, but our own will. We evaluate the situation, not in terms of a divine attraction, but in terms of human willfulness. A woman asked a prayer group to pray with her that a particular man would marry her. After many requests, she finally thanked them for their good work, for the marriage had come about. But in a few months, she was back asking for their prayer to help her "get rid of him."

If you are praying for employment, you don't have to say, "O God, I want this job. Give me this job. I won't be satisfied with anything but this job." Following Jesus' criteria under the law of compensation, you should pray only for the releasement of your creative potential and for the opportunity to fulfill it. Give thanks for employment, for the opportunity for service. When you get yourself in tune with the divine action by holding a universal thought, you will draw to you the opportunity that is the right and perfect place where you can fulfill all your needs; and the "all things added" will come too: the right salary, the right environment, even the right pensions and retirement plans.

Jesus summarizes this criterion for the universal formation of your desires in what has been called the golden rule:

Therefore, all things whatsoever ye would that men should do to you, do ye even so to them; for this is the law and the prophets [Matt. 7:12, AV].

This is the principle of action and reaction—give and receive—the law of complementarity. Do as you would be done by, think as you would like to experience, love and you shall be loved, forgive and you shall be forgiven. Jesus did not announce this as a new law. He did not create laws; He simply discovered them as part of the Divinity of Man. It is a principle as old as time, as inexorable as gravity, as impersonal as sunlight.

When we think good, speak good, do good, we not only tend to pay debts of past limitations, we prepare the way for inevitable future blessings. Call it karma, call it cause and effect, call it the law of compensation—for it is a fundamental Truth of life, and a most needed realization for all who would live life effectively.

The Sermon on the Mount ends with a stern warning:

> *Therefore whosoever heareth these sayings of mine, and doeth them, I will liken him unto a wise man, which built his house upon a rock; and the rain descended, and the floods came; and the winds blew, and beat upon that house; and it fell not: for it was founded upon a rock. And every one that heareth these sayings of mine, and doeth them not, shall be likened unto a foolish man, which built his house upon the sand: and the rain descended, and the floods came, and the winds blew, and beat upon that house; and it fell: and great was the fall of it* [Matt. 7:24–27, AV].

Jesus had seen houses built on the sands of the desert and had seen them washed away in the rain and wind. Today we have a better understanding of building, so that such mistakes are rarely made by the building industry. But, oh, how many lives are still being built upon the shifting sands of superficial ideals, materialistic goals, and in the thought of getting something for nothing.

If you purchased an electrical appliance to handle some difficult household chore for you, you might have great hopes of its usefulness in your daily life. But when you took it home, you might find to your disappointment that it didn't work. Then someone points out to you a warning on the accompanying instructions: "NOT GOOD IF DETACHED."

This is what Jesus is saying, "All these things which I have outlined for you, this philosophy or way of life, can lead you to self-discovery and to abundant living. But it doesn't work unless you use it. It must be turned on or "plugged in." He says, "If ye know these things, blessed are ye if ye do them" (John 13:17).

When you begin to catch the concept of your innate divinity, you have the means of building a life that is impervious to change and challenge. Don't be satisfied with a library of the right books, or with an accumulation of notebooks of ideas you have gleaned from reading and studying. These sayings of Jesus are practical and must be put into practice. Don't be satisfied that you have learned a lot of prayers and affirmations. *Do the thing and you shall have the power.*

To all those who are weary and sore oppressed and whose faith seems at times to prove inadequate, Jesus would say, "Lay aside your profession of faith and your creed, your religious mottoes and affirmations and devote some time to quiet meditation and contemplation of yourself as a spiritual being. Know that Truth is not something you learn or accumulate in memory, but something you unfold within yourself. Neither praying that God will make you a better person nor affirming that you are now perfect will enable you to be more than you were created to be. But you can release the hidden potential of your inmost self to give expression to the Truth that is the very law of your being."

If you insist that Truth is limitless, and if you meet all things in the consciousness of the limitless Truth of God, then the rain may descend and the floods will come and the winds will blow—but the house will not fall, for your life is built upon rock. The knowledge of "these sayings" will then be no mere platitudes or intellectual beliefs. They will become strong and vital attitudes of your being.

12 How God Forgives

His heart was as great as the world, but there was no room in it
to hold the memory of a wrong.[1]   *Emerson*

THE FORGIVENESS of sin has always been the central factor in religion.
It was a keynote of Jesus' teachings. But what do we mean by sin? It
is unfortunate that we accept words like this as having absolute
meanings, without even asking ourselves what we understand them to
mean.

The dictionary might define the word, "Transgression of divine
law." In Christian theology there is a general agreement that "Sin
occurs when man is out of harmony with the Source of his being."
Thus, sin is a sense of separation from God. We use the word "*sense
of separation*" by choice, for the separation is only in man's thought.
The finite is indissolubly linked with the Infinite. Sin is when a man,
a spiritual being and creative expression of Divine Mind, is unaware
of his divinity and acts at the level of his humanity. Thus, sin is the
major tragedy of human experience.

When man doesn't know his divinity, when he doesn't know the
depth of his own innate goodness, he does a lot of things that are the
result of the frustration of his potentiality. He thinks that he lives an
isolated life. His thoughts are completely self-regarding. His entire
experience is oriented to a selfish plane of life. The result is what has
been called *evil*—evil people doing evil deeds.

The word "evil" also needs redefinition. Evil is basically the

147

concealment of the good. The metaphysical student often declares, "There is no evil." This is about like saying there is no darkness. Of course, there is evil in the world, and there are many people expressing evil ways. However, as darkness is an absence of light, so evil is an absence of good. Actually, it might better be defined as the concealment of the depth of goodness that is in a man because God is in him. Evil is not inherent in human nature. Human nature is but the degree of consciousness of divine nature. When we see conditions of evil in the world, they have no permanency or power in and of themselves. They simply evidence the confusion that always follows the absence of the activity of God. In back of the evil condition there may always be found a man frustrating his own innate goodness and acting in the darkness of human consciousness.

It is not human nature that is at fault in evil experiences, but human *nurture*. The individual experiences darkness in his life because he has nurtured in his consciousness the thoughts of self-limitation. No one is born with negative thoughts. Wherever you find limitation of any kind, even as expressed in the most sordid evil deed, you can be sure that "somebody taught a child." This is why Jesus insists that we should turn and become as a little child—not only that we might be as receptive and teachable as the child, but also that we might return to that state of purity we had before we began to absorb and nurture all the race beliefs of our time.

In this human state of consciousness we live in a sense of separation from God and from our fellow man. We act as though we had a life of our own; as though we could have plans, purposes, and interests separate from His. This, if it were true, would mean that existence is not one and harmonious, but a chaos of competition and strife. It would mean that we are quite separate from our fellow man and can injure him, rob him, or hurt or even destroy him—without any damage to ourselves. It would mean further that the more we take from other people the more we have for ourselves. It would mean that the more we considered our own interests, and the more indifferent we are to the welfare of others, the better off we are. And it would follow that it would pay others to treat us the same way.

If all this were true—and there are many who believe it is—it would mean that the whole world is only a jungle, and that sooner or later it must destroy itself by its own inherent weakness and anarchy.

There are those who say that this is what is now happening to the world. But Jesus didn't believe such a thing, and it is completely unrealistic to believe it today.

It is more than likely that you have been raised on the teaching that God is an inhabiter of the skies, who sits on his throne recording in His big black book all of our sins—and punishing us accordingly. Under this religious discipline, you lived and worshiped in fear, fear of the wrath of God. Your churchgoing habit was more the evidence of fear than of devotion. You prayed and pledged and participated because you were afraid not to. The gates of hell yawned wide for anyone who fell down on his religious responsibilities.

What did Jesus teach? The implication that runs all through the Gospel is: *You are not punished so much* for *your sins as* by *them.* Sin is its own punishment and righteousness is its own reward. Sin is a "missing of the mark," or the failure to achieve the goal of perfection. The result is a kind of separation from God, from good, from harmony, from justice. And the punishment is that we have cut ourselves off from the source, leading to lack and limitation.

In the Bible, light is the most oft-repeated symbol for the activity of God. The process is best understood in our oft-repeated illustration of the electric light bulb. Turn the light on in your room where you are. Instantly, the room is flooded with light as the electricity is converted into light in the bulb. Now, at any moment the light will disappear if you either turn the switch "off" or if there is a break in the circuit. The break is a "sin," and the punishment for this sin is darkness. The electricity did not create the darkness. It is not even aware of the darkness. We punished ourselves as a result of the break or separation and thus we have darkness. When we turn the light on again or repair the break in the circuit, the reward is light. It is not a special gift that electricity bestows upon us because we are good enough to make the connection again. The light is its own reward. Thus sin is its own punishment and righteousness is its own reward.

Sin is cutting ourselves off from the activity of God, and the punishment is the deterioration that always follows such separation. If I were to fix a rubber band tightly around my finger, in a few minutes the finger would redden and swell and then turn blue from lack of circulation. Before long, it would reach a danger point, and serious deterioration would soon follow unless I released the band.

What has happened here? I have stopped the flow of circulation with the rubber band, which cuts off the finger and the cells of the finger from the life-sustaining forces that flow in the blood stream. However, the reddened finger is not caused by the wrath of the life force in the body. It is simply the evidence of the absence of that force. And the life force in the body won't hold anything against the finger because there is no flow. The moment I restore the flow by removing the band, forgiveness is instantaneous. Life flows into the finger and in a few moments circulation is normal.

Habakkuk refers to God as "thou that are of purer eyes than to behold evil" (Hab. 1:13). This may surprise you, even disturb you. But it is vital to you that you get this point in your consciousness and never forget it: God knows nothing of sin, nothing of want, nothing of lack of any kind. This may be hard to accept—because we have a carry-over in our consciousness of the old idea of God who sits up in the skies and who looks down upon us, changing His attitudes about us, rejoicing in our progress, angered over our weakness or indolence. But when we expand our vision to contemplate the God of Universal Mind—God as principle, God as Spirit—we see that God knows nothing of sin.

Does the principle of mathematics know anything about your mistake if you write two plus two equals five? The principle knows *four* even though you have written *five*, because the "two plus two" is an equation that means four regardless of what you think it means.

The tragedy would be if God did know sin. If God knew sin, He would be a sinner; for what Mind knows, it must be! Sin or mistakes are outside of the province of reality. Light doesn't know darkness. Light is! God doesn't know sin. God is! God is good, good is omnipresent.

However, if God does not know sin, then how can He forgive sin, or how can man find forgiveness of God? How can man find release from his feelings of guilt? We find an answer in a beautiful thought found in the Old Testament, "Behold, I have loved thee with an everlasting love" (Jer. 31:3). If God *is* love, this universal essence that is as omni-active as gravity, then the statement is simply saying, God *as* love cannot be anything else but love. God does not hold less than love for you no matter what you have done or haven't done, because God is love.

Can electricity stop being electricity? Can light stop being light?

Can gravity be less than gravity? Does gravity stop being gravity if you fall off a curb? If you are thrown to the ground, this is because gravity is at work, for that is what gravity is. Light is here when we open the window. Electricity is here at the flick of the switch. Therefore, God forever sees you as His beloved child in whom He is well pleased.

Let us turn again to the parable of the Prodigal Son. The father in the story is the divinity of you, and the prodigal son is the human side of you that forgets its divinity and experiences separation and ultimate "want." Thus the father *is* the son. When the son "comes to himself," he awakens from his ignorance of himself, realizes his innate divinity, and returns to his state of unity. He is received with open arms. There is no sense of guilt. The father doesn't say, "Now you are going to be punished for your sins." No, he showers him with blessings, and cries out, "My son who was dead is now alive again." The human consciousness has awakened to its true nature, and the very "hills clap their hands for joy." When the rubber band is released from my finger, the blood surges in with enthusiasm, and there is a veritable feast of "eat, drink, and be merry" as the cells come alive again under the influence of the life force.

How does God forgive? Our answer may seem startling, possibly even sacrilegious. God doesn't really forgive sin. Or let's take it a step further: God *cannot* forgive sin—no matter what the offense, no matter how great the guilt, no matter how much we may plead with Him for forgiveness. How can I get the forgiveness of electricity for disrupting its flow? How can I get the life force in my body to forgive me for shutting off its flow with the rubber band? By releasing the rubber band, by turning on the switch. And no one can do it for me. I must remove the band and turn the switch. And the force that surges through the finger and the switch—is it forgiving me? In a way you could say that it is. But all it is really doing is being what it is. Life can never be less than life, and electricity cannot be less than electricity—and God can never be less than God. God is love even when I am filled with hatred. God is love as the potential in me even though I am angry and bitter. The moment I release my bitterness, rise above my guilt, stop feeling sorry for myself, in that moment "God is love" sweeps through me and loves me. But that is what it has always been. I just haven't accepted it.

Thus, in a very real sense, God doesn't forgive. God is love. God hasn't held any unforgiveness. There is nothing to forgive in His sight, for "his eyes are too pure to behold iniquity." When the prodigal son wanted to come home he said, "I will arise and go unto the father." What did he mean by "arise"? "I will rise out of this limited consciousness, this faulty self-evaluation. I will stop living at the circumference of life. I will stop feeling sorry for myself in my poverty of mind and experience. I will accept the Truth about myself."

Did he have to go home and beg forgiveness? Actually in the story you will find him at first in a consciousness of begging. He rehearses a little speech that he plans to make to the father: "I will arise and go to my father, and will say unto him, Father, I have sinned against heaven and before thee, and I am no more worthy to be called thy son: make me as one of thy hired servants." But something happened to him on the way home. He dropped that servant consciousness—and perhaps there could have been no sense of union without that change. When he arrived home he said, "Father, I have sinned against heaven and in thy sight, and am no more worthy to be called thy son"—but nothing about "make me as one of thy hired servants."

It is notable that even though the son asks forgiveness, the father doesn't even acknowledge it. He simply changes the subject. He showers him with blessings. In our consciousness, we may feel guilty. We may be perfectly willing to take our punishment—to become "one of thy hired servants." The fact is we have already been receiving our punishment, for sin is its own punishment and righteousness is its own reward. In the attitude of contrition, the insistence that we become a "hired servant," we are engaging in words of futility. It is like trying to bargain with electricity to fill your room with light even though you do not turn on the switch. The moment you turn the switch you have light. The moment the prodigal really felt "I will arise and go unto the Father" and could see himself doing it, he was instantly received of the Father and showered with that which the Father is—the divinity of his own nature.

The moment I accept myself in a higher context, in that moment I have overcome, or come over, that which was the basic sin. That basic sin may have resulted in all sorts of secondary sins—but the basic sin was that I did not know who I was. The moment I come to myself, know the Truth of my innate divinity, my divine sonship, in that moment I turn on the light, and I let the flood of life and inspiration and intelligence fill me and thrill me—and I am transformed. I am forgiven, because I have forgiven myself.

"For if ye forgive men their trespasses, your heavenly Father will also forgive you. But if ye forgive not men their trespasses, neither will your Father forgive your trespasses" (Matt. 6:14, 15).

This is not saying that God is arbitrary and that He won't take the first step, but that you must show your sincerity by acting, and then He will act. This is simply a personalized way of talking about principle. It is difficult to understand the action of principle unless we relate it to things with which we can identify. This is why God is clothed in human form in the teachings of the prophets and of Jesus, and it is why we have gotten trapped in the concept of a God of the skies. God is love and He can only love you when you love. If you want forgiveness, you must express forgiveness. There is no other way.

Jesus says, "And whensoever ye stand praying, forgive, if ye have aught against any one; that your father also who is in heaven may forgive your trespasses" (Mark 11:25). The fact is, any time you feel a sense of guilt, a sense of unforgiveness—that unclean feeling in which you would like God to "create a clean heart within you"—if you take a good look at yourself, the chances are that you will find there is much you can do today by getting a new attitude toward the people around you. You can express more love, more understanding, and in this way you release the positive power of the Spirit that cleanses you—but it is the result of what *you* have done. God can do no more for you than He can do through you.

Peter once said to Jesus, "Lord, how oft shall my brother sin against me, and I forgive him? until seven times?" In other words he is saying, "You just can't go on forgiving people! How much can a man take?" Jesus replied, "I say not unto thee Until seven times; but Until seventy times seven" (Matt. 18:21). He wasn't concerned with the arithmetic here. He was indicating infinity. Forgiveness must be perpetual, a state of consciousness and not just an occasional gesture. Why? Because unforgiveness is a price that man cannot afford to pay. Forgive until seventy times seven; pray for those that despitefully use you; love your enemies—not for their sake, but for yours.

If you want light in the room, you must have the switch on. And it does you no good to sit and complain that someone else turned it off. Like little children squabbling over "who did it," we sit and suffer in the darkness. Jesus is saying, if there is unforgiveness, if there is enmity, if there is resistance in human relations, turn the light on. Don't worry about "who did it" or why. You need light; so love, forgive, bless, and release.

When Jesus stresses forgiving "until seventy times seven," He is not expecting you to live a saintly life. Actually, forgiveness is the simplest way to lighten our burdens. The man who forgives is no more saintly than one who insists upon keeping clean. In reality, the act of forgiveness constitutes a mental bath—letting go of something that can only poison us within.

The parable of the Prodigal Son reveals another great lesson that is so subtle that we might miss its great implication. When the son decides to come home, when he says "I will arise and go unto the father" (remember—the father is the divinity within him), the moment he turns toward home, the father comes forth to meet him and showers him with blessings. When you are trying to get the forgiveness of God or even a greater understanding of yourself, all you need to do is to turn in the right direction. Once you turn in the direction of the Spirit in you and have sincerely determined to "go unto the Father—once you have made up your mind that you are tired of living in materiality, in the consciousness of limitation, and that you want to rise to a new level of thinking and living—the moment you make this decision, something happens. And that something is the activity of the divine law.

Someone has said, "When you are sick of being sick you will get well." In other words, you have been involved in an experience of limitation, resisting it, talking about it, feeling sorry for yourself in it, but perhaps subtly enjoying it. But when you finally make up your mind that you have "had it," and determine that you are going to rise to a new level of consciousness, a remarkable thing happens. When you turn to God, God turns toward you. Suddenly, you have the whole universe on your side in your effort toward change.

In the parable of the Prodigal Son, which personalizes the principle, Jesus indicates that you don't have to plead and beg for forgiveness. It is instantaneous the moment you make the move to accept it. When you turn on the light switch, you do not have to pick up the phone and call the power company to say, "All right, I have the switch open, now please move the electricity into the circuits." No, the very instant the contact is made, the current flows and the light streams forth. And in the same way, the moment we turn toward God, the wisdom and love and life and peace of God shower us with the blessings of His presence. We really haven't changed God by our decision to "come to ourself," but we have brought ourselves into a state of acceptance.

There are those who consider this process unfair. Are sins so easily forgiven? Why should the sinner be showered with the blessings of the Father? What of those who have not sinned? What about the elder brother in the parable of the Prodigal Son? You may remember that when the festivities were in full swing for the return of his prodigal brother, the elder son was in the field. He heard the music and dancing, and when he discovered what was going on, he was angry. He refused to join the party. The father begged him to join in the celebration, but he said, "Lo, these many years do I serve thee, and I have never transgressed a commandment of thine; and yet thou never gavest me a kid, that I might make merry with my friends: but when this thy son came, who hath devoured thy living with harlots, thou killedst for him the fatted calf." In other words, he was saying, "A fine thing! Here I stay home and toe the mark all these years, and what does it get me? The father replies, "Son, thou art ever with me, and all that is mine is thine."

An interesting conjecture about this story is that the elder son may really have been a prodigal at heart. Perhaps he simply lacked the nerve to run off. Thus, having renounced the satisfaction of "far-country" experiences, he felt he should have a reward for his "virtue." But virtue is its own reward. If we feel the need of reward for virtue, then it is not sincere.

We can take great satisfaction in this story. There is hope for the sinner. In fact, it may well be that the person who has committed the act, and has later "come to himself," is better off than the one who has bottled up the temptation and has never really faced himself. Paul says, "My strength is made perfect in weakness" (II Cor. 12:9, AV). It is better to find the flaw in the steel, to break it, and weld it together firmly, than to allow a girder to be made of the imperfect steel. We tend to hold people to their past mistakes. Think of the prejudices society holds toward the ex-convict, the ex-alcoholic or addict, or even the divorcee. Remember, Jesus says, "He that is without sin among you, let him first cast a stone at her (John 8:7). And on that occasion they all turned away, for the light of His radiant consciousness made each man realize his own secret sins. They may not have been committed sins, but only frustrated temptations. However, in Jesus' sight they were all the same. He said, "Everyone that looketh on a woman to lust after her hath committed adultery with her already in his heart" (Matt. 5:28).

If we would follow Jesus' idealism, we would have more confidence rather than less in the overcomer. When the convict is subjected to a period of sincere re-education based on the depth potential of his innate divinity, and when he is returned to society after it has been determined that he has honestly "come to himself," then he should be given opportunity on the basis of his ability and experience. His prison record would be nothing to hide. It would simply indicate that he had taken the long route rather than the simple route to maturity. He would *graduate* from prison with a diploma that would indicate the achievement of overcoming. There are those who might scoff at such a plan. But let them come up with a constructive alternative. What is our record now of actual rehabilitation of criminals in prison, and of their readjustment to society?

Praise God there are instances, perhaps many of them, of individuals who have "come to themselves" in criminal confinement, and have returned to society to become good and useful citizens. Obviously, we must be doing something right!

There is one case that should be told. The man in his rediscovered self chose to be known as Alva Romanes. He had gotten off the path early in life, and had lived many years on the shady side of the law. After a career in crime, he found himself in a long stretch in the penitentiary. Like the prodigal son, he began to realize that there must be a better way. He became dissatisfied with himself, and over months of soul-searching, he made the discovery of his own divinity. Slowly, but surely, the prison doors of his mind opened, and he stood face to face with reality, with Truth, with his eternal self. Fortunately, he put some of his feelings into poetry. It is not great poetry, but they are great ideas. Here is my favorite of his poems—written in the hopeless atmosphere of a cell-block:

I am not the brood of the dust and sod,
    Nor a shuttled thread in the loom of fate;
But the child divine of the living God,
    With eternity for my life's estate.
I am not the sport of a cosmic night,
    Nor a thing of chance that has grown to man;
But a deathless soul on my upward flight,
    And my Father's heir in His wondrous plan.

As I weigh the suns on the rim of space,
    Who can care to doubt of my destiny?
Who can fence my feet within time and place,
    As I search the worlds of infinity?
I am man: the son of the one Most High;
    I am man, and one with the Life divine;
I am Lord of earth, and of sea and sky:
    And behold! the powers of heaven are mine.

I am man the chosen, and man the free,
    And it matters not what I may have been;
For I walk erect through eternity
    To the far-off goal that is yet unseeen.
With unswerving faith in the coming Day,
    I have turned my course from the things of time,
And with Jesus, my brother, to point the way,
    I have found my place in the Life sublime.[2]

And this man was a criminal? Could we rightly discriminate against such a man for being an ex-convict? Could such a state of consciousness have evolved for him in any way other than in his prison experience? This we cannot say. But it did evolve there. Could Paul have been the great Christian leader if he had not been at first a great persecutor of Christians? Again we do not know, but he did become the greatest of all Christian leaders.

Alva Romanes says, "I have found my place. . . . " Have you found your place? You see, obviously your "right place" is not a "place" at all, but a right attitude of mind. The right place is the state of consciousness in which we know, and know that we know, our unity with God. We know our own divinity. This man, after a life of living in the "far country" of lawless living, found his place in a new level of understanding, a new philosophy of life, a new insight that led to a wonderful new outlook on life and on people.

There are times when Jesus' teachings might seem too demanding. He tells us that it is not enough to stop hating; we must start loving. It is not enough to let a matter drop; we must actually forgive everyone involved. It is not enough even to say, "I forgive you"; we must say it and mean it and go on to prove it in action.

A little boy had hearing problems and finally was fitted with a hearing aid. This improved his attentiveness in class but it did not improve his relations with his classmates, who cruelly taunted him for his artificial ears. One day one of the youngsters was making fun of him, so he punched the boy in the nose. As the injured boy lay screaming on the ground, the teacher stepped in and insisted that the assailant apologize and also tell the other boy that he forgave him for his teasing. The hard-of-hearing lad said reluctantly, "All right, I'll tell him I forgive him, but first I am going to turn my hearing aid off."

We may think that it is too much to expect of us that we forgive, love, and pray for those who despitefully use us; but if we know ourselves in the context of our divinity, we see that we have something to live up to. Paul says, "As many as are led by the spirit of God, these are the sons of God" (Rom. 8:14). This is to say that you have the potential of being a radiant expression of light, but you must have it turned on. We may have all sorts of reasons for turning the light off. We may have a perfect justification for our bitterness and anger. We may be completely righteous in our indignation. But we will have to pay the price of the broken connection of the divine circuits. The power that goes with our divinity is only ours when we act the part. We can have our unforgiveness and bitterness and anger if we so choose, but we will also have our stomach ulcers and nervous tension and heart trouble, and mental and physical breakdowns. Turn on the light—not so much for the benefit of others, but for you. "Forgive and you shall be forgiven."

13 Jesus' Formula for Healing

Then shall thy light break forth as the morning, and thine health shall spring forth speedily.

Isa. 58:8

THERE is a strange paradox in Christianity today. While Jesus "healed all manner of diseases" and left some amazingly clear concepts by which we can follow Him in the practice of healing by spiritual means, it is rare today to find a Christian church that stresses spiritual healing, if it will admit even to the possibility. Fully one-third of the Gospel record of the public ministry of Jesus is devoted to His practice of healing and to the discourses about the cures. And yet healing by spiritual means has been frowned upon by the church and sometimes even condemned and considered sacrilegious. The church has looked upon the healing "miracles" as demonstrations of His divinity—proof that He was "very God." Thus we find such statements as this in Christian theology: "The day when God walked the earth"; "The age of miracles has passed."

The development of a church in a hostile world is a precarious business. The early Christians had a problem. On the one hand, there was the well-established religious body of the Jews, with the deep-seated commitment of most of the followers to the God of "Abraham, Isaac, and Jacob." And, on the other hand, there was the "pagan world," with its acceptance of many gods. So, they did the only thing they knew to strengthen their claim—they made a god of

159

Jesus. Thus, they had the key to theological strength—and spiritual weakness. It could be said that the "age of healing" ended with the disciples. For a millennium and a half, spiritual healing was unheard of in Christianity.

In the doctrine of the divinity of Jesus, there is no room for a healing principle. Jesus' miracles would be degraded if they could be duplicated. So, the great rationalization that sickness is God's will was developed. Man must not question God's will. He should accept his lot, even his terrible illnesses, in stoic submission. Any effort toward healing was a rebellion against God. The practice of medicine was frowned on by the early church. Emperor Justinian even closed the medical schools of Athens and Alexandria in A.D. 529. This disapproval continued through the centuries, until finally, in A.D. 1215, Pope Innocent III condemned surgery and all priests who practiced it. In 1248, the dissection of the body was pronounced sacrilegious and the study of anatomy was condemned.

And yet, "Jesus went about in all Galilee . . . healing all manner of disease" (Matt. 4:23). And He said, "All that I do you can do too, . . . and even more." Jesus proved to man for all time that man is divine, and that every man has within himself the power of healing. He can be a healing influence for others, and he can be healed. "And nothing shall be impossible to him."

The word "miracle" is a stumbling block to many. We might do well to eliminate it from our frame of spiritual ideas. The word has been used as proof of Jesus' divinity. According to Webster, a miracle is "an event or effect in the physical world deviating from the laws of nature." We live in an orderly Universe, in which deviation from law is unthinkable. If a healing is accomplished, whether by Jesus or by a medical practitioner, it is a demonstration of the remarkable wholeness of life. Exceptional as the case may be, it cannot be called a miracle. It may have dealt with the healing law on a higher level than we have heretofore known, but no laws have been transgressed. It is a natural or divinely natural phenomenon.

Jesus said that He came not to destory the law but to fulfill it (Matt. 5:17). He steadfastly refused to attempt to set aside natural law. Remember how He was taken up to the pinnacle of the Temple by the satanic influence of His own human consciousness, and tempted to throw Himself down to prove His mastery over the elements? And remember how He was tempted to try to turn stones into bread in the wilderness? In each case He refused, by saying, "Thou shalt not tempt the Lord, thy God" (Matt. 4:1–11). Jesus knew that He was not God, the Creator. He knew that He was the self-livingness of God, the activity of God in expression. His power was not in changing the laws of the Universe, but in His high consciousness *of* the law.

Jesus was not a magician. In his ministry, He simply fulfilled divine law on a higher level than anyone has before or since. The "miracle" healings were not only an evidence of the divinity of Jesus, they also evidenced the Divinity of Man—of the very person healed. The potential for healing is in every person simply because he is innately divine, innately whole and complete. Jesus' insight was so great, and He saw the divinity in the other person with such intensity, that there was a healing light. His faith quickened the sleeping potential and it sprang forth into full and perfect life.

Jesus said, "I know that His commandment is life eternal" (John 12:50). He knew that man had become drowsy in a spiritual sense. He was asleep to the Truth of his life. Jesus said, "I came that they may have life, and may have it abundantly" (John 10:10). He knew that man was an eternal being, with the power of renewal and health as a fundamental part of his divinity. Thus, the healing that resulted was a demonstration of the law of life and not a deviation from it.

Jesus said, "God is not the God of the dead but of the living" (Matt. 22:32). One of the greatest fallacies of life in our time is the belief in the certainty of death. We sometimes refer to something being "as certain as death and taxes." In our time, it may well be that taxes are pretty certain and well-nigh inevitable. But we are all due for some revision of our attitudes in this matter of the certainty of death. Medical researchers are discovering some amazing properties in "this thing called life."

In his book, *Immortality and Rejuvenation*, Matalnikov says that immortality is the fundamental property of a living organism, and that old age and death are not a state of earthly existence. Recently, a medical doctor stated that there is no reason why the human body should ever deteriorate and that, from a scientific standpoint, man should be able to live indefinitely.

One of the most "shocking" comments from members of the

medical profession was found in an editorial in the *Harvard Alumni Bulletin*. The writer is Dr. Lawrence S. Kubie, outstanding authority in the field of psychiatry and psychoanalysis, and currently director of training at the Pratt Hospital in Maryland. We quote here a few sentences from this amazing statement:

It is literally true that no man has ever used more than a small fragment of his brain power. In fact, even the most alert of us are never wholly awake, much less fully in action. . . . Why is this? It is because the brain's psychological products are so organized that almost from birth we are continuously blocked by conflicts among internal factions. This has been man's lot from the days of Adam until this moment; yet it is specifically here that we stand on the threshold of a new kind of life. The future opens up to us the possibility that we may learn to end the waste and destructiveness of this internal impasse, freeing our enormous latent creative powers from the crippling and paralyzing domination of unconscious conflicts.

. . . The infinite creative potential of the human brain is housed in a potentially indestructible body . . . which has a built-in replacement system, its own self-replenishing devices! We have learned that as long as the supply system is intact the body continuously takes itself apart and puts itself together, not merely organ by organ, or cell by cell, but literally molecule by molecule. Potentially, therefore, it is constantly renewed and never ages. Consequently, there is no reason why any human being need die. [He cites some remaining problems to be overcome, medically, which he is confident will soon be accomplished.] Someday men and women will stop dying, and will live forever.[1]

The paradox continues—in our time there is a swing back to spiritual or at least nonmaterial healing. However, it is coming in the field of medical research instead of in the Christian church. Oh, there are some individual ministers who have done amazing things in the area of spiritual healing, and there are some churches that have been "tolerant" of this heresy. But it appears that science will discover and build a system upon the Divinity of Man before the church does.

It should be pointed out here that there are a growing number of groups, such as Unity, Christian Science, Religious Science, Divine Science, which are teaching and practicing health by spiritual means. These modern "metaphysical" groups are a rapidly growing influence in the religious stream today because they deal with dynamic Truths instead of with static creeds. They have probably been the motivation or "spur" behind the recent self-evaluation that is going on through-out most denominations today. However, church mergers are only a smoke screen, and modified doctrines only a "sop." The die is cast. Man today wants to know himself, and if his church will not lead him to this self-knowledge, it will lose its place in his life.

Religion has constantly given man the promise of salvation in an afterlife. But it has sadly neglected giving him any practical, usable knowledge by which he can live this life in health and success and happiness. Neither are the great spiritual revivals any real answer to the long-term needs of man and society. The revival meeting stirs up renewed faith in the "Saviour of the world," calling attention again and again to the divinity of Jesus. But the world needs a society of saviours, individuals who come alive with the divine forces within them, and who become a saving influence by letting the light of their own divinity shine bright and clear.

Now, let us get this point straight: Jesus did not originate spiritual healing. He did not make the healing law. Nor did He heal through some magic or mystical power—or through a divine dispensation that abrogated known laws of life. Spiritual healing is possible simply because man is essentially a spiritual being, and healing is simply the art of "opening out a way whence the imprisoned splendor may escape."

Spiritual healing is not an attempt to gain special favor with God or to abrogate the divine or natural law. We do not use a different set of laws in spiritual healing than those used in medical or surgical healing. Life is the acting principle of Being, the energy that propels all forms into action. Whether the life principle's energy is activated by meditation or by medication makes no difference.

Sometimes an individual will say: "I don't go for this spiritual healing business. When a man is sick he should go to a doctor." And yet, most doctors state that a large percentage of the people who come to them for treatment are not organically ill; that their ills are emotionally induced and that their cure is more a matter of mental adjustment than of physical treatment. It is becoming commonplace for a medical doctor to refer a patient to a minister.

There is a new field of medicine that is evolving today, "The Medicine of the Whole Man." People like the distinguished Paul Tournier of Switzerland, Franz Winkler of New York City, and Evarts Loomis of the Friendly Hills Fellowship at Hemet, California, are agreeing with Socrates who said that the part can never be well unless the whole is well. Thus they are moving toward a greater recognition of the role of faith and thought and prayer in the healing art. These people may not speak in theological terms, but they are dealing with the divinity of man, the whole man. With good reason, a prince of the church made the statement, in a recent council session, that the church should adopt a new "tolerant" attitude toward modern science—recognize science and admit to some of its twentieth-century findings.

Certainly, there is a great need for communication between religionists and researchers and practitioners in the field of medical science. It is quite possible that there are more medical people than representatives of the churches who subscribe to the essentials of mental and spiritual healing. This may be because of the tendency of some theologians to live in sheltered environments, out of the mainstream of man's progress in the world about him. A not uncommon attitude is this one expressed by a minister: "God is to be worshiped, not used. He is not to be used for selfish purposes such as healing."

This would seem to indicate that God has no interest in life or in healing, that His only interest is in the church and its ministry, that He is interested in theology, but not in reality; that He is interested in congregations, but not in people. Obviously, this connotes an attitude that life and health are something that exist outside of God; that spiritual healing is degrading to the Almighty—much the same as asking God to help pick a winner at the racetrack.

Let us "look at the record." Jesus taught and practiced spiritual healing with abandon. He said, "It is not the will of your Father who is in heaven, that one of these little ones should perish" (Matt. 18:14). Even if we can come away from the Gospels with doubts concerning Jesus' philosophy of life, on one subject there can be no doubt—He believed in the right of man to be healthy, and He "healed all manner of illnesses."

Judge not according to appearances, but judge righteous judgment [John 7:24].

Jesus taught that man lives in two worlds—not in succession, but concurrently. He lives in the world of appearances, the three-dimensional world of form and shape, of time and space—the world where we have fluctuating experiences of sickness and health, of peace and war, of harmony and chaos. But man also lives in a spiritual world *as* a spiritual being.

So Jesus says, "Don't be misled in appraising yourself in life. You are whole, even if you are experiencing sickness. And you can be healed because you are whole."

When you look in the mirror you see the three-dimensional creature, the man of form and shape—and you may not be particularly happy with that shape. But you probably say, "What can I do? That's just the way I am." But if you can open your mind to consider the dynamics of Jesus' teaching, you will begin to see *through* the mirror instead of *in* it. Paul says, "We see in a mirror, darkly" but he also says we must come to "see face to face" (I Cor. 13:12). Beyond the appearances revealed in the mirror, is the total person you are in spirit.

There is that of you that is greater than your weakness, stronger than your fears, the four-dimensional creature that is whole even within your sickness. This is that of you that is the perfect idea in the Mind of God. You are simply asleep to this greater self, your innate divinity. Paul says, "Awake thou that sleepest that Christ may shine upon thee" (Eph. 5:14]. And what is Christ but your own divinity, the particularization of the Infinite source of life into the pattern of finite embodiment. It is a perfect pattern. It is whole. And it is you at the point of God.

Wordsworth says that our birth is a sleep and a forgetting. Thus the key to the demonstration of wholeness is: *awake and remember.* If you walked into a room where a man was asleep on a bed, and you had the ability to see into his dream, you might see the man out in a raging blizzard, trudging through heavy winds and hazardous snowdrifts. You might feel the urge to help him in his dilemma. What can you do? There is only one thing, since the snow experience is a dream—wake him up! Even while he is on the verge of succumbing to the elements, he is really on the bed, warm and safe. It is only a dream. Seeing him from the aspect of his dream experience, we know that there is a larger dimension of his life, and that at any time he can awake and experience the wholeness that is his.

We don't mean to imply that conscious life in three-dimensional experience is only an illusion, a dream. We simply want to provide a framework for seeing the relationship between man's spiritual wholeness and his human experience. If someone asks you, "How are you today?", you have a choice. You can answer from the standpoint of your human experience *or* your spiritual wholeness—the man in the dream *or* the man on the bed. Is the man freezing in the snow or is he warm and secure in his bed? Your answer depends on which level of his experience you focus upon.

On the physical level you might say, "I am not feeling so good today" (judging by appearances). But from the level of the divinity within you, you could reply, "I am the perfect expression of Infinite Life" (judging righteous judgment).

This is the key to affirmative prayer, often referred to as "spiritual treatment." You speak the word of Truth about the situation, which is to identify with the man on the bed instead of the man in the dream. No matter what the experience, you are a spiritual being, living in a spiritual world. You are the self-livingness of God, right now. Prayer and treatment are not attempts to make you spiritual or to bring you into unity with the wholeness of God. There is nothing you and I can do to change the nature of God, or to change our own nature as the self-livingness of God. The great Truth is: There is that in you that needs no change. There is a spiritual man of you, the divinity of you, that never gets sick; if he did, neither medicine nor surgery nor prayer could heal him.

From science today, we are getting some exciting insights into the whole man. We are coming to see that the mind is more than a brain, that the heart cannot beat without life to make it beat, and that there is something nonmaterial that determines and guides the cell-renewal process. In a film entitled *"The Development of the Chick,"*[2] we see the egg in the process of incubation. We see a strange pulsation commence in the yolk. It is the beating of the heart *before there is any heart to beat.* And then before our eyes we see the embryo form and a heart take shape and take up the beat that came first. This is an evidence that even more significant than the physical egg is the nonmaterial force that is the pattern from which the chick and the whole chicken develops.

Dr. Lewis Schreiber, eminent podiatrist, writing in the *Journal of the American Podiatry Association,* says:

The electrodynamic body is not composed of any cellular substance, but cellular substance is attracted to it and each cell falls into proper place with deadly accuracy. The pattern is a distinct entity that undergoes little change throughout life, while the cells that fill out the physical form are transitory and constantly replaced. It molds and fashions the organism after a specific predetermined pattern, and DNA can have no influence in altering the form, but must follow faithfully each minute tracing on the path, thus constantly recreating the organism.[3]

DNA, referred to here, is the deoxyribonucleic acid that we are hearing so much about today. It is the miracle catalyst of life. But life is not explained in terms of DNA, any more than healing is explained in terms of hemoglobin and red blood cells. These things are but the evidence of an activity—a "what" and a "how" but not a "why." The "why" can only be explained in terms of the unitive action of divine law.

One thing we can glean from repeated evidences in research: there is a universal tendency for everything to return to normal whenever the condition of balance has been violated. Why? Somehow there is a body that doesn't change even if the cells themselves are hurt and destroyed. Paul called it "The Lord's Body"; Jesus referred to it as the "Kingdom of heaven within," and some scientists may refer to it as an "electromagnetic-pattern body." The process of nonmaterial force directing the rebuilding of the material form is what is called the *vis medicatrix naturae* (the healing power of nature). This is a spiritual activity, whether it is evoked by medication or meditation.

Spiritual healing, then, is not based on a Pollyana philosophy that "There is no sickness, there is no pain." Anyone who has ever walked through the wards of a modern hospital knows full well that there is a lot of sickness in our world, and much of it is excruciatingly painful. Jesus was obviously aware of the widespread incidence of illness and the suffering of His fellow men. But He did not stop there. He was aware of something more—the wholeness of the individual that actually transcended the physical suffering. In other words, He taught and demonstrated that pain and sickness are only *part* of the picture of the whole man. They are appearances that can be changed if we can judge righteous judgment.

You may be living in the basement of your house, uncomfortable, cold, cramped, and hampered by darkness. But there is still a whole house. I would not say that you are not cold and uncomfortable in your basement, but I could say that this condition can be changed, and that there is a warm, comfortable, and well-lighted house that you can occupy right now—if you get out of the basement.

There is more to life than this experience. Open your eyes and see, open your mind and perceive. Realize that within you, in the Kingdom of Heaven within, there is power and life and substance that is sufficient to establish you in wholeness and abundant living. As a TV commercial once put it, "get out of the shadows into the light of new loveliness." Stop seeing yourself in part. Get out of the darkness of human thinking and living, into the light of wholeness and the fullness of life. "The people that walked in darkness have seen a great light; they that dwell in the land of the shadow of death, upon them hath the light shined" (Isa. 9:2).

If thou wilt, thou canst make me clean. . . . I will; be thou made clean [Matt. 8:2, 3].

This was a leper's appeal to Jesus and His affirmative response (Matt. 8:2-4). Here Jesus evidenced the belief that God's will is always good. God wills life and health, because God *is* Life and Wholeness. God is not, could not be, the author of sickness or affliction of any kind. If God were the author of sickness, then no one, not even Jesus would have been able to heal the sick.

A study of the evolution of religious philosophies shows that what has passed for religion has been formulated out of the prevailing thoughts and fears of man. Primitive man developed a respect for forces that he could not control. The lightning that destroyed his hut, the river that drowned his brother, the sickness that ravaged his body—all seemed to be the work of any angry god. Thus, early worship was a form of sacrifice and appeasement of the gods. Any painful or unhappy experience was regarded as a direct action of the gods.

These primitive concepts were ultimately incorporated into the more sophisticated religious teachings. Even though Jesus came, saying, "It is not the will of your Father who is in heaven, that one of these little ones should perish" (Matt. 18:14), the idea that God's anger caused sickness became part of the basis of Christian theology. Today, most Christians are taught the rationalistic doctrine that misfortune of any kind is God's will, and should be stoically accepted.

A famous healing shrine has had many remarkable demonstrations of life and health through faith, yet the following comment is included in a well-intentioned pamphlet put into the hands of pilgrims who arrive there with high hopes: "Most of you will return home without being cured just because it is your business to be ill. It is a most precious business which has come to you straight from Heaven. . . . There is no other way to heaven except suffering."[4]

If this were really true—that it is God's will for you to be sick, and that there is no other way to heaven except through suffering—then it would follow that any kind of remedial measures would be in opposition to God's will; the sicker you were, the better. It would also indicate that Jesus, who went about healing all manner of sickness, must have been the prince of sinners.

However, the person who accepts his sickness as coming through God's will usually turns immediately to medical science for help, and his religious leader usually encourages him to do so. If the patient succumbs, the eulogy might read, "God's purposes are not to be questioned." If he is healed, the comment might be, "Praise God for His wonder-working power!" If sickness is God's will, is that will turned aside by the scalpel or the medication? The doctor does not believe this. He begins on the premise that there is an ever-present force for renewal in the body cells, and he cooperates with that force.

Man has a built-in capacity for health. This is the evidence of man's divinity. Charles Fillmore says: "Health, real health, is from within and does not have to be manufactured in the without. It is the normal condition of man, a condition true to the reality of his being."[5] There is a divinity in man which is the whole and perfect activity of God. God's will is the ceaseless longing of the creator working to perfect Himself in that which He has created.

When a prayer is answered, what happens may appear to be nothing short of miraculous. However, when we understand the process, we know that the result is as normal and natural as the growth of a flower. Is it a miracle when you open a window and let in the light? A darkened room suddenly becomes cheery and bright. It is dramatic, but it is no miracle. Is it a miracle, then, when a physical body that is wracked with sickness and pain can suddenly be freed from pain and experience the fullness of life? Here we say, "Yes, of course it is a miracle!" But where is the difference?

Actually, "growth" is a good description of the process, for life is forever growing and unfolding. We lose our perspective in the bondage to time. Things take time. And if something happens instantly, it must be a miracle. Jesus indicated that anything that can evolve must first of all be involved. Thus, anything that *can be*, *already is*. Looking at a field of newly sown wheat, you would admit that in time a harvest of grain could result. But can you believe that the grain is already involved in the seed? Remember Jesus said, "Say not ye, there are yet four months and then cometh the harvest? Behold, I say unto you, lift up your eyes, and look on the fields, that they are white already unto harvest" (John 4:35).

You can't understand a concept like that in a three-dimensional consciousness. But remember, you are not a three-dimensional being. Unless you can sense what Jesus had in mind, you certainly cannot understand what life is all about. "It is the spirit that giveth life; the flesh profiteth nothing" (John 6:63).

If I cut my finger, the healing begins immediately. And what is this healing? It is the evolution of that which is involved. The finger can be healed because I am already whole. There is that of me that is changeless and perfect. It is the Christ of me, the divinity of me. This divinity of me includes a perfect finger, perfect even despite the cut on the finger. Now, in the three-dimensional human body, the cell renewal process begins, and the cut is healed in a matter of two or three days. But the cut is healed according to a nonmaterial force or pattern. How do the cells know that they should reproduce themselves in a way that will restore the finger as it was? They simply can't help themselves. There is a directive force to life that builds "according to the pattern revealed on the mount." Whether the cut is healed in three days or instantly, the same forces are involved. And that healing force is God's will—and it is always good, ceaselessly working to establish wholeness.

Wilt thou be made whole? [John 5:6, av].

Jesus wisely makes a point of man's desire. There was a man who had been lame for thirty-eight years. Jesus came upon him at the Pool of Bethesda. He asked this surprising question, "Do you really want to be healed?" Jesus was a master psychologist. He knew that "one of the minor pleasures in life is to be slightly ill." Man does not always have the courage to face up to the challenges of life. He escapes in many directions, one of which may be into sickness. He may think that he wants to be healed, and he may do everything he knows, exhaust every possibility, spend a small fortune in the process, and still find no help—because subconsciously he is finding security in his sickness.

Dr. Leslie Weatherhead, English minister, psychologist, and scholar, comments on this strange question asked by Jesus, in his book, *Psychology, Religion and Healing:*

"Disease is often—if unconsciously—an escape mechanism. It is incredible that for thirty-eight years the patient was incapable of getting himself into the moving waters if he had seriously wanted to try this treatment. . . . It is possible that the patient found it more interesting and more profitable to remain in the spotlight of publicity and in the receipt of sympathy and alms, and to maintain his illness for these reasons, than to be cured and thus to be uninteresting and compelled to earn a living or starve."[6]

Dr. Hutschnecker, in his book, *The Will to Live*,[7] points out that sickness often comes from a will to be sick, and that health must be preceded by a will to be well, a will to live, a will to overcome. He says that sickness is often a subconscious attempt to escape from life.

So, Jesus is saying to the lame man, "Do you want to be healed badly enough to give up your feelings of self-pity, to reject the long-standing habit of dwelling in despair and despondency, to be satisfied to live without the attention and assistance and sympathy of others? Are you willing to take command of the forces within you and issue an executive order?"

The force of will is almost unbelievably effective in combating physical ills. The simple statement, "I will be well," gathers the forces of mind and body around the central idea of wholeness. It is doubtful if anyone has ever died until he let go his will to live. When told by his physicians that he must die because they could do no more for him, one man said, "And leave a family of helpless children? I will not die! I will live!" And he recovered his health and lived many years.

We need to work diligently in our prayer-time to renounce any tendencies to accept and hold to less than that which is whole. "Father, let your perfect will be done in and through me. I accept your healing activity. I will to will your will. I desire healing for I believe that anything less than health and the desire for healing is a rejection of thy presence as Life in me."

Remember, this desire for healing has nothing whatever to do with influencing God that you are worthy, or urging him to come to your aid. God cannot do otherwise than come to your aid, for you are the very self-livingness of God. If you come to yourself, like the prodigal son; if you "awake and remember"; if you desire healing with all your heart; if you accept it and are willing to let go of everything less than wholeness in mind or body—then you most certainly can (and will) be healed.

Thy Faith hath made thee whole.

While on the way to Jairus' house, a woman who had suffered nineteen years with a hemorrhage, moved by great faith, made her way through the throngs of people that were following Jesus, and touched the hem of His garment. She was immediately healed. Jesus turned, and seeing what had happened, said to her, "Thy faith hath made thee whole" (Matt. 9:20–22).

Faith is the key to the fourth dimension of living, the bridge into the world of the whole man. Faith is the perception by which we can see wholeness where there appears to be sickness. It is the conviction that where lack appears, there is plenty, where pain appears, there is surcease, that in chaos there is harmony. In sickness, there is wholeness. Faith accepts wholeness. Do you have faith? You can answer this for yourself. Faith is not simply the desire to be whole. It is not just the hope that somehow, if conditions are right, God will heal you. Faith is the perception of wholeness, the intuitive sense of *being* whole even in the midst of sickness. Remember Jesus said, "Pray, believing you have received, and you will receive."

This is why the researcher spends so many long hours in the laboratory—why he is never discouraged no matter how many mistakes or failures he encounters. He believes right in the beginning that what he is reaching for is reachable. Time doesn't disturb him. He makes the investment gladly. He believes in what he is doing and that the ultimate is possible *and* inevitable.

Faith is the eye that sees the Spirit, the hand that clings to the Spirit, and the receiving power that appropriates the Spirit. Open your eyes and see. Through faith you will see beyond the appearance and accept and claim your wholeness.

Stretch forth your hand.

This was the healing word uttered to the man with the withered hand (Matt. 12:9–14). I am so very grateful that this was included in Jesus' Gospel of healing. It implies that there is always something for us to do. Often the reason we are not healed, even though we have great faith, is that we sit waiting for the miracle.

"There is a spirit in man and the inspiration of the Almighty giveth them understanding" (Job 32:8, av). Right now, no matter what the problem may be of mind, body, or affairs, there is a spirit in you, God's Spirit, the wholeness of God is in you. And the inspiration of the Almighty is whispering into your inner ear the understanding you need to take the next logical step.

Often the "sin" that has caused the separation is an unwise use of our bodies. We may be eating the wrong foods, or simply overeating. We may be sadly in need of exercise or sunshine or fresh air. Perhaps our breathing is all wrong, or our posture, or our whole way of living. There is a breath or inspiriting of God in you that will give you understanding. But you must expect to receive it. And you must be willing to "move your feet." You must expect to be guided.

An old Jewish legend vividly expresses the thought that faith cannot be passive but must be the expression of genuine inner activity. When Moses threw the wand into the Red Sea, the sea, quite contrary to the expected miracle, did not divide itself to leave a dry passage for the Jews. Not until the last man had jumped into the sea did the promised miracle happen and the waves recede.

Your miracle of healing can come to you. But be sure that you are not simply waiting for the waters to part. You are now a spiritual being. Jump into the stream and know it. Act as if you were already whole. And be humbly receptive and responsive to the inner leading that will surely come. "Stretch forth your hand."

14 The Miracle of Abundance

> Ask and it shall be given you; seek and ye shall find; knock, and it shall be opened unto you: for everyone that asketh receiveth; and he that seeketh findeth; and to him that knocketh it shall be opened.
>
> *Matt. 7:7, 8*

THIS is a great mystical Truth. The Universe in which we live is strangely and wonderfully accommodating. Because we are all unique particularizations of the Infinite, because we are all part of this accommodating Universe, asking is tantamount to receiving, seeking is actually finding, and knocking is the opening of the door. True prayer does not reach out to God "out there" in some distant place in the Universe. You simply get still and realize your unity with the whole.

In the religion *about* Jesus, there has evolved the concept that it is a Christian duty to be poor and that poverty is a virtue. This has been a corollary of the concept that wealth and possessions are somehow the evidence of sin and corruption.

This is not at all what Jesus taught. He deals not with the grace of lack or poverty, but with the grace of abundance. Study His teachings and you must conclude that He is not saying, "It is a sin to be rich." On the contrary, He strongly implies that *it is a sin to be poor*. He indicates that if you are experiencing lack, you are not accepting yourself in the fullness of your own unique relationship with the Infinite. The sin is "not to know thine own divinity."

175

Jesus taught that God is our resource and that He has provided all things for His children. He insisted that there is always abundance to meet every need—and He demonstrated it. In doing so, He was not working magic or evidencing a special dispensation from God. He was proving the Divinity of Man, showing us what man can do when he realizes his unity with the whole.

The Gospels of Jesus contain some amazing and almost unbelievable evidences of the miracle of abundance. There was the miraculous demonstration of food to feed five thousand hungry followers. There was a tremendous catch of fish that came after Jesus bade the disciples to drop their nets on the right side of the boat. There was even a gold coin found in the mouth of a fish with which to pay the Roman taxes.

It is easy to get lost in quibbling over the details. How did He feed five thousand people with one boy's lunch? How could the disciples draw such a great catch after they had fished all night and caught nothing? And whoever heard of getting money out of the mouth of a fish? To use Jesus' own metaphor, let's not "strain out the gnat and swallow the camel" (Matt. 23:24).

The feeding of the five thousand is usually considered one of the great "miracles" of the Bible. But what is a miracle? In this orderly Universe that is regulated by changeless law, it is inconceivable that natural law can be abrogated. We use the word "supernatural," but what do we mean by this? The supernatural of today becomes the natural of tomorrow. Today, an eclipse of the sun is covered by all the news media. There is little reason for anyone who has eyes to see or ears to hear to remain in ignorance of the scientific explanation of an eclipse. Yet, until comparatively recent times, an eclipse was a supernatural phenomenon that struck fear into the hearts of ignorant people.

There is no supernatural; there is only God's great natural. There is no miracle; there is only the ever-present possibility of laying hold of divine law on higher and higher levels. In a way, it is strange that we should find it difficult to think in terms of an invisible substance that is capable of manifesting itself in form and shape to fill a particular need. Consider a moment when the rain starts coming down. The air is filled with drops of water that in the city flood the yards and rage in torrents in the gutters. Where was all this water moments before

the rains came? It was present all the time in the form of unprecipi-
tated moisture in the atmosphere. Before our very eyes the invisible
became visible. A miracle? No, a perfectly natural phenomenon with
an explanation that most of us have come to accept without question.

The important lesson in the miracle stories of the Bible is that we
live in a Universe that is opulent, limitless, and accommodating. It
will manifest for us exactly what we have the consciousness to
encompass. There is a legitimate, royal abundance for every living
soul. We live and move and have our being in it. Of course at this
point, it may be nonmaterial, spiritual substance. It is an energy-
potential that requires mental and material precipitation.

However, the miracle of abundance is not the multiplication of
loaves of bread, nor the specific filling of a cruse with oil, nor the
drawing in of a mammoth catch of fish. The miracle is the all-
sufficiency and ever-availability of Infinite substance. This was Jesus'
great idea: that the Kingdom of Heaven is an opulent kingdom of
substance, of creative ideas. And the supply to meet our demands is
right *where we are*—and *what we need*.

In the story of the miraculous feeding, Jesus told the people to sit
down and then He "looked up to heaven and gave thanks." Right
away we might find ourselves "straining out the gnat," for we return
to the old concept that heaven is somewhere "out there." It would
seem that Jesus was looking up into the skies and saying, "God, you
have abundance up there. We need some of it down here." But that
isn't what is implied at all. He looked away from the appearance of
lack and emptiness, from the human feeling that "you cannot possibly feed all these people with one boy's lunch." He closed His eyes
to the lack and opened His spiritual eyes to abundance.

There is no absence of God in the Universe, and there is no
shortage in God. The only lack in life is the thought of lack. You are
always as rich as you think you are, and the only poverty is of the
spirit. You may have an empty pocketbook, and yet you may feel rich
because somewhere in a bank there are some marks on a piece of
paper that say you have abundance. The bank may not have the
money. It may be out somewhere else, as scratchings on other pieces
of paper. But you feel rich even though you have no tangible
evidence of riches at the moment. On the other hand, you may have
a pocketful of symbols of substance and still feel fearful and worried

at the fluctuations of the stock market or for the security of your job. Thus you are really poor.

Jesus is often described as being poor, without a place to lay His head. But He was welcomed into the homes of both the rich and poor all over Palestine. He dressed as a rabbi, and His clothing was so fine that the soldiers at the cross cast lots for His seamless robe. He could go forth without script or purse because He went back of money to the idea it represents and dealt with substance in the realm of ideas. He had discovered the key to releasing the tremendous power-potential within Him. He found the supernatural natural.

Let us not lose sight of the great idea that Jesus is unfolding—that man is an integral part of an opulent Universe. All we need to do is "ask" in faith, believing that we will receive, and we shall receive. Because asking is receiving. The very moment we stake our claim in Infinite Mind, that which we encompass is ours, along with the creative ability to shape it in the form of our material needs.

We should not hesitate to ask largely. God can give much as easily as He can give little. It takes no more effort for the laws of mathematics to add two million and two million to get four million, than to add two plus two to get four. At this very moment, if every man, woman, and child in the world would take a pencil and paper and write down the problem, two plus two equals four, there would be no strain on the principle, simply because it is principle.

There is no more substance in a million dollars than in a penny, for there is no quantity in spirit. What is a million dollars? To answer the question, we have to resort to quantity. It is six zeros after a one, or large quantities of bills, or the money to purchase so many barns of wheat. We still haven't defined a million dollars. It is substance that has been formed and shaped into a quantity; but the quantity is in our mind. We formed it, we shaped it, we called it a million dollars. We could have just as well called it a penny. And we could call the penny a million dollars. Each is an evidence of substance. Man forms and shapes the substance according to his need, according to his faith. And perhaps that is what faith is: the perceiving power of the mind and the ability to form and shape substance.

Looking at it in this way, the miracle begins to be more credible. Here comes a boy with five loaves and two fishes. They represent a formation of substance. There is not enough food in his lunch bag to feed five thousand people, but there is enough *substance* there, for there is no quantity in substance. If you think of the lunch in terms of the crystallization of substance as bread and fish, there is not enough. Think of it as an evidence or focal point of limitless spirit substance, and there is abundance.

The boy's lunch then could be a symbol of lack or abundance, depending upon the attitude of Jesus. "And he took the five loaves, and the two fishes, and looking up to heaven, he blessed, and brake and gave the loaves to the disciples, and the disciples to the multitudes. And they all ate, and were filled . . ." (Matt. 14:19, 20). In other words, He looked away from the appearance of lack and gave thanks for abundance. He blessed what He had, for it *was* substance. The power of blessing is not reserved for holy places or for specially ordained persons. It is an act of tremendous possibilities that should be developed by everyone. Blessing is an attitude of mind in which one may see the oak tree within the acorn, and the man of God within the newborn babe. Such an attitude lays hold of that to which it is applied on the highest possible level.

Charles Fillmore says:

God is the source of a mighty stream of substance, and you are a tributary of that stream, a channel of expression. Blessing the substance increases its flow. If your money supply is low or your purse seems empty, take it in your hands and bless it. See it filled with the living substance ready to become manifest. As you prepare your meals bless the food with the thought of spiritual substance. When you dress, bless your garments and realize that you are being constantly clothed with God's substance. . . . The more conscious you become of the presence of the living substance, the more it will manifest itself for you and the richer will be the common good of all. . . . Identify yourself with substance . . . and you will soon begin to rejoice in the ever-present bounty of God.[1]

Whatever you have, no matter how seemingly inadequate, bless it. Even if you have no money and no food, bless your hands, your mind, your skills, your friends, the air you breathe, the sun that brings light. Bless everything, and your life will be blessed with riches hitherto undreamed of.

When Jesus blessed the five loaves and two fishes, He subjected this evidence of substance to a ray as penetrating as any known to man. The symbols of bread and fish were still intact, but they were spiritually expanded far beyond the size indicated by their intrinsic worth.

We are told that Jesus "broke the bread." This is a subtle and yet all-important clue to the miracle of abundance. To break the bread is to get the attention completely away from the symbol and place it on the substance in back of the symbol. This is the break-through that ties together the fact of human need and the truth of all-sufficient supply. Though the five loaves and the two fishes materially represented an adequate lunch for one young boy, they wouldn't go far in meeting the needs of more than five thousand hungry people. As long as they remained intact, the doubting mind could always say, "You might as well face the facts. There just isn't enough to go around." Jesus broke them into small pieces. In mind, then, the substance was broken up into its invisible atomic components. Thus, when "broken," the meager supply was no longer simply loaves and fishes— it was all-sufficient substance.

What is bread? Where does it come from? We know that man forms bread from the wheat of the field, and that the wheat has grown from a tiny seed through the miracle of growth. Who can understand the mystical processes of nature whereby a tiny seed can draw upon the Universe for all that it needs to fulfill itself in growth. And if the seed can accomplish this miracle, why not man? Jesus commented on this very thing, "If God so clothe the grass of the field, which today is, and tomorrow is cast into the oven, shall he not much more clothe you, O ye of little faith?" (Matt. 6:30).

What is lack? Is it not simply an absence of faith in the miracle of abundance? Even where someone has an empty pocketbook, the trees are still drawing substance out of the air and the ground, the grass is green and the birds are clothed. You cannot really be stranded in a Universe that is so accommodating. This is what Jesus was talking about.

In other words, lack is simply a state of consciousness in man. The empty pocketbook may spell poverty to man, but it is only because he has lost sight of the universal substance back of its outer symbol. If God *is*, then substance *is*, whether we see it or not. One plus one equals two—even if we do not use the figures to express the fact. Some people can work out simple problems of arithmetic in their head. They need no pencil or paper or adding machine. Jesus went forth without script or purse for He had "meat to eat that ye know not" (John 4:32). He looked up to heaven; He looked away from the seeming absence of the symbol to the underlying substance, the resource, the universal essence. He turned to principle.

We have been conditioned to think in terms of forms and shapes, of dollars and cents. In one account, Philip, the disciple, said it would require two hundred shillings to buy bread for the multitude. A practical evaluation, but also a self-limiting one! Such an evaluation always raises a barrier of money and of time and of the means to get the supplies from the supplier to the consumer.

Paul points to a fundamental in divine law when he says, "And my God shall supply every need of yours according to His riches . . ." (Phil. 4:19). But God cannot supply lack! Lack is not a condition, but an attitude of mind. An empty pocketbook is just a need to be filled. But the fear of an empty pocket or worry about it spells the thought of lack.

Lack is really an illusion. It is the acceptance of the appearance as being real. Lack is my saying that because I do not have a pencil to write "two plus two equals four," I cannot add the figures. But the principle is true, regardless. God is substance, and substance is omnipresent whether or not man provides the consciousness through which it may manifest.

A wealthy man may fall asleep and dream that he is poor. In the dream he has all the experiences and the feelings of poverty, but it is still only a dream. Finally, he awakens and he is wealthy again. The only attainment involved in this frightening experience is the awakening. In a very real sense, man's need, in the face of apparent lack, is to awaken and realize that he is always in the opulent sea of substance. "Awake, thou that sleepest, . . . and Christ shall shine upon thee" (Eph. 5:14).

"The Kingdom of Heaven is at hand" (Matt. 3:2). Your miracle of abundance is ready for you. Awaken from the illusion of lack. Lift up your eyes. Stop seeing empty pocketbooks, unpaid bills, unemployment, or lack of opportunity. Look away from all this and know that you are living and alive in an opulent sea of substance. There is supply for you, right now, if you can accept it.

When we talk about the "miracle" of abundance, we are not implying that the demonstration of your good must come in some phenomenal manner. Not at all. The miracle is in the principle, not in any magic mode of expression. The miracle of the electromagnetic crane is the secret of electricity and the magnetic coil. When you know the secret the supernatural becomes natural and the miracle becomes commonplace.

The miracle is in the availability of substance, not particularly in the way it manifests. When Jesus was confronted with the need to pay the Roman tax, He simply told Peter to go fishing and that he would find a gold coin in the mouth of a fish (Matt. 17:27). Peter did as he was asked and he found the coin in the fish's mouth and used it to pay the tax. It is too bad that this story has been related so literally, since there is an increase in the "credibility gap" for the intellect. Actually, when we know the idiom, there is nothing unusual about this story at all. What was more natural than for Peter, who was a fisherman, to go fishing, market the fish, and pay the tax with the proceeds. This is exactly what the story says idiomatically.

In our West, the cattlemen talk about a steer being worth "forty dollars on the hoof." In the Orient, they talk about an ox having "twenty gold pieces in his horn." And in the Middle East, we find this expression among fishermen: "The fish had a gold coin in his mouth." In every case, these are figures of speech referring to the ultimate market price to be gained from the sale of the product.

Jesus is teaching the lesson that when you have a need, the answer is right where you are. The miracle may not be in the way it manifests, but in the ever-availability of ideas, of guidance, of all things working together for good. You may be guided to go fishing, or to get a job, or to "break" the loaves and fishes. But there is abundance for you—if you accept it.

We may wonder why some people have so much hardship, whereas for others everything turns to gold. The rationalization from the confused religion about Jesus is that the poor will be rewarded in some future heaven. Jesus puts it very simply: "For whosoever hath, to him shall be given, and he shall have abundance; but whosoever hath not, from him shall be taken away even that which he hath" Matt. 13:12). This is not as difficult to understand as at first it might seem. He is saying, "Hold your cup under the faucet of abundance. The empty cup is filled to running over. If the cup is held upside down, not only will it not be filled, but anything it had in it is poured out."

In this wonderfully accommodating Universe, if you have the consciousness of abundance—if you feel rich—you will claim riches and accept abundance and your cup will be filled. However, if you feel that you are discriminated against—that there are no opportunities available, that no one wants you, that you are poor and insufficient—your cup is turned upside down. All the wealth of the Universe cannot help you, and you constantly lose anything you seem momently to gain. Understanding this Truth—much as we resist the thought—"the rich *do* get richer, and the poor *do* get poorer." We may want to change this principle, but it is universal law. You may not like all the implications of gravity, but you can't change it. You can only be mighty careful that you do not step off high places.

In my experience in spiritual counseling, I see this law at work in some strange and even pitiful ways. Two men came to me for counseling in their need for employment. One man had been an executive. He had normally been in the $20,000-a-year bracket. The other man had been in various types of jobs but had averaged only about $5,000 a year. We talked at length about the law of abundance. We considered all the ramifications of the prosperity principle. We prayed for prosperity, for guidance, for a right and perfect place of employment. We used the same treatment, the same affirmation in each case. In a few days both men called back to tell me the prayer had been answered. Both were once again employed. Wonderful! It is always a blessing to witness answered prayer.

Now what sort of a job did each person get? The man who had normally been in the $20,000 bracket again received a salary in the same bracket. The man who had an average of $5,000 a year, received a job with similar pay. Why didn't they both get the same income? They both prayed the same way, used the same prayer techniques, affirmations, treatments. Both received my identical instruction and guidance. Why the wide disparity in financial results?

The answer is really quite simple, though it may not be easy to accept. *God can do no more for you than He can do through you.* The miracle of abundance works through your consciousness, in accordance with your experience, your attitudes, your self-evaluation.

If a chemist prays for guidance, ideas come about chemistry. If a physicist prays for guidance, ideas come about physics. If the poor man prays for prosperity, the answer may come in a "handout." If the rich man prays for prosperity, the answer may come in a million-dollar windfall on the stock market. The answer always comes to you in the divine prompting, "Son, thou art ever with me and all that is mine is thine." But the degree or form or shape of the manifestation depends upon your faith, your vision, your ability to accept the opulence of the Universe.

The law is, "It is your Father's good pleasure to give you the kingdom" (Luke 12:32). God is all-sufficiency—your instant, constant, and abundant supply. But you will experience only that which you can take into your consciousness. Thus any limitation must be a limitation in thought, in the faith that shapes the substance. Light streaming through a window will always assume the shape and color of the aperture through which it comes. The wealth of the universe will be yours to the degree that you can "see" it and see yourself using it.

The intellect of man, the skeptical part of your nature and mine, stands in our way. We say, "After all, you must be practical. If five thousand people are sitting on a hillside out in the country and all they have on hand is five small loaves and two fishes, those people are just not going to be fed." *But they were fed.* When Alexander Graham Bell had his telephone demonstration all set up, there were many skeptics who jeered and said, "When you have someone a hundred miles away, hooked up with only a small wire, you may talk all you want into that little black box, but they just won't hear you." *But they did hear.* And millions of times a day the same sort of hearing goes on around the world in the sophisticated telephones that have evolved from that first simple prototype.

Again let us say, don't get lost in the mechanics. The miracle is the abundance of God in terms of ideas, in terms of ways where there seems to be no way. It really doesn't matter how the multitudes were fed. All that counts is that the supply was manifest when it was needed, where it was needed, and in the amounts in which it was needed.

I once heard a woman say that she could just imagine a long fish coming down from the skies from which Jesus was able to slice off piece after piece for the multitudes. One man said it was difficult to imagine how mountain-high would be the pile of bread sufficient to serve the gathering. Some people find an explanation in the conjecture that there were many lunches lurking in the robes of this throng of people, and that the women surely brought food for the children. Dr. George Lamsa suggests that the real miracle was the timing of the arrival of a camel train laden with food, sent by a thoughtful merchant in the nearest town. He poses the question: "It says that there were twelve baskets full of food left over. Where did those baskets come from?"

All that really matters is that the people were fed. And the miracle of abundance is not the manner in which substance manifests but the ever-availability of substance in general.

Dr. Lamsa's conjecture would seem to have a modern parallel in the story that is told about George Mueller, famed director of the amazing orphanage in Bristol, England. It is said that this large institution functioned for years without any fund-raising drives or appeals. Money always came unsolicited at the time it was needed.

One of the many stories about George Mueller is apropos of the manner in which the people in the Gospel story were fed. An assistant came to George Mueller an hour before dinnertime, saying, "There is no bread for dinner." Mr. Mueller replied, "Have no fear, there will be bread." Half an hour later the assistant came again, saying, "But Mr. Mueller, there is still no bread for dinner. It is time to have the children get ready." Again the answer, "There will be bread. Have the children get ready as usual." The children filed into the dining room and stood at their places and the frantic assistant cried, "Mr Mueller, what will we do, there is no bread." Calmly, the director said, "There will be bread. Have them say grace." Almost as the children chorused their "Amen" to their prayer, there was a clatter of trucks roaring up the drive with bread. It seems that a merchant in Bristol was facing a weekend with a considerable oversupply of bread. Just about an hour before, he had a "leading" to take it out to the orphanage to feed George Mueller's children. "The Miracle of Abundance." Would it have been any more of a miracle if a few loaves had been multiplied at the tables?

There is an interesting sequel to the story of the orphanage. George Mueller called the assistant into his office and informed him that he was being dismissed. He said, "I can't afford to have in my employ someone who will doubt God three times in one hour."

Today we take for granted many things that have come out of the miracle of abundance. The electricity that lights and cooks and heats our homes was here long before man learned how to accept it. Many of us remember when women had to paint their legs because of the lack of silk hosiery during the war. They had to do this until we realized the miracle of abundance in the form of synthetic material, nylon, which proved to be superior in every way to silk. With no silk available, we might ask, how could we possibly provide the stockings for seventy-five million women? The miracle here was that we not only did find the way to make the stockings, but in so doing, we opened up a whole new world of synthetics that has changed our way of life.

The basic needs of man in the world today are about the same as they were two thousand years ago: food and water. There are hungering multitudes in such overcrowded areas as India and China. There is much concern about the population explosion and the ability of the earth to supply the food. And yet we are told that in the ocean we have all the food and water that we will need for millions of years.

What is needed? The ideas, the techniques, the means through which they may be converted into use. When such ideas come into the mind of man, isn't this an evidence of the miracle of abundance. Again, the miracle is not only the availability of supply but the availability of ideas through which the supply may be converted into use. Can anyone doubt that equipment will be developed through which fresh water may be easily and cheaply converted from sea water, that throughout all the earth all the desert places will be made to "blossom as a rose," and that food in limitless supply may be easily harnessed from the atmosphere and the ocean?

There was an announcement recently of a British scientist who had created synthetic milk. Milk that tasted in every way like cow's milk had been produced without the cow. The account told how they assembled all the feed that the cow ate and, by a special machine, were able to render from it what the cow made through its own process. The result was milk that looked and tasted like the real thing. This is automation. Perhaps it will cause the cows of the world to go on strike.

Perhaps this forecasts the ultimate development of mechanical processes for creating foodstuffs directly, without the traditional "first the grain, then the ear, then the full grain in the ear." We will simply assemble the substances that the wheat seed draws out of the elements and create wheat without planting seeds and without the growth time. Or, take it a step further, perhaps we will simply create the flour, or even the bread, synthetically. From this it is only a large step across the bridge of faith to the acceptance of the miracle of abundance that Jesus discovered and demonstrated. Is it conceivable that the time will come when man will not even have to go to his refrigerator to satisfy his hunger? Perhaps he will simply go into the inner chamber and close the door—and "be still and know" his oneness with all substance. Isn't this what the seed does? Why shouldn't man ultimately learn how? Even the thought of it taxes our imagination, but didn't Jesus say, "Man shall not live by bread alone, but by every word that proceedeth out of the mouth of God" (Matt. 4:4).

The important thing is, since substance is—opulent and limitless and everywhere present—the great miracle-working power is faith. Faith is the ability to perceive substance, to draw it forth, to form it and shape it into what we need. Paul wisely says, "Stir up the gift of God that is in thee." We need to stir up the faith to believe that we are in spiritual unity with the whole; that our mind is a channel through which great ideas flow; that we can find this substance—first in the form of ideas, guidance, and the creative skill of our hands, and second, as the outward manifestation of the means of exchange, the money to do what needs to be done.

The place to overcome lack—unemployment, financial hardship, poverty—is in the general attitudes of one's consciousness. A picture wire that is perfectly attuned to a certain note on the piano will instantly sing out when that note is struck. The person who "hath not,"—who has a consciousness of limitation, whose cup is upside down under the faucet—will always have hardship in "hard times," will always be depressed in a depression. If poverty is in the belief of man, every time that note is struck, there will be an unconscious response.

We need to change the "war on poverty" to a program of "education for abundance." We need to help people to understand their part in this great accommodating universe—help them to change their thoughts and to begin to work with ideas. We need to help people realize that they are unique expressions of the Infinite—that they can begin with themselves to give expression to new ideas, to develop new creativity and to become productive. Thus, starting with themselves, each individual will overcome first the thought and then the experience of lack. And so he will help the nation and the world itself to overcome all poverty.

The economists will often debate the question of whether everyone can have prosperity, wealth, and riches. Isn't there a limit? Economist Thomas Malthus thought so, and the Malthusian principle has predominated in the field of economics for more than a hundred and fifty years. It was and is a factual analysis of a physical world. But today, researchers of the new science realize that we cannot understand the physical world without metaphysical principles.

Charles Fillmore has said:

In the new era now at its dawn we shall have a spirit of prosperity. This principle of the universal substance will be known and acted upon, and there will be no place for lack. Supply will be more equalized. There will not be millions of bushels of wheat stored in musty warehouses while people go hungry. There will be no overproduction or underconsumption or other inequalities of supply, for God's substance will be recognized and used by all people. Men will not pile up fortunes one day and lose them the next, for they will no longer fear the integrity of their neighbors nor try to keep their neighbor's share from him. . . . Is this an impractical utopia? The answer depends upon you. Just as soon as you individually recognize the omnipresent substance and put your faith in it, you can look for others around you to do the same. 'A little leaven leaveneth the whole lump" (I Cor. 5:6). And even one life that bears witness to the truth of the prosperity law will quicken the consciousness of the whole community.[2]

This would seem to imply that it is not only a sin to be poor, but that thoughts of poverty degrade, while thoughts of abundance uplift. As more and more people lay hold of the concept of the Divinity of Man and begin to see themselves in a new context of wholeness, they will not only begin to claim their inheritance of abundance, but they will also become an uplifting influence for opulence in the world.

15 In Defense of Judas

ONE OF THE most significant events in human history took place not on a battlefield, nor in a legislative assembly, nor in a king's palace, but on the summit of a windswept hill outside the city of Jerusalem. A young man had come out of the country to set the minds and hearts of people on fire with enthusiasm for Truth. With followers growing alarmingly, the Temple rulers, fearing the weakening of the position of sacred traditions, felt that drastic action had to be taken.

Through the betrayal of one of Jesus' own disciples and after a series of trumped-up charges, Jesus was condemned to death. By law it had to be approved by the Roman authorities. However, Pilate, the local representative of Rome, was reluctant to give in to the wishes of the Sanhedrin. He talked to Jesus at length and could find no great wrong in Him. But the mobs were unruly and Pilate became fearful. He could not afford to have an uprising in his region, so he gave in to the mob and allowed Jesus to be nailed to the cross like a common thief.

Traditionally, Good Friday is set aside for the religious observance of this event, a time for reliving the pain, the suffering, the shame, the darkness of the crucifixion hour. And the disciple who betrayed Jesus, Judas Iscariot, is the villainous center of attention for this one day. It is one great and implausible drama—complicated, confusing, paradoxical.

The unfortunate thing about the Gospels is that the writers gave too much emphasis to the most impressive events. So the crucifixion and the events leading up to it are set forth in complete detail. It is almost as the life story of Abraham Lincoln might be if we were given nothing of his boyhood and young manhood, very little of his work in the White House, and every detail of his assassination. How easy it is to forget that it was Jesus' inspired life and not His agonized death that was and is the keynote of Christianity.

And yet we have been led to believe that the gruesome story of "Good Friday" is the central feature of Jesus' life and teachings. The sadness and pain and darkness of that final hour has been captured in story and picture. And the crucifix, containing a defeated and emaciated Jesus, has become the very symbol of Christianity.

Thomas Paine once said that no religion can be really divine which has in it any doctrine that offends the sensibilities of a little child. One wonders how many millions of little children have had their sensibilities offended through the years by a theology that says: "Because lambs had been put to death in the Temple as a sacrifice for the sins of the worshipers, so Jesus was the Lamb of God. His death had been planned from the beginning of the world; the human race was hopelessly wayward; God knew that it *would* be, and nothing would turn Him from His vindictive purpose to destroy it but the sacrifice of an innocent Son." What child could accept such a concept when he knows no earthly father would be so cruel?

Arnold Toynbee, in his book, *Christianity Among the Religions of the World*,[1] tells the story of an English family living in China who engaged a Chinese nurse for their small children. As soon as this Chinese woman came into their house, they saw that she was much disturbed by something. As the days passed, she showed signs of being more and more upset. They pressed her for reasons but she was too shy to tell them.

Finally, she broke down and told them, "Well, there is something that I just cannot understand. You are obviously good people. You obviously love your children and care for them; yet, in every room in this house, and on the staircase as well, I see reproductions of a criminal being put to death by some horrible form of torture that we have never heard of in China. I cannot understand how you, responsible and loving parents as you obviously are, can expose your children to the dreadful effects of seeing this awful picture at this impressionable stage of their lives."

The Christian cross is a story half-told. Paul says, "You see in part . . . but when that which is perfect is come, that which is in part shall be done away" (I Cor. 13:10). When we see the whole life of Jesus, which includes the empty tomb of Easter morning, the agonized scene of Golgotha will be done away. *And the cross will be done away!* The cross has become the symbol of depraved man, vindictive God, and unjust punishment. Where is there anything of the divine in this story, or anything worthy of our worship or emulation? Using the cross as the symbol of Christianity is the denial of the central theme of Jesus teachings: the Divinity of Man.

There is a great and meaningful lesson in this whole experience of Jesus. To understand what was really taking place, we must quickly move on to that first Easter morning. But first, let us linger long enough to meditate on some of the background of the Good Friday scene. It may help us to understand what really took place and why.

The crucifixion has been called "The Darkest Hour in Human History." The characters in the drama have been reviled and condemned: Peter for his denial of Jesus, Pilate for his weakness, and Judas for his act of betrayal. Yes, especially Judas. His name has become a synonym for the most evil of acts. Dante puts Judas the lowest of all men. In Christian dogma, Judas has been called a murderer—as if he actually drove the nails into the hands and feet of Jesus.

In our day, we take pride in a freedom that guarantees a fair trial and that insists that a man is innocent until proved guilty. However, in the Gospels, Judas is adjudged guilty long before the crime. Whenever his name is mentioned, the writers added, "who also betrayed Him." In other words, in the total Gospel story, it is almost as if Judas has a placard round his neck identifying him as the villain, as in some old-world miracle play.

To set the record straight—Judas was one of Jesus' closest friends. Jesus believed in him, saw great possibilities in him, personally selected him as one who could be of great help to the cause. And let us never forget that, like all the disciples, Judas gave up everything to follow Jesus. And because of his obvious sophistication and intelligence, he may have had to give up far more than the others of the band.

Judas was a man of strength, of vision, of dedication. He was ready to sacrifice place or position in the world for a dream. If he was ambitious or selfish, the gospel writers didn't mention it. For it was James and John who argued over who was to have the posts of leadership when Jesus "came into His kingdom." They even told Jesus they wanted to sit on His left and right hand. All the while, Judas was quietly and efficiently doing his job.

He was probably the most talented, the most educated, the most businesslike of all the disciples—and thus he was appointed treasurer for the little company and had the job of looking after their affairs and of making provision for their needs. He was the practical-minded man who was taking care of the mundane things while the remainder were building "blue-sky dreams" which they probably did not under- stand—as later events indicated.

For three years more or less, Judas lived with Jesus and in the company of the band of disciples. He had so established himself as the stable one of the group that, when Jesus announced that one of them would betray him, nobody apparently suspected Judas. He was the level-headed and steady one. Anyone but Judas!

It is important here to recognize that all the disciples had a little different shade of understanding of Jesus and what he was about. None of them at this point really understood. Even Peter, who had that flash of great insight when He saw the Christ, the divine, in Jesus, did not understand that Jesus' real mission was to bring the message of the Divinity of Man to all the world—that He was build- ing a kingdom, or new order, in the mind and affairs of man, but that it was not a political kingdom that would involve an overthrow of the government.

In the final hours, though he had been certain he would never do so, Peter denied that he had even known Jesus. Perhaps he could have saved Him, spoken in His defense, convinced the multitudes that they were being misled. But he turned away in weakness. Much is made of Peter's denial of Jesus. What of the denial of ten other disciples that is implicit in their silence and disappearance? Certainly, they had not understood Jesus' teaching of the Divinity of Man. Perhaps they were shocked by events into thinking, "If man is divine, then certainly Jesus, the best of all men, should be able to save Himself." And it may have been this very thought in the mind of the one disciple who was strong and courageous, who did not doubt that Jesus *could* save Himself, that led to the "betrayal" of Him by Judas.

When Jesus, at that last supper in the upper room, said that one of the disciples would betray Him, instead of saying, "Who is it? Who would do such a thing?" they simply and meekly said, "Is it I, Lord? Is it I?" In other words, none of the disciples was sure of himself. All were in a state of shock and weakness. Each of them actually suspected himself.

Undoubtedly, the rulers of the Sanhedrin had already approached some of the disciples, possibly all of them, looking for one who would help them trap Jesus. Perhaps they had all rejected their overtures. Perhaps even Judas had. It was almost as if a movement of destiny was in the air, and unconsciously they were all fearful that it might settle upon them.

We must note that Jesus did not condemn Judas. He seemed almost compassionate as He pointed him out—almost as if it were a matter of an assignment that someone had to have. As we read the story, Jesus seems to be almost an accessory to the "crime" of Judas. The text states that Jesus announced that he who would receive the sop was the one who would betray Him. And it says that "Satan" entered into Judas when he dipped his hand into the dish with that of Jesus. Jesus then turned to Judas and said, "What thou doest, do quickly." It was almost as if He had given him the charge: "This is your job, go and do it."

The disciples had not seemed to catch it, but Jesus had long known and often stated that this was to be his destiny. It was a destiny that He chose. He said, in effect, "I lay down my life of myself, no one taketh it from me" (John 10:18). He had a choice but He chose to go through this experience as the means of revealing the great Truth of the resurrection principle to man. More than this, it was the last lap on His own path of overcoming. His own experience of the Divinity of Man would not be complete until He could, not only go through, but grow through, the dark hour of Golgotha.

On the cross, one of the most misunderstood of the dramatic "Seven Last Words" is "Eli, Eli, lama sabachthani" (Matt. 27:46). This has always been rendered, "My God, my God, why hast thou forsaken me." How unfortunate has been this mistranslation. For if God would or could forsake this most advanced soul, then what hope is there for us? How can we or why should we worship and love a God who would ordain or even acquiesce in this horrible experience?

Now we know that Jesus' words have been misunderstood. George Lamsa, world-renowned Syrian scholar and translator of the Bible from the ancient Peshitta, says that Jesus was actually saying, "My God, my God, for this was I kept—I am fulfilling my destiny. I am on the way through the dark hour to the great demonstration of resurrection and the complete fulfillment of man's divinity."

Jesus forgave those who crucified Him, and those who taunted Him. He said, "Forgive them for they know not what they are doing" (Luke 23:34). And, of course, they didn't. How could they know that they were actually playing a role, as was Judas, in bringing about the great demonstration? So, Judas was a tool, an instrument, playing a destiny-chosen role in the dramatic portrayal of a great lesson.

Of course, there is a law of consciousness, and thus there must have been something in Judas that led him to play this role. Man is not an automaton. He has free will. Judas, then, must have had a choice. What led him to accept this role? Why not Peter? Why not the doubting Thomas? It may be that Judas accepted the role, as Jesus those many years ago accepted the mantle of the Messiah— choosing to fulfill the prophecy of man's divinity. Judas may have become the one—not because of his weakness, but because of his strength, coupled with an erroneous concept of Jesus' mission.

Judas was zealous for the Master's success. He was really convinced that Jesus intended to set up a new kingdom on earth. Jesus was to be the ruler of a new Kingdom of Judah. And He believed that Jesus would outshine David and Solomon of the earlier kingdom. He would have the riches of the world, the power of Caesar, the homage of nations. And don't forget that this thought was not completely foreign to Jesus' mind. The temptations in the wilderness indicated that He had to put these thoughts of world conquest and temporal power behind Him. Little wonder that the disciples had such thoughts.

Judas, the practical-minded man, the business head, the meticulous organizer, felt that Jesus was missing His opportunities. With the world almost in His grasp, the Master was likely to lose it from sheer inaction. Something must be done. Perhaps it was that "Satan entered into him," as the Scripture puts it. But Satan is simply the ruling force of human consciousness. The result was a materialistic and God-excluded plan, unwise, and completely inconsistent with

Jesus' goals. But remember, neither Judas nor the other disciples understood those goals.

It is conceivable that, after Jesus pointed the finger at him and said, "You are the one," he conceived the plan. "Sure—why not? I will simply betray Jesus to the Romans. This will force Him to use His powers in His own defense. I have seen evidence of that power used for others. This will spur Him to action, before it is too late." That Jesus, even under the shadow of Roman torture and death, would refuse to invoke the wrath of God upon His persecutors, probably never occurred to the worldly-minded Judas.

So he went to the chief priests and sold the Master for thirty pieces of silver. It was a ridiculously small sum. Judas came from an opulent background. Thus the money meant nothing. He could have gotten ten times the sum if money had been the object. He was simply trying to force Jesus to act. How little he understood the Master is shown in the miserable failure of his plan. But did the plan fail? How could the great demonstration be achieved unless someone played this role at this time? We are reminded of Joseph of old, who said to his brothers who had sold him into slavery, "Ye may have intended it for evil, but God intended it for good."

In 1960 I had the privilege of witnessing the grand spectacle of the Passion play at Oberammergau. Its treatment of Judas follows the theme I am setting forth here. Dramatically and articulately, the following scene unfolds:[2]

Judas is standing before Annas reporting the work is done. And Annas says, "Oh, I must embrace you, my friends! So our plan has succeeded! Judas! Thy name will have an honorable place in our annals! Even before the Feast, the Galilean shall die!" Judas is suddenly struck with what he has done: "Die, die? but I did not deliver Him to you for that! No, no, I will not have it."

Then Judas is shown in several dramatic soliloquies that tell much of his inner feelings, his remorse and his confusion. He is on this great stage alone. It is raining heavily (the stage is out of doors and it just happened to be a rainy day—which actually added to the credibility of the scene). Judas says:

"Sinister forebodings persecute me! The word of Annas! *He must die*—oh, this word torments me wherever I go and stand! It would be terrible—terrible. If they would . . . my Master . . . and I, the cause of it! If the Master wished to save Himself, He would have let them feel His power a second time in the Garden of Olives. As He did it not then, He will not do so now. And what can I do for Him? I, most miserable man, that have delivered Him into their hands? They shall have back the money. I will go and put in my claim— But—will He be saved by that? O vain and foolish hope! They will mock at my offer."

He bursts into the council chambers and accuses the priests of tricking him. He throws the money down and runs out. And then, in the most eloquent and dramatic part of the entire play, Judas covers the entire stage, beating his breast, on his knees, standing, running, crying, shouting . . .

"Where can I go to hide my fearful shame, to get rid of the tortures of my conscience? Earth! Open thou and swallow me! I can not, can not live! My Master, the best of men, have I sold, given Him up to ill-treatment and to the tortures of a martyr's death—I, detestable betrayer! Oh! where is there a man on whom such guilt rests! How good He always was to me! How sweetly did He comfort me when dark gloom lay on my soul! How wondrously happy I felt when I sat at His feet, and heavenly teachings, dropped like honey from His mouth! . . ." And he winds a cloth about his neck and hangs himself.

Does this sound like a man who cooked up a ruthless scheme to betray Jesus for money? Can we find anything in this other than the remorse of a man who tried to speed up the process of Jesus' mission and simply miscalculated what that mission was?

Much has been made in recent years over the guilt of the Jews for murdering Jesus. How easily and rationalistically we forget history! Judas was a Jew, as were all the disciples. And Jesus was a Jew. So why should we make so much of the fact that the Sanhedrin rulers were Jews? Do the people of Dallas deserve eternal condemnation because one Dallas man shot President Kennedy? John Wilkes Booth, who shot Lincoln, was an American. Must Americans throughout time bear the stigma of the murder of this great man?

And we must return to Jesus' own testimony, "I lay down my life of myself, no one taketh it from me." Judas was playing a role in this cosmic drama, as were the priests of the Sanhedrin, as was Pilate and the disciples and the screaming throngs of people and the soldiers who drove in the nails.

John Ruskin once said that the sin of the world is essentially the sins of Judas, and that men do not disbelieve in Christ, but they sell Him! There is something of Judas in you and me, and it is a very real influence in our lives. We believe in the things of the Spirit, but we desire the things of the flesh. Though we are all divine in potential, yet we often act the part of our humanity. We frustrate our potentialities. We conceal our innate goodness. Thus we betray the Christ for the gratification of human desires. And, as the poet says, "sole root of sin in thee is not to know thy divinity."

From a metaphysical point of view, there is rich meaning in the crucifixion story. The whole Gospel account is a story within a story. Incidentally, it tells of the overcoming and regeneration of one man into the perfection of the Christ. But fundamentally it tells of the processes of the struggle of finite man into his infinite oneness. It is your story and my story. Thus, in the crucifixion, we see that the personal ego, the material-centered thoughts must go, must die so that the true essence of the divine in man may live.

Jesus made no effort to defeat the act of Judas, for He knew that the sense consciousness is not to be destroyed; it must destroy itself. This must take place before the soul can make its demonstration of eternal life. Judas, along with all the disciples, was part of the consciousness of Jesus. There was that in Jesus, the human self, the ego, the personal, the material-centered (seen in the wilderness experience) that had to be crossed out completely. Jesus *had* to go to the cross to prove His freedom from the sense man; and Judas, the ego, *had* to destroy himself so that the full demonstration of eternal life could manifest. To the mind familiar with the language of mysticism, this is an absolutely essential sequence of events.

Don't be too hard on Judas—for there is a Judas' state of mind in us all. Let us work diligently to lift up our motives, our goals and aspirations, so that we can say: "I came to bear witness to the Truth." And anyway—according to George Bernard Shaw—they crucified Him on a stick, but by some means He managed to get hold of the right end of it.

16 The Great Demonstration

That God which ever lives, and loves,
One God, one law, one element,
And one far-off divine event
To which the whole creation moves.[1]

IMAGINE the news coverage of that event of the first Easter, if it had taken place in modern times. The *Jerusalem Daily News* might have a banner headline: "NAZARENE'S TOMB FOUND EMPTY." Secondary headlines might read: "Earthquake rends city as prophet dies. . . . Crucified king of Jews seen alive is report." Can't you hear the newsboys of Jerusalem on the streets crying out: "Read all about it. . . . Tomb empty. . . . Crucified one seen alive."

We might read the front-page editorial: "Last Friday the city of Jerusalem witnessed what we believe will go down in history as one of the most bizarre spectacles of all time. A simple preacher from the country was nailed to a cross as a common thief. Everywhere people were asking themselves, 'Why? How could this have happened in this country and in these times?' . . . And today there is a mysterious sequel to the story. The prophet's tomb has been found empty. *What does this empty tomb mean?*"

A man once stood looking at the Grand Canyon. As he gazed out at the breathtaking immensity and beauty of this wonder of nature, he remarked, "Something must have happened here." Obviously, something happened, and it wasn't just an Indian dragging a stick along behind him as he walked. Something happened! As we contemplate the mystery and miracle of the resurrection story of that first Easter, we may not understand what happened. Perhaps we do not have the faith to accept the possibility that what appeared to happen did, in fact, happen. But something happened!

Did Jesus actually rise bodily from the dead? It is unthinkable, unscientific, impossible! The man in the street insists, "When you die, you are a long time dead." What happened then? Was there some great hoax perpetrated, some vicious "Passover Plot" engineered to lend authority and mystery to a new religion? Have we then built a Christian dogma upon a lie?

Maybe the problem is in trying to understand the phenomenon in the framework of human experience. Spiritual things must be spiritually discerned. Man lives in a human body and in a physical world. The Easter mystery must lie in another dimension. How can we be expected to understand when most of us are still struggling to understand life in a three-dimensional world?

We wouldn't expect to understand calculus until we had learned to add two plus two and multiply three times three. As we progress in our knowledge and experience of mathematics, gradually we can apply the principles on higher and higher levels. Few of us understand the principles involved in modern computers, but a skilled mathematician understands them—and even creates them.

What does that empty tomb mean? *Incidentally*, it must mean that there is something eternal about life that can transcend even death, and that the chain reaction of Jesus' great discovery, those many years before, triggered the releasement of pent-up energies that recharged the cells of His body so that "death was swallowed up in victory." In the years to come, new discoveries in science will probably reveal the actual process. But something happened!

However, *fundamentally*, the implications of that empty tomb are great and far-reaching. It evidences the function of a principle that we may have overlooked in our study of the Universe and in our evaluation of ourselves. Easter is not a passport to another world, it is a quality of perception for this one. It is not just a day when we recall how Jesus rose from the dead. It is a time to take a new look at ourselves and contemplate the Divinity in us, the depths of our own innate God-potential. It is a time to reappraise the principle that makes all overcoming possible.

Let us take a closer look at that tomb. Too often the account is shrouded in mystery, obscured and overshadowed by angels and robes and a general aura that makes it completely unrelated to life as we know it. A Sunday School teacher, who taught high school physics, walked into his church one Sunday morning, musing over the problem of class attendance. Suddenly he looked up into a large picture of an angel that dominated the narthex. He had seen this picture many times before. He found himself saying, "How can we expect young people to come to church when it involves believing in anatomical monstrosities like that?"

"And entering into the tomb, they saw a young man sitting on the right side, arrayed in a white robe; and they were amazed. And he saith unto them, Be not amazed: ye seek Jesus, . . . who hath been crucified: he is risen: he is not here: behold, the place where they laid him! But go, tell his disciples and Peter, He goeth before you into Galilee: there shall ye see Him, as He said unto you" (Mark 16:5-7).

In effective Oriental imagery, what this is really saying is this: "And entering into the sepulcher, and failing to find the body of Jesus lying where they had placed it, they were filled with fear, but instantly the thoughts came to mind of the teachings of Jesus pertaining to this very event, and the realization that Jesus had completed the demonstration over so-called death came fully to their consciousness. And their fear subsided as they comprehended the Truth of the matter, and to convince themselves yet more fully, they went again to the place where He had been laid. And the women said, 'we will go quickly and tell the disciples and Peter, and call to their mind that Jesus said He would meet them in Galilee.' "

Why this insistence that we eliminate angels from the story? Simply because it complicates credibility in a manifestation that the human mind is already struggling to understand. Angels are referred to in the original manuscripts as "messengers," and messengers are essentially divine ideas. They always refer to inspiration, to an experience in consciousness rather than in physical sight.

In Luke 24:23—where it tells of the women coming to the disciples with their story of the resurrection—it clearly says, "They came, saying that they had also seen a *vision* of angels. . . ." It was something that happened within Mary Magdalene and Mary, the mother of James. It was a vision so real that they could almost see it. When the writers wrote this story many years later, how could they emphasize this unusual insight which the women experienced? The personalization in the form of angels was an effective means, but a misleading one.

Let us view this Easter "happening" against the backdrop of Jesus' teaching of the Divinity of Man. Remember, Jesus taught that life is for living, not dying; that life is lived from within out, and that there is great depth to the life within you. We may not understand that depth. Perhaps it is unknowable. However, in the context of that depth as a very real part of man's life-potential, we can know that the resurrection did not involve magic or trickery or even outside angelic help. The Lord's body, the electrodynamic body, which is eternal and indestructible, simply specialized itself anew in the corporeal body of Jesus. I can't really understand it. But then I don't really understand the mystery of the seed and the renewal of spring. However, I accept it and I am inspired by its annual pageantry.

Someone has said that there are three classes of people: those who see, those who see when they are shown, and those who do not see. Jesus saw; the disciples saw when they were shown, but there were and are multitudes of people who never see. I am not sure that I accept the limitation of the last grouping. I am certain that everyone *can* see if he is properly shown, *and* if there is an inner awakening.

Some may "see" the resurrection "happening" with a perception that gives great meaning to life. Perhaps this is what Jesus meant when He said: "Except one be born anew, he cannot see the kingdom of God" (John 3:3). However, this experience is not a special dispensation given to a few, but a level of spiritual evolution that will ultimately happen to everyone. Perhaps it is like the voice change of an adolescent boy. He may try to deepen his voice in the years he is striving to appear manly, but to no avail. But suddenly a change begins. There is a time of vocal uncertainty when he may oscillate between bass and soprano in one sentence. But eventually the change is complete and a new depth is heard in his voice. He is still the same person, and he may still talk and sing about the same things—but the voice deals with them on a different octave level.

The kingdom that Jesus talks about is all about us and within us. When we are "born again," nothing really happens to us in a three-dimensional sense. Everything is really the same, but we see it differently, we see a new spiritual dimension. Perhaps there is no true understanding of ourselves or of life in general until this awakening takes place.

The wonderful part of life is that there is meaning on every level, and there are points of growth and fulfillment on every level. And the Bible is all things to all people. It has a message for you, no matter on what level of consciousness or spiritual evolution you may be. That is the amazing thing about Scripture. Perhaps that is the criterion by which it became Scripture. The resurrection story meets this qualification. There is a deep and important meaning for you right where you are.

It is important to remember that Jesus was on the road of overcoming right up to the very end (which was a new beginning). When He said, "follow me" and "come after me," He was talking as a big brother who knew He was not only pursuing His goal but making a trail for us to follow, "that where I am, there ye may be also" (John 14:3). He is saying, "Follow me into a greater awareness of the Truth by which you can see and demonstrate higher and higher overtones of the law."

It is unfortunate that we have put Jesus on a cloud, where we cannot understand Him or identify with Him. Jesus was a man, "one that hath been in all points tempted like as we are, yet without sin" (Heb. 4:15). He made the overcomings along the way of His life, not because He *could not* sin, but because He *would not*. He was no ordinary man, but He *was* a man. He was called "Master," not because of the manner of His birth, but because of the victorious overcoming through His life. All along the way, even while teaching and healing, He was engaged in His own work of self-mastery.

So Easter morning was a commencement day for Jesus. He had made the "Great Demonstration." He had proved Himself by journeying into the beyond and return. It is beyond comparison, but we can find a parallel on a lower level of experience in the first space flight which sent John Glenn into orbit on the theory that it was feasible to bring him back. The return of that space capsule was a great moment in science. However, much more was accomplished than the act of bringing John Glenn safely back to earth. That was done, and millions cheered and uttered prayers of thanksgiving for his safety. But the important thing was that this demonstrated a new application of universal law by which space research could go forward. In future years, when flights into far-off points of the heavens have become commonplace, John Glenn may be thought of as the Columbus of outer space.

Thus, when Jesus returned "from the dead," He had demonstrated more than the overcoming in His own life. He did that. He rose again. And this was and is good reason for rejoicing for those who love Him. But the most important factor, and one that has been almost universally overlooked, is that He had verified His teaching of the Divinity of Man. He had proved in the most dramatic manner that there is a depth within man beyond the human. He not only achieved a victory for Himself but He became the greatest explorer of "inner space." We downgrade Jesus and the Great Demonstration when we think of the Easter "happening" as a miracle of God instead of the revelation of the depth-potential of man.

The great pianist, Paderewski, was giving a command performance for a royal family in Europe. After his concert a duchess came to him, bubbling with enthusiasm, and said, "Maestro, you are a genius!" He replied, "Ah yes, but before I was a genius I was a clod." In other words the moment of genius was the result of years of discipline and overcoming and practice, practice, practice. In the same sense, we might say of Jesus on that resurrection morn, "Master, you are the Christ." And He could well have replied, "Ah yes, but before I demonstrated mastery, I was a humble carpenter in Nazareth."

Never forget this—for it is the important reminder of the repeatability of the Great Demonstration. Perhaps as yet we cannot "see." But remember His words: "Verily, verily, I say unto you, He that believeth on me [the Christ indwelling], the works that I do shall he do also; *and greater works* than these shall he do; because I go unto the Father [Because I have made the break-through and have proved the Divinity of Man]" (John 14:12).

Jesus said, "I came that they may have life, and may have it abundantly" (John 10:10). He wanted to show us what life really is. Life to the average person consists of birth, emotions, eating, drinking, education, business, pleasure, hoping, wishing, sleeping, worrying, hating, fighting, hoarding, dominating, disappointment and death. We often say, in the face of some limitation, "Well, that's life for you!" But it is not life at all. It is but a small fragment of life whose full potential has been frustrated. Life is God and life is boundless.

Looking at the empty tomb, the resurrected Jesus, and the great possibilities of life that they revealed for all of us, we could say (and we should), "*That's* life for you!" That is the life that Jesus is revealing. Through the resurrection, Jesus proved conclusively that the life of God is indestructible, changeless and eternal—and not just for Himself, but for you and me.

Easter deals not only with the passing into death and return, but with the power to go beyond the end of things to a new opportunity and a new vision for overcoming. Through the resurrection principle man *can* overcome death. We may not understand it or even believe it, but some of our scientists today are hinting at such a possibility. But what is more important and can happen now, a man can rise above limited experiences and he can go forward through any dark hour to a new beginning. This is pointed up by another facet of Jesus' diamondlike lesson-story of the Prodigal Son.

You will recall that when the son finally came to himself out in the "far country," he suddenly saw himself in a larger context, and he came home. He was free. He had released his greater potential. The father received him with open arms and cried out, "Rejoice . . . for my son who was dead is now alive again." This was a very real resurrection. It didn't involve dying and returning from the grave, but it did involve waking up to the awareness of his true being.

One of the tragedies of war is the large number of amputees who are faced with a lifetime of handicapped living. And yet, it is often true that the handicap proves to be the catalyst to release the innate potential. There are cases of bodies so broken and maimed that to go on at all would seem beyond endurance. And yet, many do go on and live victorious lives, proving the Divinity of Man in a dramatic way.

One young man was returned from the war without his legs. When the healing of the body had completed itself, he was still far from returning to civilian life. Something had died in him when he found he would never walk again. He lay in his hospital bed, staring blankly at the ceiling. He refused to talk to anyone who tried to help him. He refused to cooperate with doctors or nurses who wanted to help him to make the great adjustment.

One day another inmate of the hospital strolled in and sat down on a chair near the bed. He drew a harmonica from his pocket and began to play softly. The patient looked at him for a second, then back to the ceiling. That was all for that day. Next day the player came again. For several days he continued to come and to play quietly. One day he said, "Does my playing annoy you?" The patient said, "No, I guess I like it." He talked a little more each day.

One day the harmonica player was in a jovial mood. He played a sprightly tune and began to do a tap dance for his friend. The other looked on but was apparently unimpressed by the exhibition. "Hey, why don't you smile once and let a guy know you're alive!" The dancer was smiling as he gave the gentle rebuke. But the amputee said, "I might as well be dead as in the fix I'm in." "Okay," answered the happy one, "so you're dead. But you're not as dead as a fellow who was crucified two thousand years ago, and He came out of it all right." "Oh, it's easy for you to preach," replied the patient, "but if you were in my fix, you'd sing a different tune." With this the dancer stood up, saying, "I know a two-thousand-year-old resurrection is pretty far in the dim past. So maybe an up-to-date example will help you to believe it can be done." With that he pulled up his trouser legs and the boy in the bed looked and saw *two artificial limbs*. Needless to say, his own resurrection began that moment. Today he is living a normal life and helping other people to look up, to find the Easter of their own soul.

This is the keynote of the Great Demonstration of Easter: You are divine. No matter what you have thought of yourself, no matter what you have done in your life or with it, no matter how limited your experience has seemed to be—you are divine. Like the prodigal son, you may have been living off in the "far country." You may have come to know want in the form of obstacles, handicaps, or inharmonious experiences. You must wake up. You must realize the depth of your own divine potential.

The divinity of you is that of you that is eternal, ageless, deathless, whole and complete. It is that of you that is perfect even when you seem to be imperfect. It is that of you that knows even when you are facing indecisiveness and fear. It is that of you that can never be alone. It is that of you that can never really be sick. It is that of you that can never be frustrated. For it is the true God-self of you. We must say to ourselves, with Paul, "Awake thou that sleepest . . . and Christ shall shine upon thee" (Eph. 5:14). Every one of us must come to himself and take the giant step from here to eternity.

This is not the impossible thing that it may appear to be. We do it every time we pray. This is what prayer is. This is what faith is. All spiritual qualities are rooted in the eternal of you, the divinity of you. Jesus said, "When thou prayest, enter into thine inner chamber, and having shut thy door, pray to thy Father who is in secret, and thy Father who seeth in secret shall recompense thee (Matt. 6:6). In a very real sense this door divides the mortal from the immortal, the three-dimensional experience from the eternity domain. Jesus is telling us to close the physical eyes that are affixed on the appearances of human experience, and to open the spiritual eyes to behold the depths of spirit. Dwell in this consciousness for even a few moments and wonderful things happen. In that moment, we transcend time. In that moment we dwell in the healing of wholeness. There is a recharging of the very cells of the body. And if we are really still, and if we really believe, "all things are possible." At least that is what Jesus taught.

Christianity has tried and failed miserably to comprehend immortality in terms of time. It has been a matter of the future located in a place called "heaven." It has been tomorrow, another life, a future existence. But the great Truth that Jesus teaches is that you do not have to die to be immortal. You are immortal right now. Immortality has nothing to do with time. It is beyond time. It is in and of another dimension. We all live in immortality and can't get out of it. The Christ of you, the divinity of you is immortal. That not only means that you will live forever—it does mean that, but it also means that you live in the deep foreverness of now. This means that in the midst of any experience, at any time, you can be still and take the step into eternity. In that instant the part becomes immersed in the whole, the limited becomes limitless. You may feel a new burst of confidence, a new surge of faith, a new flow of ideas, a new releasement of strength. You are awake and whole, and you can go on.

After this "inner-chamber" prayer experience, you may return to your three-dimensional, time-bound experience still facing the things that need to be done. But you will have a new consciousness, a new fearlessness, a new confidence. Intuitively, you will know that you are immortal. And it has nothing to do with living forever in time. It will be a dawning consciousness that you are living in a depth of the spirit, in which you are alive for the first time with what Jesus called "life more abundant."

Jesus demonstrated that life is not an experience of dying. One of the most hideous doctrines of Christian theology is that which cries, "From the day you are born you begin to die." In this concept, life is constantly on the wane, and time is running out, and we all eventually die and go to meet our maker "up there." The moment we think of life in terms of time, we have lost the real Truth of the greatness of life. Life is not for dying—Life is for living! Life is for growing and unfolding, for experiencing a deeper and deeper awareness of the *ISness* of God and of His perfect life. Anything you will ever be, you already are. The greatness of the Infinite is already involved in you. Sleeping within you is a strong, capable, confident, dynamic person—the person you long to be. No matter what obstacles may beset you, there is the seed potential within you of the giantlike man or woman who can conquer and overcome.

"And looking up, they saw that the stone was rolled back." Of course they did! Whenever we look up, we wake up. When we are mesmerized by the appearance, we look at the job or the person or the obstacle before us and say, "It is too much. I can't handle it. It is impossible. I can't go on." The strength and courage and ability and goodness is within us, but we have forgotten it. We see only the stone. But when we look up, we wake up, we look away from the problem. Suddenly, we are "born from above." We realize something greater about ourselves and about life. We know that there is a presence, there is a power, there is an intelligence. And we know our oneness with it. "I am in tune with the Infinite and I can do what needs to be done. Through the power that indwells me I can succeed, I can overcome, I can be what I want to be."

The great need in life for all of us is not so much to achieve the ability to set all things right, but to gain the perception to see them rightly. In human consciousness, man is forever trying to adjust things, to change people, to manipulate events. He even tries to use prayer to assist him in setting things right. He wants his daughter to marry this man. He wants his son to take this job or go to this school and get that result. In his own job, he is forever trying to make his co-workers fall into a mold that he has created for them. And, of course, these goals never quite materialize as he hopes. He doesn't give up easily. He even prays long and hard for "my will not thine." It is like trying to put some iron filings in a certain order when they are being influenced by a magnet. They must find their own pattern.

Life is for living! And living is an experience in growth and unfoldment. It is not so important what happens around us or even to us. What counts is what happens *in* us. Problem situations and problem people may stand in our way. We may be tempted to try to set them right and it is possible to do so—to an extent. But we still haven't solved our own problems, which are: that in us that drew the experiences; and the level of consciousness that sees them. Maybe the important thing is not to solve problems but to be solved by them. Could this have been what Jacob meant when he said, "I will not let thee go, except thou bless me" (Gen. 32:26)?

Look up and live! This is a dimension of life that man has lost sight of. This is the thing we need more than anything else. Not so much to find the way to change people or even to change ourselves, but to lift up our eyes and see deeply—to see the immortal, to see the divine. This is the way from "here to eternity," the gateway to the kingdom and the practical technique for demonstrating "life more abundant." Suddenly, the former things—too late, too old, too little, too big—are passed away. They are now irrelevant. "All things are become new." We are resurrected into a new consciousness of peace and power and plenty.

Every year on Easter morning, millions of people throughout the Christian world proclaim the words, "He is Risen, Hallelujah, He is Risen." If only every devotee could catch the deep implications of Easter and of his own statement, "He is risen." If everyone would realize that "He is risen in me, which enables me to see that which is risen in every person in the world," we would see a manifestation of "peace on earth, good will toward men." If He is risen (and Christians all build their faith on this acceptance), then He has demonstrated the divine of you and the divine of every person in the world. Dwelling on that first Easter in the right spirit, looking toward the dawn, and "looking up" to the Spirit indwelling, we can see beyond appearances—the stones of human limitations are rolled away. We no longer see the barriers of prejudice or class distinction; we are no longer hampered by the iron curtains between nations or minds. We may see from the divinity in ourselves; and we can see that same divinity in other people—all people.

The usual celebration of Easter—spending an hour hearing about the exciting event of two thousand years ago—is much like contemplating for one day the mysteries of calculus without ever having conditioned ourselves to understand the basic two plus two. We take out our calculus book and we read it over (with no real comprehension) and we say, "It is so beautiful." Then we return it to the high place on the bookshelf where it will remain for another year. We tell ourselves that it was a wonderful experience to think about it for a day.

There is an urgency about the underlying science of the Great Demonstration. The world needs this Truth today. It cannot be allowed to catch dust on the shelf until the next once-a-year contemplation. It is not enough to parrot the resurrection story. We need to reduce it to the least common denominator and then put the principles to work. Easter deals with the Divinity of Man, of you, and of people everywhere—on every side of the iron and bamboo curtains, on every side of wars and feuds, on every side of labor-management disputes, and all around the conference tables.

There are stones in the world—many of them—and some are quite mammoth. Let us lift up our eyes, and the stones will be rolled away. Let us not try to set things right but to see them rightly. Right seeing is our eternal passport from the illusions of human sense to the heaven of accomplishment.

17 Did Jesus Teach Reincarnation?

> Our birth is but a sleep and a forgetting.
>   The soul that rises with us, our life's star,
> Hath had elsewhere its setting,
>   And cometh from afar.
> Not in entire forgetfulness
>   And not in utter nakedness
> But trailing clouds of glory do we come
>   From God who is our home.
>
>   *Wordsworth*[1]

THROUGH THE AGES there have been many philosophies of the heretofore and the hereafter. Man has forever been searching his soul and the world about him for answers to his questions: "Why am I here? Why am I like I am? Why am I one thing and another a different thing? Where is the justice in the inequities of life?"

The materialist has insisted, "This is all there is. You are like the tree or the animal. You come into life because the seed was planted. You leave this life if and when life is either accidentally or naturally taken from you. You only live once, enjoy yourself."

Yet, a study of what passed for religion back in its most primitive forms indicates that there has always been a belief that this life is but one part of the whole, that there is a something, usually referred to as the soul, that survives death. What happens to this soul after death? Man has entertained all sorts of possibilities: a place of eternal rest in the skies, the "Valhalla" of Scandinavian mythology. And at death the truly good Polynesians "go West." Often there is a twofold path: one up and one down—the happy place for the good, while the rest suffer eternal torment. But at death the chance is over, the case is rested.

Orthodox Christianity has taught that birth is the beginning of life, but that death is but a step into our eternal existence, which is the real purpose of it all. Life "down here" is only a preparation for a future bliss to come "up there." But this leaves a host of unanswered questions.

The church has tended to envelop itself in a veil of infallibility. The pilgrim of the way has been warned: "Do not reason! To reason, to think, to question, to analyze is the path which leads to hell. Believe or be damned." It was just such an implication in the Christian position that led Robert G. Ingersoll to proclaim, "Believe and be damned—I will find out." We will not comment here on his findings, but we do heartily applaud his courage and defend his right to ask the questions.

Let us courageously ask some questions for ourselves—not in criticism of any theological position, but through an earnest desire to find a framework for a workable faith. Have you not at some time wondered:

1. If this life is but the preparation for another to come, how do we account for the inbred desire to live? Why are we not anxious to get into the next life? Even the most rabid Fundamentalist, who believes in the glories of heaven, leaves no stone unturned in trying to heal an illness.

2. How do we account for the seemingly unfinished pattern of individual lives and the constantly progressive pattern of the civilization that man builds?

3. How do we account for the great inequality among men, while we are told that all men are created equal? Is God then not a God of justice and fairness? Are we all supposed to arrive at the same goal even though we start on different levels? It would appear that some have a head start, while others commence with a handicap. Some are born with a silver spoon in their mouths, while others are born on the wrong side of the tracks. Some are born with normal healthy minds and bodies, while others are born crippled or blind or with brain damage. Where is the justice?

4. How can we say that a soul is created at a point in time and then survives the death of the physical body and goes on living forever? Isn't it illogical and unscientific to say that we survive the body but did not pre-exist it, that we have a beginning, but no end?

Jesus said, "Ye therefore shall be perfect, as your heavenly Father is perfect" (Matt. 5:48). In these few words, He unequivocally establishes the ultimate goal of life. But how can we achieve perfection in the span of life that we experience. Look around you today and see if anyone gives evidence of reaching this ultimate in this lifetime. Doesn't it seem somewhat illogical that Jesus would expect us to reach this goal of perfection in one lifetime that begins with birth and ends with death?

And yet, He clearly commands, "Ye therefore *shall* be perfect." If Jesus meant this seriously (and how can we doubt that?) then isn't it possible and quite logical that He is talking about an ultimate goal whose attainment might take many successive existences—perhaps even hundreds, as the rate at which most of us appear to develop and grow? Certainly, the idea of reincarnation gives a credible answer to the questions that most of us might logically ask of life.

What of the amazing feats of child prodigies? Is there any other explanation for Mozart who played a concert on the harpsichord at the age of five and toured Europe at six? Sir William Hamilton learned Hebrew at three and at thirteen could speak thirteen languages. Is it an accidental grouping of genes that makes a child far in advance of men and women who have slaved for years in the field? If so, life seems surely to be whimsical as well as unjust.

Or is it, as the theory of reincarnation might suggest, that they have been here before and bring with them a development gained in previous lives. The sophisticated intellectual who brushes aside all religious theories in a devotion to the concepts of the ancient Greek philosophers might be shocked to find that Plato was an out-and-out believer in reincarnation. In his famous "Theory of Reminiscence" he said, "Knowledge easily acquired is that which the enduring self had in an earlier life, so that it flows back easily."

And what of the strange phenomena such as this one which I experienced some years ago: My wife and I were driving into Chicago through a very old section. I had never been in Chicago before and had had no occasion to learn about the city. Suddenly, I found myself calling off the names of cross streets before we came to them. After doing this for about twenty blocks, my wife remarked, "I see you have been here before. You have a good memory." At that moment, I realized what I had been doing. "But," I protested, "I have never been here before." We were silent for a while, and then my wife said, "Perhaps you *have* been here before."

John Buchan tells of finding himself in a scene which he could not have visited before and yet was perfectly familiar. He says he is certain it was the stage of an action in which he once took part.

We have all had those occasions when we have met someone and have had the strange feeling that we have known them before. Of course, these strange phenomena can be brushed aside as hallucinations or clairvoyance or some kind of extrasensory perception. Many will want to take this recourse. Others will want to press on to consider more of the growing weight of evidence.

In this work we are not espousing the cause of reincarnation. Nor are we equipped at this time to lead such a cause. We simply want to consider, in the light of Jesus' teachings of man and of life, what He had to say about all this. Did Jesus teach reincarnation?

We must recognize that all Jesus taught or did was certainly not incorporated into the Gospel record. The four Gospels came into being as the remembered influence of Jesus upon these writers, who did not write until many years later. Obviously, they wrote about the things that impressed them the most, the things that seemed most important and most revolutionary in terms of the old Law. The fact that the concept of reincarnation is not mentioned could be explained in either of two ways: Either it was no part of the belief of Jesus, or it was such a generally accepted belief that there was no reason to comment upon it. We can take our choice of possibilities.

It is known today that the theory of reincarnation was a commonly held belief in Jesus' time. We don't know that it was accepted by the Pharisees. It probably was not. It may have been on a par with the contemporary interest in flying saucers and ESP. Jesus does, at times, seem to recognize that reincarnation was a prevailing belief of the times. Yet He did not comment upon it, although He was courageously outspoken when He felt that what prevailed was wrong. It would appear to be more significant that He said nothing against reincarnation than that He didn't actually speak in favor of it.

What did Jesus mean in Matthew 11:14 when, speaking of John the Baptist, He said, "This is Elijah, that is to come"? Or again, in Mark 9:11, "They asked Him saying, the scribes say that Elijah must come first. And He said unto them, Elijah indeed cometh first, and restoreth all things: and how it is written of the Son of man, that he should suffer many things and be set at nought? But I say unto you that Elijah is come, and they have also done unto him whatsoever they listed, even as it is written of him." It would be hard to state any more clearly that John the Baptist was the reincarnation of Elijah. And this was Jesus speaking!

In Matthew 16:13 we read that Jesus asked His disciples, "Who do men say that the Son of man is?" and they said, "Some say Elijah; and others, Jeremiah, or one of the prophets." In other words, "What are the people saying about me?" And they answered in effect, "The people are talking among themselves, saying that you are the reincarnation of Elijah or Jeremiah or one of the prophets." True, Jesus did not accept or reject this information. But isn't it interesting that He did not rebuke them for talking nonsense? The fact that Jesus did not make an issue of it might indicate that He shared the belief in reincarnation, or at least accepted it as a possibility.

There is an interesting passage for study found in John 9:2, where we read that a man "born blind" was brought to Jesus with the question: "Master, who did sin, this man or his parents, that he was born blind?" If one wanted to analyze this with the intensity and depth of a legal mind, he might "have a ball" thinking about it. Certainly, we cannot help but admit that the question itself indicates a prevailing belief in reincarnation. Now, if it were contemplated that a man born blind was being punished by his blindness for sin committed, then the sin must have been in an earlier life before he was born into this world.

Note carefully Jesus' answer: "Neither did this man sin nor his parents: but that the works of God should be made manifest in him." It would appear that He concedes that both theories were reasonable because He did not reject or ridicule them. He could have said, "Don't be ridiculous! How could a man sin before he was born?" But He didn't do this. He simply stated that neither of the theories posed applied in this case. He had a third answer, that the affliction was simply a process of growth for the individual, the soul choosing a challenge through which to grow in this life experience.

Jesus does not reject the idea of reincarnation, which may mean that He accepted it or at least was open-minded about it. But, in this instance, He introduces another very significant concept which might answer many of man's puzzling questions. Life is an experience in growth. Living as he so often does in the "far country," man tends to think of life as an opportunity for self-indulgence. Thus his goals are most often in the direction of acquisition of things and the achievement of a placid kind of joy and peace of mind. He often reaches his materialistic goals at the expense of his life, rather than in the *expanse* of it. So, like the prodigal son, he "comes to know want."

Jesus knew that life is lived from within out, and "the Kingdom of God is within." He knew that life is an opportunity to discover our divinity and release our "imprisoned splendor." He knew that, as a student enrolls in difficult courses of study so that he can further his education, so man, in his eternal unfoldment, often draws the most challenging experience to him because of the opportunity it affords for personal growth. Thus, in His analysis of the man born blind, He said, "This is not a case of punishment for previous wrongs. This is a case of a man moving on to the next grade, ready for the more difficult tests that will lead to his greater development—if he can pass the tests."

Let us not overlook this casual statement of Jesus. It indicates that one should never glibly comment on the shortcomings of another by saying, "Well, it is the result of wrong thinking, or previous sin." Judge not according to appearances! The blind, the lame, the unfortunates we find along life's way could conceivably be farther along the way of spiritual unfoldment than their more fortunate brothers. One may be working out his karma, while another may be taking the tests of a higher level of living. Perhaps only the insight of the Christ can rightly discern.

Christians often tend to think of the theory of reincarnation as a cultish idea that has come out of the thinking of weird religious bands. The truth is that a majority of the human race believes in one or another of the philosophies relating to reincarnation. It may not be palatable for modern Christian theologians to accept, but it is a matter of recorded church history that primitive Christianity entertained the idea of reincarnation as a doctrine of the church all the way up until the Council of Constantinople in A.D. 553.[2]

This council was, in reality, only the last phase of the violent ten-year conflict brought on by the edict of the Roman Emperor Justinian against the teachings of Father Origen. This was a stormy period in Christian history. Historians refer to Justinian's government as a caesaropapacy—one in which the emperor became the pope, with no religious background. Justinian ruled the church by imperial law and dictated her theological doctrines. Church doctrines have been pieced together through the centuries like an unfolding mosaic, as conferences and councils and "holy bodies" have developed the religion *about* Jesus.

Without the stabilizing influence of the total life concept in Christianity, individuals are led to feel, "Oh well, what's the difference? Have fun! You only live once, and when you are dead, you are a long time dead." It is entirely possible that the loss of the idea of reincarnation and its related law of cause and effect may be the greatest single reason for the rise of what is called "Western Materialism."

Within the very church that rejected the theory of reincarnation have been many believers, among them St. Augustine and St. Francis of Assisi. Add to these the long list of intelligent people in all fields who have endorsed the concept, and you have a mighty convincing argument. There were Cicero, Seneca, Pythagoras, and Plato in early times; more recently, Maeterlinck, Ibsen, Lavater, Schopenhauer, Hume, Goethe, and Emerson, and among the poets, Walt Whitman, Longfellow, Tennyson, Browning, Swinburne, W. E. Henley, and Kipling. Who has not felt, with Tennyson:

> So friend, when first I looked upon your face,
> Our thoughts gave answer each to each, so true
> Opposed mirrors each reflecting each,
> Although I knew not in what time or place,
> Me thought that I had often met with you,
> And each had lived in others' mind and speech.[3]

You may wonder, "But if I have lived before, why don't I remember my past lives?" You do. Character is memory. It is the cumulative distilled essence of your previous experience. Genius is memory. The child prodigy reveals a prodigious memory of cumulative development.

All this is certainly not proof that reincarnation is a fact. I say there is no proof. But neither is there proof against it. We can neither prove it nor disprove it. In a debate on the subject of reincarnation, I think I would find it easier to take the negative position than the positive one, because I could think of many more reasons why it could not be true from an intellectual point of view. And yet, in my heart I feel that it is the only credible explanation of life, from an eternal standpoint. Jesus very definitely taught the Divinity of Man. Man is divine and must ultimately unfold his potential and achieve the fulfillment of the Christ. Reincarnation would seem to indicate a way in which it can be done.

But there is really nothing imperative about accepting the idea. Whether or not you accept it is a matter of your choice. If it doesn't appeal to you, don't worry about it. Just let the matter drop. You may occasionally find some puzzling questions or gaps in your philosophy of life. The idea of reincarnation may well fill these gaps for you and cause life to make a little more sense.

The important thing is that man was born to live and not to die. "Verily I say unto you, if a man keep my word, he shall never see death" (John 8:51). Paul says, "The wages of sin is death" (Rom. 6:23). This is the sin of wrong thinking—of thinking in terms of separation from God, of failing to embrace the allness of God in thought and faith. And, most important, it is the sin of not knowing your divinity. All this seems to be the cause of the ills to which the flesh is heir.

However, man is a living soul. He is not a body. He *has* a body. If the body is laid aside, this in no way spells the end of man. It simply means that the eternal self, the soul, moves on to be clothed according to God's purpose.

Charles Fillmore says:

God did not create man to die: death is a result of transgression of the law. . . . When man loses his body by death, the law of expression works with him for re-embodiment, and he takes to himself a new body. The Divine Law allows him to keep trying until he learns to live aright. And man will do this by overcoming sin, sickness, old age, and finally death. When these are eliminated "reincarnation" will be no more.[4]

The Book of Revelation would seem to imply the same thing: "He that overcometh, I make him a pillar in the temple of my God, and he shall go out thence no more" (3:12). Reincarnation is not God's final plan for man. It is a token of God's love for us whereby, if through sin and missing the mark of perfection we lose the body, we may be reclothed. We may try again to complete the great work that the Father has given us to do.

The oft-heard cry of man is, "Oh, if I only had my life to live over again." Reincarnation might be an answer to that eternal hope. It is not a punishment, but the mark of God's forgiving love, the eternal provision for fulfilling the goal of perfection.

However, there are dangers in the contemplation of the idea of reincarnation. If you have lived a continuous round of previous lives, it is difficult to repress a curiosity about what and where you might have been before. This would be another form of living in the past. Jesus said, "No man, having put his hand to the plow, and looking back, is fit for the kingdom of God" (Luke 9:62).

In my book, *Life Is for Living*, I liken life to a wave in the ocean, pointing out that a wave is not a body of water, not even a movement of water. It is a movement of an intangible force upon the water.

A wave is the ocean expressing itself as a wave. It has form and shape and movement. It has an identity, a uniqueness; yet it is nothing less and nothing more than the ocean. It is not even limited to a particular segment of ocean. It is a movement within the ocean, a projection of the ocean, which at the same time moves on and through the ocean. When the wave eventually crashes on the shore, where is the ocean water that formed the first swell? It is right back in the deeps where it always was. And this leads to a key fact about life.

. . . Your life that seems to begin with birth and end with death is like one instant in the movement of the wave. In that instant the wave is a particular part of the water. In your present life experience, at this moment, life for you is your body, and the particular cells of life that make up the organs and functions of your body. Life is not limited to your body. If the body temple should be laid aside in the experience we call death, this is not the end of you or of the movement of life that is being projected through you and *as* you. The wave moves on.

. . . Where is the wave that appeared a hundred yards farther out? You may find the water that was at one moment expressing as the wave, but it has simply returned to placid ocean. The only place to find the wave that *was* is in the wave that *is*. I am certain that man's memory mind may retain the vibrational patterns of a distant past (even as a magnetic tape sometimes retains some of the electronic patterns of a previous recording while a new recording is being made). But I believe we should let the scientists make careful explorations in this area of consciousness.

The life you once lived can only be found in the life you now express. You could conceivably find a long chain of tombstones and possessions and niches in history, but the wave has moved, . . . looking at the water that once was the wave really tells us nothing about the wave. Launching into an "age-regression" search into our past could conceivably produce evidence of a past life or lives, but it could not really tell me anything about the moving projection of life into visibility that passed through each point and is now manifest *as* me.[5]

We have touched on the concept of reincarnation simply because it seems to be a natural corollary to Jesus' concept of the Divinity of Man. It offers a credible explanation of how and when the "imprisoned splendor may escape." We have tried to point out the inference of this concept in Jesus' teachings. But we have proved nothing. Nor do we suggest that you get involved in a deep study of the subject. Charles Fillmore warns: "The study of reincarnation is not profitable to the student of higher thought. . . . Not what you have been but what you now are is the issue."[6]

Jesus tried to urge us to look to the heights of God-consciousness, to sense a life that is not a matter of time or a collection of things or experiences or even people—to awaken to a greater purpose in life than mere existence, to know that life is so much more than that which begins with birth and ends with death. When we know this Truth, really know it, then we are free from fear, from anxiety, from the awful resistance toward and grief over death.

There is no doubt about it—Jesus taught that death is not an ultimate, not a goal, not a final experience. Death settles nothing, and there is no escape from problems or limitations through its portals. Unfinished business must be carried over in some way. Unsolved problems must eventually be worked out. Spiritual development and "treasures in heaven" cannot be lost.

For every end there must be a beginning; for every death there must be a birth. In the larger view, perhaps birth and death are but two sides of one door, two ways of viewing one experience, one frame of a motion picture of the ocean wave that relentlessly moves toward the distant shore.

You are living and alive within an eternal experience, without beginning and without end. Resolve to live this day and every day as if it were the only day there is—because in fact it is. Yesterday no longer exists, and tomorrow and the days of the future will simply unfold out of the continuous movement of the existence that is "now" in its unfoldment.

In time, "life" and "death" as opposite sides of each other will fade into nothingness. Neither have any reality in that context. Life that is but the prelude to death, and death that is but the postlude to life, have existence only in the consciousness of man. It is true, "Life *is* consciousness." Let us work for the consciousness that, with O'Neill's Lazarus, looks upward to eternal life, to the fearless and deathless, to the everlasting, to the stars.

In its complete sense, life simply is. Let us accept it, live it, rejoice in it. We have all eternity to achieve that ultimate goal of perfection. And for those who wonder how that can be, there is the possibility of reincarnation. Jesus didn't directly teach it. But He certainly seems to have strongly implied it. And the Divinity of Man, which He most certainly did teach, seems to call for it as an important process.

18 When Shall the Kingdom Come?

IN CHRISTIAN THEOLOGY there is an interesting word that is rarely heard by the layman. It relates to an area of Christian preaching that is constantly heard throughout the land. The word is "eschatology." It is the doctrine of the final judgment and the future state of mankind, and of the second coming of Christ. Tomes upon tomes of doctrine and dogma have been formulated about the literal and physical coming of the Kingdom. And millions of followers, from the days of the disciples down to present times, have been hopefully or fearfully looking for an event to happen.

There are those who preach that we are now entering the final stages of a civilization that will ultimately be destroyed, ushering in "a new heaven and a new earth," when "former things are passed away. And . . . I make all things new" (Rev. 21:1, 4, 5, av). These voices cite the secularization of life, the atomic bomb, the growing emphasis upon sex, violence, and materialism.

However, civilizations have never been destroyed by outer conquest or by divine fiat. Civilizations have risen and fallen by the rise and fall of human consciousness. The fall of Rome, for instance, was an inside job. If mankind is in trouble today, it is not because of the wrath of God, but because of the darkness in the minds of men. The danger is not in the atom, but in the Adam man who is frustrating his inherent potential. The Kingdom of Heaven is still within man, and "the mind that was in Christ Jesus" is in every one of us.

A young lad, trying to discredit the wisdom of a wise man, asked the old man, "Is this bird in my hand alive or dead?" The wise old man knew that if he said it was dead the boy would show him the live bird, and if he said it was alive the boy would crush it and produce a dead bird. So he replied, "It is as you will it, my son."

So it is with atoms, and machines, and nations, and liberties, and inner potentialities. It is as we will it. In our quest for understanding we are gradually stockpiling the tools and building materials we need to make a heaven of our earth. Potentially, man is stronger than his fears and greater than his weaknesses. The role of teachers and preachers and philosophers is to help people, all people, to know this basic fact of life. The future of our civilization may depend upon whether we can succeed in helping men everywhere to know and relate to the "beyond within."

Since primitive times men have rationalized the inequities of this life by the dream of a future life where all things are made right. In all cultures we find reference to such places as "beyond the blue," "the happy hunting grounds," "the Elysian fields." But what did Jesus teach about this? He often referred to "the Kingdom of Heaven" and "the Kingdom of God." Where did He locate them? Did He talk about golden streets and harps and white robes?

Jesus was quite specific. He said the Kingdom of Heaven is "at hand." This indicates that the time is *now*. "And being asked by the Pharisees when the Kingdom of God cometh, he answered them and said, The Kingdom of God cometh not with observation: neither shall they say, Lo, here! or, There! for lo, the Kingdom of God is within you" (Luke 17:20). This indicates that it is not a place in space.

The "green pastures" kind of heaven has evolved as a result of man's speculation upon Jesus' concept. It has always been a problem for man to understand nonmaterial things from a material frame of reference, to contemplate a fourth-dimensional experience in a three-dimensional outlook on life.

Ouspensky, in his *New Model of the Universe*, says,

The world is a world of infinite possibilities. Every moment contains a large number of possibilities. And all of them are actualized, only we do not see it and do not know it. We always see only one of the actualizations, and in this lie the poverty and limitation of the human mind.

. . . Time is not a passing phenomenon, but an unfoldment of the infinite possibilities of an expanding universe.[1]

This could very well be a description of the Kingdom of Heaven. With this insight we may see that Jesus is not talking about a place to which we go; nor is it an experience in time. It is not of the future. It is not somewhere to go, but *something to be*. There is no point in looking for it, for it comes not with observation. It is a potentiality that is always present within or on the spiritual level of life.

Tradition holds that the disciples once asked Jesus, "When shall the Kingdom come?" and He answered, "When the without shall become as the within." In other words—when you become in expression what you were created to be. Or, from the world view, when the race of man is elevated to the level of universal perfection. Such a possibility is beyond imagination for most of us. There is so much weakness, so much apparent evil!

Robert Browning dreamed of the development of a perfect race of man. He saw the entire race of mankind as in the preparatory stages of evolving this perfection. To him, the "end of the world" would be that point where all men are finally perfected. I hold this to be one of the loftiest visions of man ever penned:

> Man's self is not yet man,
> Nor shall I deem his object saved, his end attained,
> His genuine strength put fairly forth,
> While only here and there a star dispels the darkness,
> Here and there a towering mind o'erlooks its prostrate
> Fellows. When the host is out at once, to the despair of night:
> When all mankind alike is perfected,
> Equal in full-blown power,—then, not till then I say,
> Begins man's general infancy.[2]

What a difference it would make if more people could catch this vision of life! The average person thinks of life as static rather than dynamic. He thinks of his traits or characteristics as a kind of fingerprint of his life. He may not like what he is. He may resent it and even rebel against it. But how often he will conclude, "But that's just the way I am."

The more we understand the concepts of Jesus, the more we realize that the only time we can truthfully say, "That's just the way I am," is when we are referring to the divinity within us. You have a great potentiality, a divine self within you that needs to be released. This is what Jesus really taught.

The story is told of a precocious young lad standing on a street corner. A minister, passing by, stopped for a moment to play his role. Patting the lad on the head he said, "Sonny boy, who made you?" The young fellow looked up and said, somewhat impatiently, "Well, to tell you the truth sir, I ain't done yet." And that is the Truth about you. You are not done yet. No matter what may be the level of your experiences at the moment, you are not done yet. There is more in you. And the experience itself is an opportunity to *grow* through as you *go* through the challenge.

Many people refer to heaven as "upstairs." God is often said to be "the man upstairs." I can remember as a child saying, "Cross my heart and point to heaven." There was no question about it—it was right "up there." And God was up there, too. We looked up there as we talked about Him. We prayed up to Him.

In a very real sense, heaven *is* "upstairs"—but it is the upper level of man's total consciousness. Perhaps it would help to think of your life as a great house. Jesus used this illustration, "In my Father's house are many mansions" (John 14:2). In other words, there are many levels at which we can experience life. There are numerous upper floors—and there is a basement. It may be said that most people live much of their lives in the basement of existence, unaware that there are rooms upstairs for happy and successful living.

No matter where a man may be or on what level he may be expressing, the Kingdom of God is within him. He may be living out his life in the basement or even in a subbasement. He may be sick in mind or body. He may be deprived or depraved. But there are still upper floors in the house of his life even if he has never known them. His sin is simply the frustration of his potentiality. He is living in a veritable hell. Interestingly, the words "hades," which is usually erroneously translated as "hell," literally means "not to see." The man in the basement is not able to see the fullness of life. But there is more in him, there is God in him. Bergson agrees with this when he says that an intelligent being carries within him the means to surpass himself.

The word "heaven" comes from the Greek word, *ouranos*, which literally means "expanding." The Kingdom of Heaven, then, is the principle of expansion. Life is a limitless experience in an expanding Universe. The very nature of life is growth. This is why Jesus, in trying to explain the Kingdom of Heaven, uses such illustrations as the sower going forth to sow, the mustard seed, the "little leaven that leaveneth the whole lump." A strange lot of illustrations if He is talking about some place in the skies to which we go at some future time!

Life is growth and unfoldment, and life is lived from inside out. How few people really know this! The average person lives his life from outside in. He frustrates his potential when he lets his level of consciousness be determined by what people say, what conditions appear to be, what he reads in the newspapers. He becomes little more than a barometer that registers the conditions of his world. Then he is caught up in the dilemma of whether to conform to the world around him or to spend his life resisting it.

Jesus came declaring, "Ye shall know the truth, and the truth shall make you free" (John 8:32). It really doesn't matter what happens around you or to you. These things are in the world, and you *can* overcome the world. All that really matters is what happens *in* you—your thoughts about conditions and people. And you can control your thoughts, for you are the master of your mind—or you can be.

There is a belief deeply rooted in the collective unconscious of the race that "you can't teach an old dog new tricks"—you can't change human nature. Reject this for the great lie that it is. When you catch Jesus' concept of the Divinity of Man, you see that you not only *can* change human nature, but this is the whole object of the Christian teaching. "As Moses lifted up the serpent in the wilderness, even so must the Son of man be lifted up" (John 3:14). And you are that son of man and you *can* transcend your basement experiences and come to live in the upper rooms of life.

Jesus' message of the Kingdom is the message of wholeness. We are forever seeing only part of life and concluding that the part is the whole. This is a great problem in formulating religious views. Shelley says that religion is the perception of the relation in which man stands to the universe. But that perception is an individual experience. Someone communicates *his* perception to another and we are on the way toward the creation of dogma. In time whole bodies of people accept a "perception" that is given to them secondhand. They might even insist that there is no individual perception, or think of such an inner awareness, or firsthand experience, as a "work of the devil."

Jesus recognized that the greatest foe of the great idea of the Kingdom of Heaven as an inner potential in man was Pharisaism. He was merciless in His denunciation of the Pharisees, for they symbolized the crystallized preoccupation with externals, with custommade convictions. He said, "Woe unto you, scribes and Pharisees, hypocrites! because ye shut the kingdom of heaven against men" (Matt. 23:13). Today Pharisaism is the greatest obstacle in man and in the world to the full realization of the Truth.

To many people religion is synonymous with a church service—a spectacle to witness, a ritual to employ, a prayer book to use once a week. Religion is a badge of conventional respectability. Belonging to the right kind of church is often more important than *being* the right kind of person.

The word "religion" means "to bind together." It is a relationship, an awareness of man's unity with the great creative force of God. Ancient religions had no formal doctrine. They were simply a way to strengthen the individual's relationship with the Infinite. Prayer was a spontaneous expression of finite man seeking to feel his unity with the Infinite. It was only as religions became corporate bodies that dogma and ceremony took precedence over the individual quest. In time the purpose of religion, from the standpoint of its work with the individual, was unity with the church rather than unity with God.

The church has a vital place in the life of man—but not as a supermarket in which to pick up take-out orders of faith and prayer. The church must be a school in which the individual learns the Truth of his unity with God, of his own divine sonship, and of the Kingdom of Heaven within him. Like any place of learning the church must seek to make itself progressively unnecessary, to help people to become self-reliant. In other words, if the church is doing its job sincerely, it will be forever trying to put itself out of business. In the Book of Revelation there is an interesting insight into a great dream: "The holy city, new Jerusalem, coming down out of heaven from God. . . . *And I saw no temple therein*" (Rev. 21:2, 22). In other words, the vision of the future reveals a God-inhabited society of God-intoxicated people.

This doesn't mean that we shouldn't have churches. Without a doubt the churches of our land are still the greatest sources of good men. But churches must change their self-image and begin seeing themselves, not as repositories of Infinite Truth, but as centers engaged in research into man and the Universe—laboratories in which people may search out the deep things of God in themselves. In the future the only church worthy of the name will be such a center, open in mind and in doctrine, helping all people to find the Spirit within themselves.

There are some healthy signs in religion today. Individual pastors, and whole denominations, are checking up on themselves in terms of a realistic faith sufficient to meet the problems of today. Perhaps you were shocked when you heard the first theologian announce that "God is dead." Actually, there is much to rejoice about in such a disclosure. Theologians, who have been in the Pharisaical stream for so long, with all their religion contained in a neatly packed box, have suddenly found the courage to lift the lid and look in. Now they are humbly admitting that the box is empty. This can only be the prelude to a widespread quest for deeper Truth. Of course, this quest is painful to both the suppliers and the consumers of custom-made Truth. But who can say that it is not a step along the way toward a revitalization of a dying church and toward an increasing awareness of the Divinity of Man?

To the Pharisees, Jesus seemed to be saying, "God is dead," when He said, "God is spirit, and those who worship him must worship in spirit and truth" (John 4:24, RSV). Didn't this deny the personal God of the skies and the authority of "His" priesthood? "Silence him! Put him out of the way!" they cried, "For he denies the God of our fathers, and puts himself in His place!"

In his fine book, *Cosmic Consciousness*, Richard M. Bucke suggests a hopeful development in man's collective quest for Truth. He seems to feel that religions will decrease, but that the influence of religion will increase. He says:

The immediate future of our race is indescribably hopeful. . . . In contact with the flux of cosmic consciousness all religions known and named today will be melted down. The human soul will be revolutionized. Religion will absolutely dominate the race. . . . The evidence of immortality will live in every heart as sight in every eye. Doubt of God and of eternal life will be as impossible as is now doubt of existence; the evidence of each will be the same. . . . Each soul will feel and know itself to be immortal, will feel and know that the entire universe with all its good and with all its beauty is for it and belongs to it forever.[3]

Charles Fillmore, too, reflects the optimism of Browning and Bucke. He says, "The time is ripe for the advent of a new race, the advent of the spiritualized man. This will be brought about, not by a miracle or the fiat of God, but by the gradual refinement of the man of the flesh into the man of Spirit."[4]

The time is more than ripe. Many people are disturbed by the trend of things in the world. What can be done about the division of men and nations, about man's inhumanity to man? Certainly there is a need for the advent of a new race, but a race of men is made up of individuals. Every person must ultimately face this fact and direct his desire for world peace through the ideal, "Let it begin with me."

No matter what condition the world is in, you can find and express peace within yourself, for the Kingdom of God is within you. And it is not enough to isolate yourself in peace away from the world. You must become a peacemaker, an influence for peace among men. Christians have talked about being "saved." This usually implies being saved from society, from the rest of the pagan and evil world. But no man can be saved *from* society; he must be saved *with* it, if at all. For he is society and society is him.

Herbert Spencer says profoundly that no one can be perfectly moral until all are moral; no one can be perfectly free till all are free; no one can be perfectly happy till all are happy.

This might lead us to re-examine the age-old question of Cain, "Am I my brother's keeper?" The United States has tried to be a keeper to brothers around the world, but has found that being a keeper arouses the resentment of the "kept." So the answer is: No, I am not my brother's keeper. I am my brother's *brother*. And more than that, in the cosmic perception of the Divinity of Man, I *am* my brother and my brother is me.

When we begin to treat people, individually and in groups, as spiritual beings, saluting the divinity within them, then we will give and receive and do business on the level of love and mutual trust. We will begin to expect far more of ourselves and of others. And we will treat people as if they already were what our faith reveals they can be. In this way we will actually become an influence to help them get out of the basement of limited thinking and living and express more of the divine potential within them.

There is so much negative talk about the deteriorating morality of mankind today. It is refreshing to read the optimism of Albert Schweitzer:

Our humanity is by no means so materialistic as foolish talk is continuously asserting it to be. I am convinced that there is far more in people than ever comes to the surface of the world. Just as the water of the stream we see is small in amount compared to that which flows underground, so, the good that men do is small in amount compared with what men and women bear locked in their hearts. . . . To unbind what is bound, to bring the underground waters to the surface, mankind is waiting and longing for such as can do that. . . . We ourselves must try to *be* the water which does find its way up; we must become a spring at which men can quench their thirst for gratitude.[5]

We may say, "If only we had a giant of a man to lead us!" People have always looked for a saviour or messiah. Plato looked for a god or a God-inspired man to teach us our duties and take away the darkness from our eyes. That Messianic hope sings all through the Old Testament. The religion *about* Jesus insists that this hope was fulfilled *in* Jesus, that Jesus is the hope of mankind for all time, that man must believe on Him to be saved. However, in the context of Jesus' discovery of the Divinity of Man we see that this great hope was not fulfilled *in* Jesus, but revealed *through* Him. The true hope of mankind is the Christ-Spirit in the heart of all men, which Jesus in His illumined consciousness revealed. Paul puts it in true perspective when he says, "Christ in you, the hope of glory" (Col. 1:27).

The Christian church has preached about the saving of society, but Jesus called for a society of saviours. You must be a saviour. Don't stand looking to the heavens. Stir up the gift of God within you. You can be a saving influence. You can be a peacemaker. Declare your unity with God and with mankind by affirming: "I am now established in spiritual unity with God and with all the people of the earth."

And then let your thoughts reach out in love and prayer to all people on every side of the iron and bamboo curtains. See the good in them. Salute the divinity in them. Affirm for all those involved in positions of leadership around the world who have in their hands the privilege and responsibility of making peace or war: "Through the Christ-Mind you are unified in thought, purpose, and understanding, and inspired to right action for the security and freedom of all mankind."

We hear much talk about the depraved generation of young people. I have observed their antics on Sunset Strip, in Greenwich Village, at a "BE-in" in Central Park, and in a great war protest parade to the United Nations Building. I do not claim to understand these things or the people involved in them. I am not sure they are looking in the right direction. But they *are* looking, they are searching. They are the most serious young generation the world has ever known. And they may well be the most spiritual.

The latter point will be debated. Certainly they do not seem to conform to the traditional concepts of religon or morality. They too may have opened the "box" of custom-made convictions that we have handed down to them and have found it empty of anything meaningful to them in terms of today's needs. But they are searching for meaning, for Truth, and for a nonmaterial absolute in a perilously material world.

The young people of today are rebelling against my generation. And why not? After all—we created the bomb, provoked several horrible wars, and at least acquiesced in unspeakable racial and relious persecutions. They are caught up in a great ferment of values. They are seeking love, and often settling for its undisciplined perversion. They are seeking the expansion of consciousness, and often settling for an illusionary psychedelic experience.

Not all the young people of today are in the parades or the coffee-houses, or sporting long hair and weird clothes. But the extreme ones are symptomatic of a subtle revolution that is in the process. They caricature a very serious and important development in man.

One thing is certain. The world will never be the same again. We would do well to recognize this and even to rejoice in it. For the world of yesterday produced the confused world of today. It might help to contemplate the possibility that when Jesus made His "triumphal entry" into Jerusalem on that first Palm Sunday, He might well have appeared to the staid and conservative Jerusalemites of that time very much as the hippies appear to us today.

What can we do for our young people? Love them and let them know that we do. Believe in them and act as if we do. Respect their maturity and listen to them. Salute the divinity in them and believe that there is something wonderful seeking meaningful expression in each one. Who can say but that the great ideas that will shape the world of tomorrow may not come from those very troubled young people of today?

One of the heart-warming stories coming out of the darkness of Nazi terror in World War II is the story of Philippe Vernier, who was subjected to just about every form of indignity because he was a man of peace. He rotted in prison, and his family were harassed and starved. But he had awakened to the dynamics of the Kingdom within him and none of these things had any influence on his faith. An American officer who called upon him afterward reported that the visit with this great soul was the greatest inspiration of his life. Here are some of the words from a letter in Vernier's hand:

If you are a disciple of the Master, it is up to you to illumine the earth. You do not have to groan over everything the world lacks; you are there to bring it what it needs. . . . There where reign hatred, malice, and discord you will put love, pardon, and peace. For lying you will bring Truth; for despair, hope; for doubt, faith; there where is sadness you will give joy. If you are in the smallest degree the servant of God, all these virtues of light you will carry with you. Do not be frightened by a mission so vast! It is not really you who are charged with the fulfillment of it. You are only the torch-bearer. The fire, even if it burns within you, even when it burns you, is never lit by you. It uses you as it uses the oil of the lamp. You hold it, feed it, carry it around; but it is the fire that works, that gives light to the world, and to yourself at the same time. . . . Do not be the clogged lantern that chokes and smothers the light; the lamp, timid, or ashamed, hidden under a bushel; flame up and shine before men; lift high the fire of God.[6]

How important is this realization! You do not have to groan over what the world lacks. Flame up and shine! This could be an answer to our young people, and also to their troubled parents. "In the world ye have tribulation: but be of good cheer; I have overcome the world" (John 16:33). This was the key to Jesus' approach to the world. "I have gone upstairs. I have found the higher regions of my own nature. Here I can keep my mind peaceful and I can also be an influence for peace in the world around me." This doesn't mean that He went off on a cloud. It means that He had wisely taken the high road instead of the low road, that He had determined to act from greatness rather than from weakness. This is the trail He blazed for us, and over which we must follow Him.

When shall the Kingdom come? Whence comes the millennium? When shall Christ come into His Kingdom? When is the day of judgment? Theology may give profound eschatological answers. Perhaps we should all demand, as do our young people today, "Tell me like it is." And the answer that fits this question: "When the without shall become as the within."

The great sin of mankind is not to know the divinity that lies unexpressed within every individual. Perhaps the millennium that man has looked forward to must come to individuals one by one. We must stop thinking in terms of futurity. The time is now! The Kingdom of God may begin its unfoldment into the world right at this moment, and it may find in you its starting point.

Make the great discovery for yourself. Knowledge of the divine potential in you will not only lead to great new things for you. It will also help you play a great role in the "next development in man."

"Namaskar!" Behold yourself in a mirror and say, "Namaskar!" (I salute the divinity in you.) And then go out and act the part. Behold all the people of your world—friends and enemies, neighbors and strangers—"Namaskar!" And then treat them as if they were what they should be. You will be an influence in making them what they can be. In this way, your life will have meaning.

No matter where you are on the ladder of life, no matter what you may be experiencing, no matter how many heartaches you have had or how many conflicts you have right now—there is more in you, there is a divinity in you, the Kingdom of God is within you. You can release your potential, for Jesus proved that you have it, and that you *can* release it. This is what Jesus *really* taught.

Notes

Unless otherwise indicated, all Scripture quotations are from the American Standard Version of the Bible, copyright 1901 by Thomas Nelson & Sons, 1929 by International Council of Religious Education.

Special thanks to Dr. George M. Lamsa for much material giving insight into Biblical idiom—from his *"Gospel Light"* (Philadelphia, Pa.: A. J. Holman Co., 1936).

INTRODUCTION

1. Oliver L. Reiser, *Cosmic Humanism* (Cambridge, Mass.: Schenkman Publishing Co., 1966). pp. 406, 407.

1. THE ETERNAL QUEST

1. William Wordsworth, "Lines Composed a Few Miles Above Tintern Abbey," from *Masterpieces of Religious Verse* (New York: Harper & Brothers, 1948), p. 65.
2. Alfred Tennyson, "OEnone," Stanza 12, from John Bartlett, *Familiar Quotations* (Boston: Little, Brown and Co., 11th ed., 1941), p. 462.
3. Jane Dunlap, *Exploring Inner Space* (New York: Harcourt, Brace & World, 1961), pp. 207, 208.
4. Robert Browning, "Paracelsus," Part I, from *Masterpieces of Religious Verse* (New York: Harper & Brothers, 1948), p. 431.

2. THE GREAT DISCOVERY

1. Charles Fillmore, *Talks on Truth* (Lee's Summit, Mo.: Unity School of Christianity, 1926), p. 169.
2. Ralph Waldo Emerson, *The Complete Writings of Ralph Waldo Emerson* (New York: Wm. H. Wise & Co., 1929), p. 40.

3. THE GREAT DECISION

1. H. Emilie Cady, *How I Used Truth* (Lee's Summit, Mo.: Unity School of Christianity, 1950), p. 21.

235

2. Henry David Thoreau, *Walden* (New York: New American Library of World Literature, Signet Books, 1942), p. 215.
3. H. Emilie Cady, *God a Present Help* (Lee's Summit, Mo.: Unity School of Christianity, 1940), p. 30.

4. JESUS' UNIQUE CONCEPT OF GOD

1. John A. T. Robinson, *Honest to God* (London: SCM Press Ltd., 1963), p. 14.
2. Paul Tillich, *The Shaking of the Foundations* (New York: Charles Scribner's Sons, 1948), p. 57.
3. Alfred Tennyson, "The Higher Pantheism," stanza 6, from *John Bartlett, Familiar Quotations* (Boston: Little, Brown and Co., 11th ed., 1941), p. 467.
4. Walt Whitman, *Leaves of Grass* (New York: Doubleday, Doran & Co., 1940), p. 55.
5. Charles Fillmore, *Unity Magazine*, Dec. 1901 (published by Unity School of Christianity, Lee's Summit, Mo.).

5. FROM MISERABLE SINNERS TO MASTERS

1. Walt Whitman, *Leaves of Grass* (New York: Doubleday, Doran & Co., 1940), p. 24.
2. Charles Fillmore, *Atom-Smashing Power of Mind* (Lee's Summit, Mo.: Unity School of Christianity, 1949), p. 122.
3. Oliver Wendell Holmes, "The Voiceless," Stanza 1, from John Bartlett, *Familiar Quotations* (Boston: Little, Brown and Co., 11th ed., 1941), p. 451.
4. Ernest Holmes, *Science of Mind Magazine*, Dec. 1966 (published by Institute of Religious Science, Los Angeles, Calif.).
5. Ella Wheeler Wilcox, *Collected Poems of Ella Wheeler Wilcox* (London: Leopold B. Hill, n.d.), p. 91.

6. THE AMAZING BE ATTITUDES

1. Emmet Fox, *Sermon on the Mount* (New York: Harper & Brothers, 1934), p. 6.

7. YOUR THOUGHT IS YOUR LIFE

1. Charles Fillmore, *Keep a True Lent* (Lee's Summit, Mo.: Unity School of Christianity, 1957), p. 147.
2. Geoffrey Chaucer, "Canterbury Tales," Prologue, l. 500, from John Bartlett, *Familiar Quotations* (Boston: Little, Brown and Co., 11th ed., 1941), p. 5.

8. THE LAW OF NONRESISTANCE

1. T. S. Eliot, *The Cocktail Party, The Complete Poems and Plays of T. S. Eliot* (New York: Harcourt, Brace and Co., 1952), p. 364.

Used by permission of Harcourt, Brace and Co., and of Faber and Faber Ltd., London.
2. William Shakespeare, Sonnet 116, *Dictionary of Shakespeare Quotations* (New York: E. P. Dutton & Co., 1963), p. 457.

9. THE FORGOTTEN ART OF PRAYER

1. Clarence Day, *God and My Father* (New York: Alfred A. Knopf, 1941), p. 14.
2. John A. T. Robinson, *Honest to God* (London: SCM Press Ltd., 1963), p. 93.
3. Ralph Waldo Emerson, *The Complete Writings of Ralph Waldo Emerson* (New York: Wm. H. Wise & Co., 1929), p. 148. (Italics added.)
4. Kahlil Gibran, *The Prophet* (New York: Alfred A. Knopf, 1941), p. 74.
5. Charles Fillmore, *Prosperity* (Lee's Summit, Mo.: Unity School of Christianity, 1953), p. 113.
6. Kahlil Gibran, *op. cit.*, p. 76.

10. SUFFICIENT UNTO TODAY

1. Charles Fillmore, *Keep a True Lent* (Lee's Summit, Mo.: Unity School of Christianity, 1953), p. 102.
2. Lloyd C. Douglas, *The Robe* (Boston: Houghton Mifflin Co., 1942), p. 365.
3. William James, *Varieties of Religious Experience* (New York: Longmans, Green & Co., 1904), p. 323.
4. Henry David Thoreau, *The Journal of Henry D. Thoreau*, Vol. 2, 1850–Sept. 15, 1851 (Boston: Houghton Mifflin Co., 1949), p. 66.

12. HOW GOD FORGIVES

1. Ralph Waldo Emerson, *Forty Thousand Quotations* (New York: Halcyon House, 1917), p. 760.
2. Alva Romanes, *Weekly Unity*, May 31, 1931 (published by Unity School of Christianity, Lee's Summit, Mo.), uncopyrighted.

13. JESUS' FORMULA FOR HEALING

1. Dr. Lawrence S. Kubie, *Harvard Alumni Bulletin*, Sept. 29, 1956 (an editorial).
2. "The Development of a Chick," Coronet Films, Chicago, Ill.
3. Dr. Lewis Schreiber, *Journal of the American Podiatry Association*, Vol. 55, No. 12, Dec. 1965.
4. Father Vernon Johnson, "Suffering and Lourdes," Catholic Tract Society, 1950, quoted by Leslie Weatherhead in *Psychology, Religion, and Healing* (New York: Abingdon Press, 1951), p. 153.

5. Charles Fillmore, *Keep a True Lent* (Lee's Summit, Mo.: Unity School of Christianity, 1953), p. 173.
6. Leslie Weatherhead, *Psychology, Religion, and Healing* (New York: Abingdon Press, 1951), p. 47.
7. Arnold A. Hutschnecker, *The Will to Live* (New York: Thomas Y. Crowell, 1951).

14. THE MIRACLE OF ABUNDANCE

1. Charles Fillmore, *Prosperity* (Lee's Summit, Mo.: Unity School of Christianity, 1953), p. 24.
2. *Ibid.*, p. 23.

15. IN DEFENSE OF JUDAS

1. Arnold Toynbee, *Christianity Among the Religions of the World* (New York: Charles Scribner's Sons, 1957), p. 26.
2. *The Passion Play at Oberammergau* (Official Text for 1960, published by the Community of Oberammergau, Germany).

16. THE GREAT DEMONSTRATION

1. Alfred Tennyson, "In Memoriam," *The Complete Poetical Works of Tennyson* (Boston: Houghton Mifflin Co., 1898), p. 198.

17. DID JESUS TEACH REINCARNATION?

1. William Wordsworth, "Intimations of Immortality," from *Masterpieces of Religious Verse* (New York: Harper & Brothers, 1948), p. 267.
2. *Catholic Encyclopedia*, 1909 ed., Vol. 10, pp. 236–37, Chapter on "Re-embodiment as Taught Through the Ages."
3. Alfred Tennyson, "Sonnet to ———," from *The Complete Poetical Works of Tennyson* (Boston: Houghton Mifflin Co., 1898), p. 24.
4. Charles Fillmore, *Unity Magazine*, Sept. 1948, p. 1 (published by Unity School of Christianity, Lee's Summit, Mo.).
5. Eric Butterworth, *Life Is for Living* (Lee's Summit, Mo.: Unity School of Christianity, 1965), pp. 158–59, 167–68.
6. Charles Fillmore, *Unity Magazine*, Sept. 1948, p. 1 (published by Unity School of Christianity, Lee's Summit, Mo.).

18. WHEN SHALL THE KINGDOM COME?

1. P. D. Ouspensky, *A New Model of the Universe* (New York: Alfred A. Knopf, 1931), p. 139.
2. Robert Browning, "Paracelsus," Part V, from *Masterpieces of Religious Verse* (New York: Harper & Brothers, 1948), p. 320.
3. Richard Maurice Bucke, *Cosmic Consciousness* (New York: E. P. Dutton & Co., 1962), p. 4.

4. Charles Fillmore, *Keep a True Lent* (Lee's Summit, Mo.: Unity School of Christianity, 1953), p. 190.
5. Albert Schweitzer, *Memoirs of Childhood and Youth* (New York: The Macmillan Company, 1955), p. 66.
6. Philippe Vernier, quoted by Lewis L. Dunnington in his book, *The Inner Splendor* (New York: The Macmillan Company, 1954), pp. 104–5.